Apache Karaf Cookbook

Over 60 recipes to help you get the most out of your Apache Karaf deployments

Achim Nierbeck

Heath Kesler

Jamie Goodyear

Johan Edstrom

[PACKT] open source *
PUBLISHING   community experience distilled

BIRMINGHAM - MUMBAI

Apache Karaf Cookbook

First published: August 2014

Production reference: 1180814

Published by Packt Publishing Ltd.
Livery Place
35 Livery Street
Birmingham B3 2PB, UK.

ISBN 978-1-78398-508-1

www.packtpub.com

Credits

Authors
Achim Nierbeck

Heath Kesler

Jamie Goodyear

Johan Edstrom

Reviewers
Ladislav Gažo

Sachin Handiekar

Arun Manivannan

Charlie Mordant

Commissioning Editor
Usha Iyer

Acquisition Editor
Meeta Rajani

Content Development Editor
Mohammed Fahad

Technical Editor
Taabish Khan

Copy Editors
Deepa Nambiar

Stuti Srivastava

Laxmi Subramanian

Project Coordinator
Wendell Palmer

Proofreaders
Maria Gould

Paul Hindle

Indexers
Tejal Soni

Priya Subramani

Graphics
Ronak Dhruv

Production Coordinator
Nitesh Thakur

Cover Work
Nitesh Thakur

Cover Image
Sheetal Aute

About the Authors

Achim Nierbeck has more than 14 years of experience in designing and implementing Java enterprise applications. He is a committer and PMC at the Apache Karaf project and member of the ASF. Besides working on Apache Karaf, he is also the project lead of the OPS4j Pax Web project. Since 2010, he has enjoyed working with OSGi enterprise applications. He holds a Diploma in Computer Engineering from the University of Applied Sciences in Mannheim.

When not working on enterprise or integration projects or open source development, he enjoys spending time with his family and friends.

He can be reached at `notizblog.nierbeck.de`.

> I'd like to thank my wife, Doro, and my kids for their support while writing this book and in my career. I'd also like to thank the open source communities at Apache and OPS4j, who made this book possible.

Heath Kesler is an Apache developer and committer, has spoken at conferences around the world, and is a senior SOA architect with Savoir Technologies. He has architected and developed scalable, highly available SOA systems for large corporations around the globe.

He currently helps corporations implement and develop enterprise integration systems using messaging and web services with a focus on maintainability and scalability. He gives training classes on complex concepts and frameworks that provide functionality to large-scale enterprise solutions. He has bootstrapped development on mission critical systems for several Fortune 500 companies.

He has reached committer status on Apache Karaf and is a contributor to Camel. He received a Bachelor of Science degree from DeVry University after his tour in the army.

> I'd like to thank my wife, Christina, and kids for their unending support throughout my career. Thanks also to the open source communities for making high-powered software accessible to the masses.

Jamie Goodyear is an open source advocate, Apache developer, and computer systems analyst with Savoir Technologies; he has designed, critiqued, and supported architectures for large organizations worldwide. He holds a Bachelor of Science degree in Computer Science from Memorial University of Newfoundland.

Jamie has worked in systems administration, software quality assurance, and senior software developer roles for businesses ranging from small start-ups to international corporations. He has attained committer status on Apache Karaf, ServiceMix, and Felix, and is a Project Management Committee member on Apache Karaf. His first printed publication was co-authoring *Instant OSGi Starter*, *Packt Publishing*, with Johan Edstrom followed by *Learning Apache Karaf*, *Packt Publishing*, with Johan Edstrom and Heath Kesler.

Currently, he divides his time between providing high-level reviews of architectures, mentoring developers and administrators with SOA deployments, and helping the Apache community grow.

To Laura and caffeine, my companions through many a long night of writing.

I'd like to thank my family and friends for all of their support over the years. I'd also like to thank all the open source communities that have made Apache Karaf possible.

Johan Edstrom is an open source software evangelist, Apache developer, and seasoned architect; he has created Java architectures for large, scalable, high transaction monitoring, financial, and open source systems. He is a trained electronics engineer with a penchant for fractal geometry.

He has worked as a development lead, infrastructure manager, IT lead, and programmer, and has guided several large companies to success in the use of open source software components. Lately, he has been helping some of the world's largest networking companies and medical start-ups achieve high availability, scalability, and dynamically adapting SOA systems.

Johan divides his time between writing software, mentoring development teams, and teaching people how to use Apache ServiceMix, Camel, CXF, and ActiveMQ effectively and in a scalable way for enterprise installations.

Johan is the co-author along with Jamie Goodyear of *Instant OSGi Starter, Packt Publishing*.

Johan is a committer on Apache Camel and Apache ServiceMix and is a Project Management Committee member for Apache Camel.

I'd like to thank my wife, Connee, my daughter, Annica, and my parents, Bengt and Birgitta, for supporting me and cheering us on while writing this book as well as making it possible to work through quite a few nights.

I'd like to thank the Apache Software Foundation, a fantastic place fostering open source development.

About the Reviewers

Ladislav Gažo is a long-time computer enthusiast who has enjoyed digging into the software world from a very young age. He has more than 12 years of professional experience in development and software engineering. While experimenting with computer graphics and network administration, he realized that his true path is in the combination of software engineering and business. He has been developing, analyzing, and architecting Java-based, desktop-based, and modern web-based solutions for several years. The application of the agile approach and advanced technology is part of his hobby and day-to-day job.

Rich experience with various technologies led Ladislav to cofound Seges—a software development company based in Slovakia. He actively participates in start up events and helps building development communities, namely Google Developer Group and Java Group, in Slovakia. With his colleagues, he designed and spinned off an interactive content management solution called Synapso, utilizing contemporary technologies combined with the user experience in mind.

> I would not have been able to materialize my knowledge as part of the review process of this book without the support of all my colleagues, friends, and family. Creating a good long-term environment helped me gain the experience that I can pass on.

Sachin Handiekar is a senior software developer with over five years of experience in Java EE development. He graduated in Computer Science from the University of Greenwich, London, and currently works for a global consulting company, developing enterprise applications using various open source technologies such as Apache Camel, ServiceMix, ActiveMQ, and ZooKeeper.

He is very interested in open source projects and has contributed code to Apache Camel and developed plugins for Spring Social, which can be found at GitHub (`https://github.com/sachin-handiekar`).

He also actively writes about enterprise application development on his blog (`http://sachinhandiekar.com`).

Arun Manivannan has been trying hard to write better programs for over 10 years, with little luck. His languages of choice are Java and Scala, but he meddles around with various others, just for kicks. He is one of DZone's Most Valuable Bloggers and blogs at http://rerun.me. His interests include enterprise integration, information retrieval, and NoSQL databases.

Arun holds a Master's degree in Software Engineering from National University of Singapore. He also holds a Bachelor's degree in Commerce, a Master's degree in Computer Applications, and a PG Diploma in Human Resource Management from a business school.

I am deeply indebted to my dad, who taught me the value of persistence and determination in life, and my mom, without whose prayers and boundless love, I'd be nothing.

There are simply no words to thank my loving wife, Daisy. Her humongous faith in me and her support and patience make me believe in life-long miracles. She simply made the man I am today.

I can't finish without thanking my five-year old son, Jason, enough, for kissing me goodnight even if I couldn't read him his bedtime story. He's the greatest inspiration in my life.

Charlie Mordant is an experienced JEE software architect, enterprise architecture and Eclipse Modeling consultant, and is also an OSS contributor (OPS4J and an unlimited number of tickets to Apache, JBoss, Linux, and Eclipse).

He is a polyglot programmer and DevOPS enthusiast (Java, OSGi, EMF, AngularJS, Maven, Chef, and Docker) and also the creator of an Apache-licensed OSGi to roughly-EE bridge (the Osgiliath enterprise framework). He does his best to encourage large companies to embrace modularity.

Currently, he is working at Obeo, the Eclipse Modeling leaders.

I would like to thank my girlfriend, Anne, for her support.

www.PacktPub.com

Support files, eBooks, discount offers, and more

You might want to visit www.PacktPub.com for support files and downloads related to your book.

Did you know that Packt offers eBook versions of every book published, with PDF and ePub files available? You can upgrade to the eBook version at www.PacktPub.com and as a print book customer, you are entitled to a discount on the eBook copy. Get in touch with us at service@packtpub.com for more details.

At www.PacktPub.com, you can also read a collection of free technical articles, sign up for a range of free newsletters and receive exclusive discounts and offers on Packt books and eBooks.

http://PacktLib.PacktPub.com

Do you need instant solutions to your IT questions? PacktLib is Packt's online digital book library. Here, you can access, read and search across Packt's entire library of books.

Why Subscribe?

- ▸ Fully searchable across every book published by Packt
- ▸ Copy and paste, print and bookmark content
- ▸ On demand and accessible via web browser

Free Access for Packt account holders

If you have an account with Packt at www.PacktPub.com, you can use this to access PacktLib today and view nine entirely free books. Simply use your login credentials for immediate access.

Table of Contents

Preface   **1**

Chapter 1: Apache Karaf for System Builders   **7**
  Introduction   7
  Configuring production-ready logging in Apache Karaf   8
  Creating our own custom Karaf command using a Maven archetype   12
  Branding the Apache Karaf console   14
  Deploying applications as a feature   18
  Using JMX to monitor and administer Apache Karaf   23
  Reconfiguring SSH access to Apache Karaf   25
  Installing Apache Karaf as a service   27
  Setting up Apache Karaf for high availability   29

Chapter 2: Making Smart Routers with Apache Camel   **33**
  Introduction   34
  Installing Apache Camel modules into Apache Karaf   34
  Listing Camel Contexts in Karaf   36
  Displaying Camel Context information in Karaf   38
  Starting and stopping Camel Contexts in Karaf   41
  Listing routes in Karaf   42
  Displaying route information in Karaf   43
  Starting, stopping, suspending, and resuming routes in Karaf   44
  Listing endpoints in Karaf   46
  Making a pure Java-based Camel Router for deployment in Karaf   47
  Creating a Blueprint-based Camel Router for deployment in Karaf   52
  Adding Configuration Admin to a Blueprint-based Camel Router   54
  Creating a managed service factory implementation of a Camel Router   59

Chapter 3: Deploying a Message Broker with Apache ActiveMQ — 69

Introduction — 69
Installing Apache ActiveMQ modules into Apache Karaf — 71
Using the ActiveMQ query command — 73
Using the ActiveMQ list command — 78
Using the ActiveMQ dstat command — 79
Using the ActiveMQ purge command — 81
Using the JMS connection factory commands — 82
Using the JMS send command — 85
Using the JMS browse command — 86
Configuring and deploying a master/slave broker with Apache Karaf — 87
Configuring and deploying a Network of Brokers with Apache Karaf — 92

Chapter 4: Hosting a Web Server with Pax Web — 97

Introduction — 97
Installing Pax modules in Apache Karaf — 98
Installing extended Http Service in Apache Karaf — 100
Configuring Pax Web modules deployed in Apache Karaf — 102
Building a Http Service project to host in Apache Karaf — 104
Building a Http Service with the Whiteboard pattern in Apache Karaf — 107
Building an application with custom HttpContext with Apache Karaf — 113
Building a standard web project to host in Apache Karaf — 117
Configuring security for a web application in Apache Karaf — 120
Binding a web project to a specific host in Apache Karaf — 124
Building a Servlet 3.0 annotated web application with Apache Karaf — 126
Creating a CDI web application with Apache Karaf — 128

Chapter 5: Hosting Web Services with Apache CXF — 131

Introduction — 131
Installing Apache CXF modules in Apache Karaf — 131
Using the CXF list-endpoints command — 134
Using the CXF stop and start commands — 136
Building and deploying a RESTful service in Karaf — 138
Building and deploying a Camel CXF web service in Karaf — 142

Chapter 6: Distributing a Clustered Container with Apache Karaf Cellar — 149

Introduction — 149
Installing Apache Karaf Cellar modules in Apache Karaf — 150
Using Apache Karaf Cellar commands — 152
Building and deploying a distributed architecture with Cellar — 158

Chapter 7: Providing a Persistence Layer with Apache Aries and OpenJPA   163

Introduction	163
Installing OpenJPA modules in Apache Karaf	164
Installing Apache Aries JTA modules in Apache Karaf	166
Building a project with a persistence layer for deployment in Karaf	167
Building a project with a persistence layer and transaction support for deployment in Karaf	182

Chapter 8: Providing a Big Data Integration Layer with Apache Cassandra   187

Introduction	187
Installing Cassandra client bundles in Apache Karaf	188
Modeling data with Apache Cassandra	189
Building a project with a persistence layer for deployment in Karaf	192

Chapter 9: Providing a Big Data Integration Layer with Apache Hadoop   203

Introduction	203
Starting a standalone Hadoop cluster	204
Installing Hadoop client bundles in Apache Karaf	206
Accessing Apache Hadoop from Karaf	209
Adding commands that talk to HDFS for deployment in Karaf	211

Chapter 10: Testing Apache Karaf with Pax Exam   221

Introduction	221
Setting up a Pax Exam test environment	222
Testing Apache Karaf features	225
Testing commands with Apache Karaf	229
Coverage with Apache Karaf Pax Exam tests	231
Testing Apache Camel with Blueprint and Apache Karaf	233

Index   237

Preface

Welcome to *Apache Karaf Cookbook*. This Cookbook has been created to provide you with best practices and lessons learned from working with Apache Karaf in the trenches.

The recipes in this book are not to be read in a serial manner. Readers are expected to pick and choose recipes as per their needs. We've taken the greatest care to make sure it's possible to refer to foundational knowledge wherever applicable. However, we do expect our audience to have some background in OSGi, Karaf, and the packages each recipe focuses on. Readers requiring more background information on Karaf and OSGi might seek out the following books:

- *Learning Apache Karaf, Johan Edstrom, Jamie Goodyear, and Heath Kesler, Packt Publishing*
- *Instant OSGi Starter, Johan Edstrom and Jamie Goodyear, Packt Publishing*

What this book covers

Chapter 1, Apache Karaf for System Builders, covers recipes on how to make Apache Karaf more production ready. Topics such as improved logging, custom commands, branding, management, and high availability are explored.

Chapter 2, Making Smart Routers with Apache Camel, introduces Apache Camel commands, and then discusses how to build recipes for a Camel Router using Plain Old Java Objects (POJO), Blueprint, Blueprint with the Configuration Admin support, and finally, using a managed service factory.

Chapter 3, Deploying a Message Broker with Apache ActiveMQ, explores how to use Apache ActiveMQ in an embedded fashion and walks through the different commands for monitoring and interacting with the embedded ActiveMQ broker.

Chapter 4, Hosting a Web Server with Pax Web, explains how to configure and use Apache Karaf with Pax Web. It starts with basic Http Service to full web application support.

Chapter 5, Hosting Web Services with Apache CXF, shows how to set up Apache CXF endpoints in Karaf for both RESTful- and WSDL-based web services.

Chapter 6, Distributing a Clustered Container with Apache Karaf Cellar, explains the setup of Cellar and introduces the usage of its commands.

Chapter 7, Providing a Persistence Layer with Apache Aries and OpenJPA, explores adding Java persistence and transaction support to your OSGi environment.

Chapter 8, Providing a Big Data Integration Layer with Apache Cassandra, shows how to install Cassandra client bundles into Karaf, set up modeling data, and build your project to take advantage of a Cassandra-backed persistence layer.

Chapter 9, Providing a Big Data Integration Layer with Apache Hadoop, shows you how to integrate all of the Hadoop dependencies into a feature file, deploy them correctly into Karaf while managing resources, and use HDFS to store and retrieve data.

Chapter 10, Testing Apache Karaf with Pax Exam, explains how to perform integration tests with OSGi in general and shows how to use Apache Karaf in your integration test.

What you need for this book

The authors have taken great care to keep the quantity of software required to explore Apache Karaf to a minimum. You will need to obtain the following before trying out the recipes included in this book:

- Apache Karaf 3.0
- Oracle Java SDK 1.7
- Apache Maven 3.0
- Git Client
- Any text editor

Who this book is for

Apache Karaf Cookbook is a collection of recipes for developers and system administrators looking to apply best practices when developing and deploying their applications. Readers will discover many recipes that pertain to service-oriented architectures and managing Big Data, as well as several libraries that require some experience with OSGi to fully utilize their potential.

Conventions

In this book, you will find a number of styles of text that distinguish between different kinds of information. Here are some examples of these styles, and an explanation of their meaning.

Code words in text, database table names, folder names, filenames, file extensions, pathnames, dummy URLs, user input, and Twitter handles are shown as follows: "We append `jmxRole` to the admin group."

A block of code is set as follows:

```
<resource>
 <directory>
  ${project.basedir}/src/main/resources
 </directory>
 <filtering>true</filtering>
 <includes>
  <include>**/*</include>
 </includes>
</resource>
```

When we wish to draw your attention to a particular part of a code block, the relevant lines or items are set in bold:

```
log4j.appender.out.append=true
log4j.appender.out.maxFileSize=10MB
log4j.appender.out.maxBackupIndex=100
```

Any command-line input or output is written as follows:

```
karaf@root()> feature:repo-add mvn:com.packt/features-file/1.0.0-
  SNAPSHOT/xml/features
```

New terms and **important words** are shown in bold. Words that you see on the screen, in menus or dialog boxes for example, appear in the text like this: "The **QueueSize** column shows the number of messages that are currently in the queue waiting to be consumed."

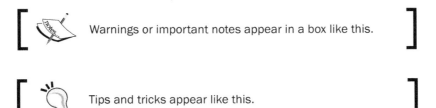

Warnings or important notes appear in a box like this.

Tips and tricks appear like this.

Reader feedback

Feedback from our readers is always welcome. Let us know what you think about this book—what you liked or may have disliked. Reader feedback is important for us to develop titles that you really get the most out of.

To send us general feedback, simply send an e-mail to feedback@packtpub.com, and mention the book title via the subject of your message.

If there is a topic that you have expertise in and you are interested in either writing or contributing to a book, see our author guide on www.packtpub.com/authors.

Customer support

Now that you are the proud owner of a Packt book, we have a number of things to help you to get the most from your purchase.

Downloading the example code

You can download the example code files for all Packt books you have purchased from your account at http://www.packtpub.com. If you purchased this book elsewhere, you can visit http://www.packtpub.com/support and register to have the files e-mailed directly to you.

Errata

Although we have taken every care to ensure the accuracy of our content, mistakes do happen. If you find a mistake in one of our books—maybe a mistake in the text or the code—we would be grateful if you would report this to us. By doing so, you can save other readers from frustration and help us improve subsequent versions of this book. If you find any errata, please report them by visiting http://www.packtpub.com/submit-errata, selecting your book, clicking on the **errata submission form** link, and entering the details of your errata. Once your errata are verified, your submission will be accepted and the errata will be uploaded on our website, or added to any list of existing errata, under the Errata section of that title. Any existing errata can be viewed by selecting your title from http://www.packtpub.com/support.

Piracy

Piracy of copyright material on the Internet is an ongoing problem across all media.
At Packt, we take the protection of our copyright and licenses very seriously. If you come across any illegal copies of our works, in any form, on the Internet, please provide us with the location address or website name immediately so that we can pursue a remedy.

Please contact us at `copyright@packtpub.com` with a link to the suspected pirated material.

We appreciate your help in protecting our authors, and our ability to bring you valuable content.

Questions

You can contact us at `questions@packtpub.com` if you are having a problem with any aspect of the book, and we will do our best to address it.

1

Apache Karaf for System Builders

In this chapter, we will cover the following topics:

- ▶ Configuring production-ready logging in Apache Karaf
- ▶ Creating our own custom Karaf command using a Maven archetype
- ▶ Branding the Apache Karaf console
- ▶ Deploying applications as a feature
- ▶ Using JMX to monitor and administer Apache Karaf
- ▶ Reconfiguring SSH access to Apache Karaf
- ▶ Installing Apache Karaf as a service
- ▶ Setting up Apache Karaf for high availability

Introduction

Experienced users of Apache Karaf will tell you that out of the box, Karaf provides you with the features and tools you'll need to deploy your application. However, to build a production-ready environment, you'll want to tweak things.

The recipes in this chapter are devoted to systems builders, the people who need to make their Apache Karaf instance production-ready and applications within it manageable.

New to Apache Karaf and OSGi?

Readers interested in obtaining a deeper understanding of Apache Karaf and its underlying technologies should consult Packt Publishing's *Instant OSGi Starter, Jamie Goodyear and Johan Edstrom*, and *Learning Apache Karaf, Jamie Goodyear, Johan Edstrom, and Heath Kesler*.

Configuring production-ready logging in Apache Karaf

One of the first tasks administrators of Apache Karaf undertake is changing the default logging configuration to more production-ready settings.

To improve the default logging configuration, we'll perform the following tasks:

- Update the logfile location to be outside the data folder. This helps administrators avoid accidentally wiping out logfiles when deleting runtime data.
- Increase the logfile size. The default size of 1 MB is too small for most production deployments. Generally, we set this to 50 or 100 MB, depending on the available disk space.
- Increase the number of logfiles we retain. There is no correct number of logfiles to retain. However, when disk space is cheap and available, keeping a large number of files is a preferred configuration.

How to do it...

Configuring Karaf's logging mechanism requires you to edit the `etc/org.ops4j.pax.logging.cfg` file. Open the file with your preferred editor and alter the following highlighted code entries:

```
# Root logger
log4j.rootLogger=INFO, out, osgi:*
log4j.throwableRenderer=org.apache.log4j.OsgiThrowableRenderer

# File appender
log4j.appender.out=org.apache.log4j.RollingFileAppender
log4j.appender.out.layout=org.apache.log4j.PatternLayout
log4j.appender.out.layout.ConversionPattern=%d{ISO8601} | %-5.5p |
    %-16.16t | %-32.32c{1} | %X{bundle.id} - %X{bundle.name} -
    %X{bundle.version} | %m%n
```

```
log4j.appender.out.file=${karaf.base}/log/karaf.log
log4j.appender.out.append=true
log4j.appender.out.maxFileSize=10MB
log4j.appender.out.maxBackupIndex=100
```

In the preceding configuration, we instruct Karaf to write logs to a log folder in the base installation directory, increase the logfile size to 10 MB, and increase the number of retained logfiles to 100.

When finished editing the file, save the changes. They will take effect shortly.

 We can change the verbosity of logging by altering the `log4j.rootLogger` entry from INFO to DEBUG, WARN, ERROR, or TRACE.

How it works...

The logging system for Karaf is based on **OPS4J Pax Logging** with the `log4j` library acting as its backend. The configuration file, `etc/org.ops4j.pax.logging.cfg`, is used to define appenders, log levels, and so on. Let's take a look at the following default appender configuration and how we'll tweak it to become more production-ready:

```
# Root logger
log4j.rootLogger=INFO, out, osgi:*
log4j.throwableRenderer=org.apache.log4j.OsgiThrowableRenderer

# File appender
#log4j.appender.out=org.apache.log4j.RollingFileAppender
#log4j.appender.out.layout=org.apache.log4j.PatternLayout
#log4j.appender.out.layout.ConversionPattern=%d{ISO8601} | %-5.5p
  | %-16.16t | %-32.32c{1} | %X{bundle.id} - %X{bundle.name} -
  %X{bundle.version} | %m%n
#log4j.appender.out.file=${karaf.data}/log/karaf.log
#log4j.appender.out.append=true
#log4j.appender.out.maxFileSize=1MB
#log4j.appender.out.maxBackupIndex=10
```

In the previous code, the `File appender` configuration sets up the default Karaf logging behavior. The initial configuration sets `RollingFileAppender` and constructs a log entry pattern. The remaining options dictate the location of the logfile, its size, and the number of logfiles to retain.

Karaf monitors the configuration file in the KARAF_HOME/etc folder. When the updates to the configuration file are read, the logging service is updated with the new value(s). The mechanism that allows this behavior is provided by File Install (available at http://felix. apache.org/site/apache-felix-file-install.html) and the OSGi Configuration Admin service. Have a look at the following figure:

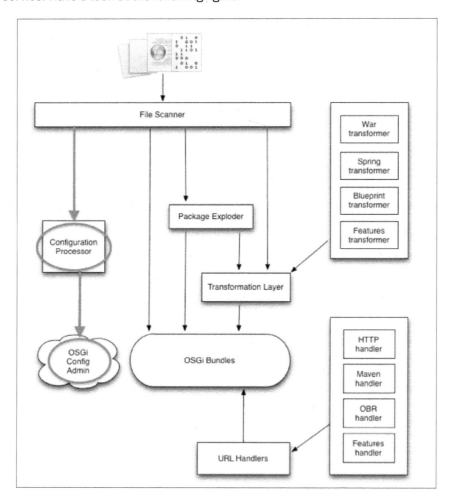

As illustrated in the preceding figure, when a file in the KARAF_HOME/etc directory is created, deleted, or modified, the file scanner will pick up on the event. Given a configuration file change (a change in the file format of the Java properties file), a configuration processor will process the entries and update the OSGi Configuration Admin service.

Downloading the example code

You can download the example code files for all Packt books you have purchased from your account at http://www.packtpub.com. If you purchased this book elsewhere, you can visit http://www.packtpub.com/support and register to have the files e-mailed directly to you.

There's more...

To further improve logging, you can provide the log4j library with an external logging location, separating the I/O requirements of logging from the base system at the expense of increased network traffic. This architecture is shown in the following figure:

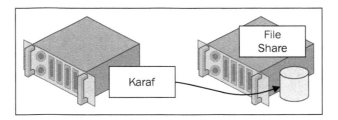

To achieve this logging architecture, you'll need to mount the external volume on the server on which Karaf is running.

See also

▶ The *Creating our own custom Karaf command using a Maven archetype* recipe.

Creating our own custom Karaf command using a Maven archetype

The Karaf console provides a multitude of useful commands to interact with the OSGi runtime and manage deployed applications. As a systems builder, you may want to develop custom commands that integrate directly into Karaf so that you can automate tasks or interact directly with your applications.

Custom Karaf commands will appear in your container as a fully integrated component of the console, as shown in the following screenshot:

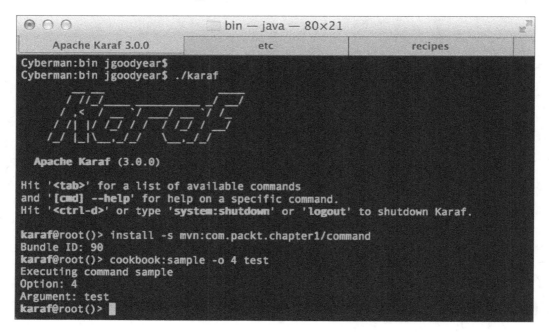

The previous screenshot illustrates our sample cookbook command accepting an option flag and an argument. Let's dive into building your own command.

Getting ready

The ingredients of this recipe include the Apache Karaf distribution kit, access to JDK, Maven, and a source code editor. The sample code for this recipe is available at https://github.com/jgoodyear/ApacheKarafCookbook/tree/master/chapter1/chapter1-recipe2.

How to do it...

1. The first step is generating a template command project. To encourage building custom commands, the community has provided the following Maven archetype invocation to generate Karaf command projects:

```
mvn archetype:generate \
  -DarchetypeGroupId=org.apache.karaf.archetypes \
  -DarchetypeArtifactId=karaf-command-archetype \
  -DarchetypeVersion=3.0.0 \
  -DgroupId=com.packt.chapter1 \
  -DartifactId=command \
-Dversion=1.0.0-SNAPSHOT \
-Dpackage=com.packt
```

In the preceding archetype invocation, we supply the Maven project group and artifact names. The process will request you to supply a command name. Maven then generates a project template for your command.

2. The next step is implementing your custom code. The custom command template project will supply you with a Maven POM file, Blueprint wiring (in the `src/main/resources/OSGI-INF/blueprint` directory), and custom command stub implementation (in the `src/main/java/` directory). Edit these files as required to add your custom actions.

3. The last step is building and deploying the custom command in Karaf. We build our command via the Maven invocation `mvn install`. Deploying it in Karaf only requires issuing a well-formed install command; to do this, invoke `install -s mvn:groupId/artifactId` in the Karaf console. Consider the following invocation:

```
karaf@root()> install -s mvn:com.packt.chapter1/command
  Bundle ID: 88
karaf@root()>
```

The preceding invocation has the `groupId` value as `com.packt.chapter1` and the `artifactId` value as `command`.

How it works...

The Maven archetype generates the POM build file, Java code, and Blueprint file for your custom command. Let's take a look at these key components.

The generated POM file contains all of the essential dependencies a Karaf command requires and sets up a basic Maven Bundle Plugin configuration. Edit this file to bring in additional libraries your command requires. Make sure that you update your bundle's build parameters accordingly. When this project is built, a bundle will be produced that can be installed directly into Karaf.

Our custom command logic resides in the generated Java source file, which will be named after the command name you supplied. The generated command extends Karaf's `OSGICommandSupport` class, which provides us with access to the underlying command session and OSGi environment. A `Command` annotation adorns our code. This provides the runtime with the scope, name, and description. Karaf provides the `Argument` and `Option` annotations to simplify adding a command-line argument and option processing.

The Blueprint container wires together our command implementation to the commands available in Karaf's console.

For more information on extending Karaf's console, see
`http://karaf.apache.org/manual/latest/`
`developers-guide/extending.html`.

There's more...

Thanks to Apache Karaf's SSHD service and remote client, your custom commands can be leveraged to provide external command and control of your applications. Just pass your command and its parameters to the remote client and monitor the returned results.

See also

 ► The *Branding the Apache Karaf console* recipe

Branding the Apache Karaf console

Apache Karaf is used as the runtime environment for production application platforms. In such deployments, it is common to have Karaf sporting a custom branding.

The Karaf community has made rebranding the runtime a simple task. Let's make our own for this book.

Getting ready

The ingredients of this recipe include the Apache Karaf distribution kit, access to JDK, Maven, and a source code editor. The sample code for this recipe is available at `https://github.com/jgoodyear/ApacheKarafCookbook/tree/master/chapter1/chapter1-recipe3`.

How to do it...

1. The first step is generating a Maven-based project structure. For this recipe, we need to only create the bare of Maven POM files, set its packaging to `bundle`, and include a `build` section.

2. The next step is adding a resource directive to our POM file's build section. In our POM file, we add a resource directive to our build section, as shown in the following code:

```
<resource>
  <directory>
    ${project.basedir}/src/main/resources
  </directory>
  <filtering>true</filtering>
  <includes>
    <include>**/*</include>
  </includes>
</resource>
```

We add a resource directive to our build section to instruct Maven to process the contents of our `resources` folder, filter any wildcards, and include the result in the generated bundle.

3. Next, we configure the Maven Bundle Plugin as shown in the following code:

```
<configuration>
  <instructions>
    <Bundle-SymbolicName>
      ${project.artifactId}
    </Bundle-SymbolicName>
    <Import-Package>*</Import-Package>
    <Private-Package>!*</Private-Package>
    <Export-Package>
      org.apache.karaf.branding
    </Export-Package>
```

```
        <Spring-Context>
          *;publish-context:=false
        </Spring-Context>
      </instructions>
    </configuration>
```

We configured the Maven Bundle Plugin to export `Bundle-SymbolicName` as the `artifactId` and set the `Export-Package` option to `org.apache.karaf.branding`. The symbolic name as the project's `artifactId` variable is a common convention among Karaf bundle developers. We export the Karaf branding package so that the Karaf runtime will identify the bundle as containing the custom branding.

4. The next step is creating our custom branding resource file. Returning to our project, we'll create a `branding.properties` file in the `src/main/resource/org/apache/karaf/branding` directory. This `.properties` file will contain ASCII and Jansi text characters, organized to produce your custom look. Using Maven resource filtering, you can use variable substitutions in the `${variable}` format, as shown in the following code:

```
##
welcome = \
\u001B[33m\u001B[0m\n\
\u001B[33m        _            ___    ____       _____        \u001B[0m\n\
\u001B[33m       / \\         |_   ||_   _|   .'   ___  |   \u001B[0m\n\
\u001B[33m      / _ \\          | |_/ /    / .'     \\_|  \u001B[0m\n\
\u001B[33m     / ___ \\         |  __'.    | |           \u001B[0m\n\
\u001B[33m   _/ /   \\ \\_      _| |  \\ \\_  \\ '.___.'\\   \u001B[0m\n\
\u001B[33m  |____| |____|    |____||____|   '.____ .'   \u001B[0m\n\
\u001B[33m                                              \u001B[0m\n\
\u001B[33m        Apache Karaf Cookbook              \u001B[0m\n\
\u001B[33m Packt Publishing - http://www.packtpub.com\u001B[0m\n\
\u001B[33m        (version ${project.version})\u001B[0m\n\
\u001B[33m\u001B[0m\n\
\u001B[33mHit '\u001B[1m<tab>\u001B[0m' for a list of available
  commands\u001B[0m\n\
\u001B[33mand '\u001B[1m[cmd] --help\u001B[0m' for help on a
  specific command.\u001B[0m\n\
\u001B[33mHit '\u001B[1m<ctrl-d>\u001B[0m' or
  '\u001B[1mosgi:shutdown\u001B[0m' to shutdown\u001B[0m\n\
\u001B[33m\u001B[0m\n\
```

In the preceding code, we use a combination of ASCII characters and Jansi text markup in the `branding.properties` file to produce simple text effects in Karaf, as shown in the following screenshot:

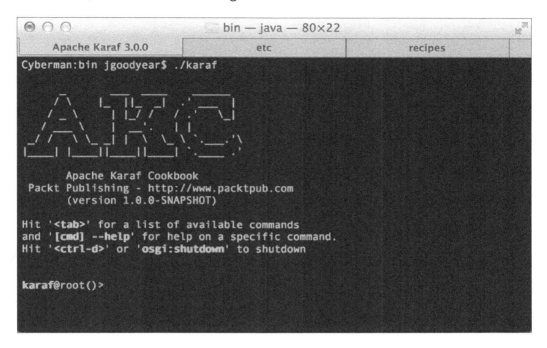

5. The final step is building and deploying our custom branding. We build our branding via the Maven invocation `mvn install`. After we build our branding bundle, we place a copy inside Karaf's `KARAF_HOME/lib` folder and then start the container. Upon the first boot, you will see our custom branding displayed.

How it works...

At the first boot, Apache Karaf will check for any bundle in its `lib` folder and will export the `org.apache.karaf.branding` package. Upon detection of this resource, it will access the `branding.properties` file content and display it as part of the runtime startup routine.

There's more...

The Apache Karaf community maintains a web console that may also be branded to reflect your organization's branding. See `https://karaf.apache.org/index/subprojects/webconsole.html` for more details.

Deploying applications as a feature

Managing the assembly and deployment of repository locations, bundles, configuration, and other artifacts quickly becomes a major headache for system builders. To combat this, the Karaf community has developed the concept of *features*. The following figure describes the concept of features:

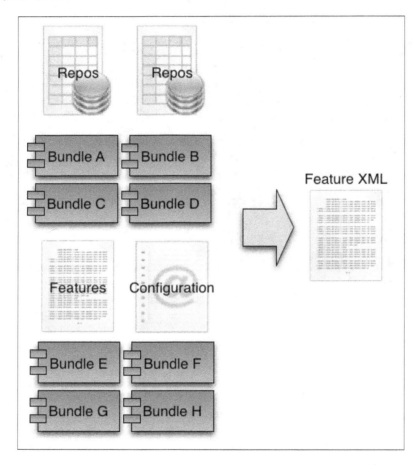

A feature descriptor is an XML-based file that describes a collection of artifacts to be installed together into the Karaf container. In this recipe, we'll learn how to make a feature, add it to Karaf, and then use it to install bundles.

Getting ready

The ingredients of this recipe include the Apache Karaf distribution kit, access to JDK, Maven, and a source code editor. The sample code for this recipe is available at `https://github.com/jgoodyear/ApacheKarafCookbook/tree/master/chapter1/chapter1-recipe4`.

How to do it...

1. The first step is generating a Maven-based project. For this recipe, we need to create a Maven POM file, set its packaging to `bundle`, and include a `build` section.

2. The next step is editing the POM file's `build` directives. We add a `resources` directive to our POM file's `build` section and `maven-resources-plugin` and `build-helper-maven-plugin` to its plugin list. Consider the following code:

```
<resources>
    <resource>
        <directory>src/main/resources</directory>
        <filtering>true</filtering>
    </resource>
</resources>
```

In the preceding code, the `resources` directive indicates the location of the features file we'll create for processing. Now, consider the following code:

```
<plugin>
    <groupId>org.apache.maven.plugins</groupId>
    <artifactId>maven-resources-plugin</artifactId>
    <executions>
        <execution>
            <id>filter</id>
            <phase>generate-resources</phase>
            <goals>
                <goal>resources</goal>
            </goals>
        </execution>
    </executions>
</plugin>
```

In the preceding code, `maven-resources-plugin` is configured to process our resources. Now, consider the following code:

```xml
<plugin>
    <groupId>org.codehaus.mojo</groupId>
    <artifactId>build-helper-maven-plugin</artifactId>
    <executions>
        <execution>
            <id>attach-artifacts</id>
            <phase>package</phase>
            <goals>
                <goal>attach-artifact</goal>
            </goals>
            <configuration>
                <artifacts>
                    <artifact>
                        <file>
                          ${project.build.directory}
                          /classes/${features.file}</file>
                        <type>xml</type>
                        <classifier>features</classifier>
                    </artifact>
                </artifacts>
            </configuration>
        </execution>
    </executions>
</plugin>
```

Finally, `build-helper-maven-plugin` completes the build of our `features.xml` file as described in the preceding code.

3. The third step is creating a `features.xml` resource. In the `src/main/resources` folder, add a file named `features.xml` with the details of your bundles, as shown in the following code:

```xml
<?xml version="1.0" encoding="UTF-8"?>

<features>

  <feature name='moduleA' version='${project.version}'>
    <bundle>
      mvn:com.packt/moduleA/${project.version}
    </bundle>
  </feature>
```

```
<feature name='moduleB' version='${project.version}'>
  <bundle>
    mvn:com.packt/moduleB/${project.version}
  </bundle>
</feature>

<feature name='recipe4-all-modules'
  version='${project.version}'>
  <feature version='${project.version}'>moduleA</feature>
  <feature version='${project.version}'>moduleB</feature>
</feature>

</features>
```

We provide each feature with a name that Karaf will use as a reference to install each element specified in the named feature's configuration. Features may reference other features, thus providing fine-grained control over installation. In the preceding features file, we can see three named features: moduleA, moduleB, and recipe4-all-modules. The recipe4-all-modules feature includes the content of the other two features.

 If you need to include a JAR file that is not offered as a bundle, try using the wrap protocol to automatically provide the file with the OSGi manifest headers. For more information, see https://ops4j1.jira.com/wiki/display/paxurl/Wrap+Protocol.

4. The final step is building and deploying our feature. Using our sample recipe project, we will build our feature by executing mvn install. This performs all of the feature file variable substitutions and installs a processed copy in your local m2 repository.

To make our feature available to Karaf, we'll add the feature file's Maven coordinates as follows:

```
karaf@root()>feature:repo-add mvn:com.packt/features-
  file/1.0.0-  SNAPSHOT/xml/features
```

Now, we can use Karaf's feature commands to install moduleA and moduleB, as shown in the following command-line snippet:

```
karaf@root()>feature:install recipe4-all-modules
Apache Karaf starting moduleA bundle
Apache Karaf starting moduleB bundle
karaf@root()>
```

Using `feature:install` in this fashion helps to promote repeatable deployments and avoid missing component installations that are not caught by the OSGi environment (if no bundle dependencies are missing, then as far as the container is concerned, all is well). We can verify whether our feature is installed by invoking the following command:

```
karaf@root()>feature:list | grep -i "recipe"
```

We can then observe whether our feature is listed or not.

How it works...

When Karaf processes a feature descriptor as a bundle, hot deployment, or via a system start-up property, the same processing and assembly functions occur, as shown in the following figure:

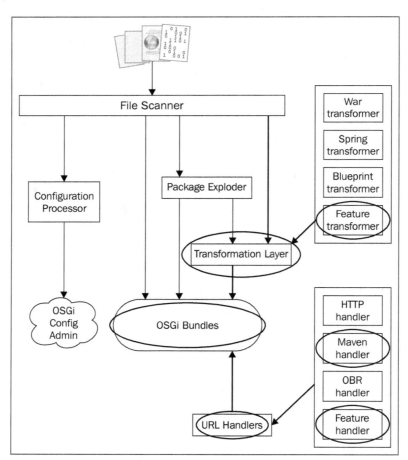

The feature descriptor invocation is transformed into a list of artifacts to be installed in the OSGi container. At the lowest level, individual elements in a feature have a handler to obtain the described artifact (such as a bundle, JAR file, or configuration file). Our sample feature uses Maven coordinates to obtain bundles, and the Maven handler will be called to process these resources. If an HTTP URL was specified, then the HTTP handler is called. Each artifact in the specified feature will be installed until the entire list is processed.

There's more...

The *How to do it...* section of this recipe outlines a general methodology to produce a feature file for your projects and automate the filtering of resource versions. From Apache Karaf's point of view, it just processes a well-formatted features file so that you can handwrite the file and deploy it directly into Karaf.

Feature files have additional attributes that can be used to set bundle start levels, flag bundles as being dependencies, and set configuration properties. For more information, visit `http://karaf.apache.org/manual/latest/users-guide/provisioning.html`.

An advanced use case of Karaf feature files is to build a **KAraf aRchive** (**KAR**). A KAR file is the processed form of a feature file, collecting all the required artifacts into a single deployable form. This archive is ideal for deployment when your Karaf instance will not have access to remote repositories, as all required resources are packaged in the KAR file.

See also

- We'll be using the features concept of Apache Karaf in several chapters of this book to simplify the installation of Apache Camel, ActiveMQ, and CXF among other projects.

Using JMX to monitor and administer Apache Karaf

By default, Apache Karaf can be administered via Java Management Extensions (JMX). However, systems builders often need to tweak the default configurations to get their deployment integrated into their network. In this recipe, we'll show you how to make these changes.

Getting ready

The ingredients of this recipe include the Apache Karaf distribution kit, access to JDK, and a source code editor. The sample configuration for this recipe is available at `https://github.com/jgoodyear/ApacheKarafCookbook/tree/master/chapter1/chapter1-recipe5`.

Administrators should take care when exposing JMX access to their Karaf instance. Enabling of SSL and use of strong passwords is recommended.

How to do it...

1. The first step is editing the management configuration. Apache Karaf ships with a default management configuration. To make our modifications, we update the `etc/org.apache.karaf.management.cfg` file. Consider the following code:

    ```
    #
    # Port number for RMI registry connection
    #
    rmiRegistryPort = 11099


    #
    # Port number for RMI server connection
    #
    rmiServerPort = 44445
    ```

    The default ports, 1099 and 44444, are usually fine for general deployment. Change these ports only if you are experiencing port conflicts on your deployment. Now, consider the following snippet:

    ```
    #
    # Role name used for JMX access authorization
    # If not set, this defaults to the ${karaf.admin.role} configured
    in etc/system.properties
    #
    jmxRole=admin
    ```

    Towards the bottom of the configuration file, there will be a commented-out entry for `jmxRole`; enable this by removing the hash character.

2. The next step is updating the user's file. We must now update the `etc/users.properties` file with the following code:

    ```
    karaf = karaf,_g_:admingroup
    _g_\:admingroup = group,admin,manager,viewer,jmxRole
    ```

    The `users.properties` file is used to configure users, groups, and roles in Karaf. We append `jmxRole` to the admin group. The syntax for this file follows the `Username = password, groups` format.

3. The last step is testing our configuration. After making the previous configuration changes, we'll need to restart our Karaf instance. Now, we can test our JMX setup. Have a look at the following screenshot:

After restarting Karaf, use a JMX-based admin tool of your choice (the previous screenshot shows JConsole) to connect to the container. Due to image size restrictions, the full URL couldn't be displayed. The full URL is `service:jmx:r mi://127.0.0.1:44445/jndi/rmi://127.0.0.1:11099/karaf-root`. The syntax of the URL is `service:jmx:rmi://host:${rmiServerPort}/jndi/ rmi://host:${rmiRegistryPort}/${karaf-instance-name}`.

Reconfiguring SSH access to Apache Karaf

Using Apache Karaf via its local console provides the user with superb command and control capabilities over their OSGi container. Apache Karaf's remote console extends this experience to remote consoles, and as such, presents systems builders with an opportunity to further harden their systems. In this recipe, we'll change Karaf's default remote connection parameters.

Getting ready

The ingredients of this recipe include the Apache Karaf distribution kit, access to JDK, and a source code editor. The sample configuration for this recipe is available at `https://github.com/jgoodyear/ApacheKarafCookbook/tree/master/chapter1/chapter1-recipe6`.

How to do it...

1. The first step is editing the shell configuration. Apache Karaf ships with a default shell configuration file. It's a good practice to edit entries in the `etc/org.apache.karaf.shell.cfg` file to point to the non-default ports as a security precaution. Consider the following code:

   ```
   #
   # Via sshPort and sshHost you define the address you can login
   into Karaf.
   #
   sshPort = 8102
   sshHost = 192.168.1.110
   ```

   In the preceding sample configuration, we defined the port for SSH access to `8102` and set `sshHost` to an IP address of the host machine (the default value, 0.0.0.0, means the SSHD service is bound to all network interfaces). Restricting access to particular network interfaces can help reduce unwanted access.

2. The next step is restarting Karaf. After editing the configuration, we must restart Karaf. Once restarted, you'll be able to connect to Karaf using an SSH client command as follows:

   ```
   ssh -p 8102 karaf@127.0.0.1
   ```

   Upon connection, you'll be prompted for your password.

There's more...

Changing the default remote access configuration is a good start. However, system builders should also consider changing the default `karafuser/password` combination found in the `users.properties` file.

You might also decide to generate a server SSH key file to simplify remote access. Information regarding this configuration can be found at `http://karaf.apache.org/manual/latest/users-guide/remote.html`.

Installing Apache Karaf as a service

When we install Apache Karaf, we'll want it to operate as a system service on our host platform (just like Windows or Linux). In this recipe, we'll set up Karaf to start when your system boots up.

Getting ready

The ingredients of this recipe include the Apache Karaf distribution kit, access to JDK, and a source code editor. The sample wrapper configuration for this recipe is available at https://github.com/jgoodyear/ApacheKarafCookbook/tree/master/chapter1/chapter1-recipe7.

How to do it...

1. The first step is installing the service wrapper feature. Apache Karaf utilizes a service wrapper feature to handle gathering and deploying of the required resources for your host operating environment. We begin its installation by invoking the following command:

   ```
   karaf@root()>feature:install service-wrapper
   ```

   The service wrapper feature URL is included in Karaf by default; so, no additional step is required to make it available.

2. The next step is installing the wrapper service. Now, we must instruct the wrapper to configure and install the appropriate service scripts and resources for us. Consider the following command:

   ```
   karaf@root()>wrapper:install -s AUTO_START -n Karaf3 -D
     "Apache Karaf Cookbook"
   ```

   The preceding `wrapper:install` command invocation includes three flags: `-s` for the start type, `-n` for the service name, and `-D` for the service description. The start type can be one of two options: `AUTO_START`, to automatically start the service on boot, and `DEMAND_START`, to start only when manually invoked. The service name is used as an identifier in the host's service registry. The description provides system administrators with a brief description of your Karaf installation. After executing the `install` command, the Karaf console will display the libraries, scripts, and configuration files that the wrapper generates. You'll now need to exit Karaf to continue the service installation.

3. The final step is integrating it in to the host operating system. This step will require administrator level permissions to execute the generated Karaf service wrapper installation scripts.

The following command installs the service natively into Windows:

```
C:> C:\Path\To\apache-karaf-3.0.0\bin\Karaf3-service.bat
   install
```

The following `net` commands allow an administrator to start or stop the Karaf service:

```
C:> net start "Karaf3"
```

```
C:> net stop "Karaf3"
```

Linux integration will vary based on distribution. The following commands will work on Debian- or Ubuntu-based systems:

```
jgoodyear@ubuntu1204:~$ ln -s /Path/To/apache-karaf-
   3.0.0/bin/Karaf3-service /etc/init.d
jgoodyear@ubuntu1204:~$ update-rc.d Karaf3-service defaults
jgoodyear@ubuntu1204:~$ /etc/init.d/Karaf3-service start
jgoodyear@ubuntu1204:~$ /etc/init.d/Karaf3-service stop
```

The first command creates a symbolic link from the service script in Karaf's `bin` folder to the `init.d` directory and then updates the startup scripts to include the Karaf service to automatically start during boot. The remaining two commands can be used to manually start or stop the Karaf service.

How it works...

The wrapper service feature integrates Karaf into the host operating system's service mechanism. This means that on a Windows- or Linux-based system, Karaf will avail of the available fault, crash, processing freeze, out of memory, or similar event detections and automatically attempt to restart Karaf.

See also

▶ The *Setting up Apache Karaf for high availability* recipe

Setting up Apache Karaf for high availability

To help provide higher service availability, Karaf provides the option to set up a secondary instance of Apache Karaf to failover upon in case of an operating environment error. In this recipe, we'll configure a **Master/Slave** failover deployment and briefly discuss how you can expand the recipe to multiple hosts.

Getting ready

The ingredients of this recipe include the Apache Karaf distribution kit, access to JDK, and a source code editor. The sample configuration for this recipe is available at `https://github.com/jgoodyear/ApacheKarafCookbook/tree/master/chapter1/chapter1-recipe8`.

How to do it...

1. The first step is editing the system properties file. To enable a Master/Slave failover, we edit the `etc/system.properties` file of two or more Karaf instances to include the following Karaf locking configuration:

```
##
## Sample lock configuration
##
karaf.lock=true
karaf.lock.class=org.apache.karaf.main.lock.SimpleFileLock
# specify path to lock directory
karaf.lock.dir=[PathToLockFileDirectory]
karaf.lock.delay=10
```

   The previous configuration sample contains the essential entries for a file-based locking mechanism, that is, two or more Karaf instances attempt to gain exclusive ownership of a file over a shared filesystem.

2. The next step is providing locking resources. If using a shared locking file approach is suitable to your deployment, then all you must do at this time is mount the filesystem on each machine that'll host Karaf instances in the Master/Slave deployment.

 If you plan to use the shared file lock, consider using an NFSv4 filesystem, as it implements flock correctly.

Each Karaf instance will include the same lock directory location on a shared filesystem common to each Karaf installation. If a shared filesystem is not practical between systems, then a JDBC locking mechanism can be used. This is described in the following code:

```
karaf.lock=true
karaf.lock.class=org.apache.karaf.main.DefaultJDBCLock
karaf.lock.delay=10
karaf.lock.jdbc.url=jdbc:derby://dbserver:1527/sample
karaf.lock.jdbc.driver=org.apache.derby.jdbc.ClientDriver
karaf.lock.jdbc.user=user
karaf.lock.jdbc.password=password
karaf.lock.jdbc.table=KARAF_LOCK
karaf.lock.jdbc.clustername=karaf
karaf.lock.jdbc.timeout=30
```

The JDBC configuration is similar to the SimpleFileLock configuration. However, it is expanded to contain the JDBC `url`, `driver`, `timeout`, `user`, and `password` options. Two additional JDBC options are included to allow for multiple Master/Slave Karaf deployments to use a single database. These are the JDBC `table` and `clustername` options. The JDBC `table` property sets the database table to use for the lock, and the JDBC `clustername` property specifies which pairing group a Karaf instance belongs to (for example, hosts A and B belong to a cluster prod group, and hosts C and D belong to a cluster dev group).

When using the JDBC locking mechanism, you'll have to provide the relevant JDBC driver JAR file to Karaf's `lib/ext` folder. For specific database configurations, consult Karaf's user manual (`http://karaf.apache.org/manual/latest/index.html`).

3. The final step is verifying the lock behavior. Once you have configured each Karaf instance to be a participant of the Master/Slave deployment and ensured that any locking resources have been made available (mounted filesystems or database drivers/connectivity), you must now validate that it is all working as desired. The general test to perform is to start one instance of Karaf, allow it to gain the lock (you'll see this recorded in the logfile), and then start all additional instances. Only the first instance should be fully booted; the others should be trying to gain the lock. Stopping this first instance should result in another instance becoming the Master. This verification step is vital. Most Master/Slave deployment failures occur due to misconfigurations or shared resource permissions.

How it works...

Each instance of Apache Karaf contains a copy of the locking configuration in its `etc/system.properties` file. This is described in the following figure:

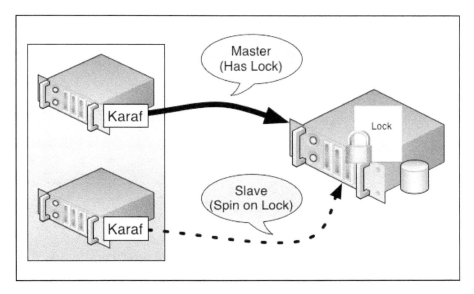

In the case of a SimpleFileLock configuration, Karaf attempts to utilize an exclusive lock upon a file to manage which Karaf instance will operate as a live (Master) container. The other instances in the set will try gaining lock file access for `karaf.lock.delay` seconds each. This can be easily simulated on a single host machine with two Karaf installations both configured to use the same locking file. If the lock file is located on a shared NFSv4 filesystem, then multiple servers may be able to use this configuration. However, a JDBC-based lock is the most often used in multihost architectures.

There's more...

Karaf failover describes an active/passive approach to high availability. There is also a similar concept that provides active/active architecture via Apache Karaf Cellar.

2
Making Smart Routers with Apache Camel

In this chapter, we will cover the following topics:

- ▶ Installing Apache Camel modules into Apache Karaf
- ▶ Listing Camel Contexts in Karaf
- ▶ Displaying Camel Context information in Karaf
- ▶ Starting and stopping Camel Contexts in Karaf
- ▶ Listing routes in Karaf
- ▶ Displaying route information in Karaf
- ▶ Starting, stopping, suspending, and resuming routes in Karaf
- ▶ Listing endpoints in Karaf
- ▶ Making a pure Java-based Camel Router for deployment in Karaf
- ▶ Creating a Blueprint-based Camel Router for deployment in Karaf
- ▶ Adding Configuration Admin to a Blueprint-based Camel Router
- ▶ Creating a managed service factory implementation of a Camel Router

Introduction

Apache Karaf provides a friendly OSGi-based container environment to deploy, manage, and most importantly, enjoy your applications. One of the more common projects to be hosted on Karaf is the Apache Camel-based router. In this chapter, we'll explore recipes to help make using Camel on Karaf quick, easy, and fun.

Before we proceed, let's take a closer look at Apache Camel.

Apache Camel provides a rule-based routing and mediation engine for Java, implementing **Enterprise Integration Patterns (EIPs)** as described in *Enterprise Integration Patterns: Designing, Building, and Deploying Messaging Solutions, Gregor Hohpe and Bobby Woolf, Addison Wesley*. One of the key features of the Camel library is its domain-specific language to configure routers and mediation. This allows for type-safe completion of rules in an integrated development environment, thereby greatly saving time and reducing complexity.

> The purpose of this chapter is to explore the Apache Camel-Apache Karaf integration. For more in-depth exploration of Enterprise Integration Patterns and Camel, read *Apache Camel Developer's Cookbook*, *Instant Apache Camel Messaging System*, or *Instant Apache Camel Message Routing*, all by Packt Publishing.

Installing Apache Camel modules into Apache Karaf

Before we can begin to explore how to build Camel-Karaf smart routers, we must first install all the required Camel modules into the Karaf container.

Getting ready

The ingredients of this recipe include the Apache Karaf distribution kit, access to JDK, and Internet connectivity.

How to do it...

1. First, we add an URL to the Camel feature to our Karaf installation feature repository using the following command:

```
karaf@root()> feature:repo-add mvn
  :org.apache.camel.karaf/apache-camel/2.12.2/xml/features
```

```
Adding feature url mvn:org.apache.camel.karaf/apache-
   camel/2.12.2/xml/features
karaf@root()>
```

 Alternatively, you can use the `feature:repo-add camel 2.12.2` command.

Upon adding the feature URL, Karaf will then be ready to install all Apache Camel dependencies. If you'd like to see all of the install targets, issue the `feature:list | grep -i camel` command.

2. The next step is installing the base Camel feature into Karaf. We install a feature by executing the `feature:install` command and the feature's name, as shown in the following command:

```
karaf@root()>  feature:install camel
```

We can verify the installation by executing the `list -t 0 | grep camel` command, which will list all the installed Camel components in Karaf (camel-core, camel-karaf-commands, camel-spring, and camel-blueprint).

How it works...

The Apache Camel community maintains an Apache Karaf features descriptor for each release of their project. When the descriptor file is added (using the `feature:repo-add` command) to Karaf, the container processes its content, making each feature's target available to be installed. The following diagram shows how various Camel bundles are deployed on top of a base Karaf system:

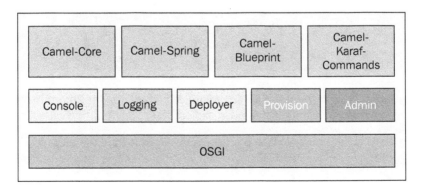

When a particular feature, in this case Camel, is installed (using the `feature:install` command), Karaf will use the appropriate URL handlers to obtain the required resources and install them into the container, and will then attempt to bring them to a `Started` state. If you execute `list -t 0` on the Karaf console, you will see Camel and all other artifacts deployed into the container. We can depict the integration of Camel components into Karaf more simply by illustrating the key Camel artifacts being deployed atop a standard Karaf installation.

See also

▶ The *Deploying applications as a feature* recipe of *Chapter 1, Apache Karaf for System Builders*

Listing Camel Contexts in Karaf

The installation of Apache Camel into Apache Karaf includes a set of custom Camel commands as part of the `camel-karaf-commands` bundle. The Camel community has developed and maintained these commands for the benefit of Karaf users, and as such have helped to fully integrate Camel into the Karaf experience. These commands are listed in the following screenshot:

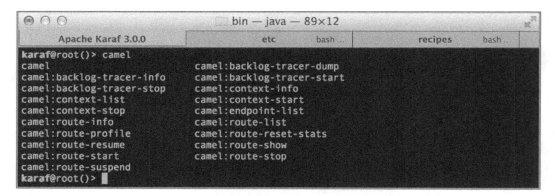

As of Apache Camel 2.12.2, there are 18 Camel-Karaf commands (as shown in the previous screenshot), and in the following recipes, we'll explore the most commonly used commands.

One common task Camel users want to perform is to list all of the Camel Contexts deployed into a Karaf container.

Getting ready

The ingredients of this recipe include the Apache Karaf distribution kit, access to JDK, Maven, and a source code editor.

A sample Camel application has been developed for this recipe, and is available at `https://github.com/jgoodyear/ApacheKarafCookbook/tree/master/chapter2/chapter2-recipe2`. Building the application requires executing a Maven install and then deploying the assembled bundle into Karaf (using the `install -s mvn:com.packt/sample` command).

Follow the instructions in the *Installing Apache Camel modules into Apache Karaf* recipe to provide the base requirements to operate the sample code. We'll reuse this recipe's resources several times.

How to do it...

To list all of the Camel Contexts deployed in Karaf, execute the `camel:context-list` command:

```
karaf@root()> camel:context-list
  Context              Status        Uptime
  -------              ------        ------
  CamelCommandContext  Started       1 hour 44 minutes
karaf@root()>
```

In the previous command invocation, we observe the sample Camel Router's context name displayed (in this example, the context name was set in Blueprint—see the recipe's source code for details).

How it works...

When the `camel-karaf-commands` bundle is installed into Karaf via the Camel feature, the Camel commands become automatically available on the Karaf console. Under the hood, the Camel command Blueprint descriptor is instantiated and the various Camel-Karaf commands are wired into the container.

When the `context-list` command is executed, the context IDs of each Camel Context deployed is displayed along with their current status, and if available, their uptime.

There's more...

The Apache Camel community maintains updated information on their commands, which you can find at `http://camel.apache.org/karaf.html`.

See also

▶ The *Displaying Camel Context information in Karaf* recipe

Displaying Camel Context information in Karaf

Karaf can display detailed information about individual Camel Contexts deployed in the container using the `camel:context-info` command. Context-wide statistics, behaviors, contained components, and more can be discovered using this command.

Getting ready

Follow the instructions in the *Listing Camel Contexts in Karaf* recipe's *Getting ready* section for this recipe.

How to do it...

Use the following `camel:context-info` command on the Karaf console to retrieve context information—a small warning, there may be a lot of output generated:

```
karaf@root()> camel:context-info CamelCommandContext
```

The output will be as follows:

```
Camel Context CamelCommandContext
  Name: CamelCommandContext
  ManagementName: 123-CamelCommandContext
  Version: 2.12.2
```

```
  Status: Started
  Uptime: 1 hour 50 minutes
Statistics
  Exchanges Total: 1321
  Exchanges Completed: 1321
  Exchanges Failed: 0
  Min Processing Time: 0ms
  Max Processing Time: 6ms
  Mean Processing Time: 0ms
  Total Processing Time: 1110ms
  Last Processing Time: 1ms
  Delta Processing Time: 0ms
  Load Avg: 0.00, 0.00, 0.00
  Reset Statistics Date: 2014-02-27 16:01:41
  First Exchange Date: 2014-02-27 16:01:42
  Last Exchange Completed Date: 2014-02-27 17:51:43
  Number of running routes: 1
  Number of not running routes: 0


Miscellaneous
  Auto Startup: true
  Starting Routes: false
  Suspended: false
  Shutdown timeout: 300 sec.
  Message History: true
  Tracing: false


Properties
```

```
Advanced
  ClassResolver:
    org.apache.camel.core.osgi.OsgiClassResolver@2ffd5a29
  PackageScanClassResolver:
    org.apache.camel.core.osgi.OsgiPackageScanClassResolver@222a525c
  ApplicationContextClassLoader: BundleDelegatingClassLoader(sample
    [123])
Components
  mock
  bean
  timer
  properties

Dataformats

Languages
  simple

Routes
  CamelRoute-timerToLog
```

The preceding `camel:context-info` invocation demonstrates that a large quantity of data is available about each context; it is not uncommon for users to capture this output for analysis.

How it works...

The `context-info` command hooks into Camel's own facilities to access context information. Upon retrieval, the data is then formatted for display on Karaf's console.

See also

 ▶ The *Starting and stopping Camel Contexts in Karaf* recipe

Starting and stopping Camel Contexts in Karaf

Starting and stopping the bundle that contains a Camel Context can be very clumsy; you can use the `camel:context-start` and `camel:context-stop` commands to manage specific contexts.

Getting ready

Follow the instructions under the *Listing Camel Contexts in Karaf* recipe's *Getting ready* section for this recipe.

How to do it...

Managing Camel Contexts in Karaf is easy, but requires you to become familiar with two commands, which are as follows:

- ► `camel:context-start contextName`: This command is used to start a context
- ► `camel:context-stop contextName`: This command is used to stop a context

The following Camel command invocations demonstrate the result of stopping a context:

```
karaf@root()> camel:context-list
 Context                Status        Uptime
 -------                ------        ------
 CamelCommandContext    Started       3.139 seconds
karaf@root()> camel:context-stop CamelCommandContext
karaf@root()> camel:context-list
karaf@root()>
```

How it works...

The context commands operate on the Camel framework and do not represent the OSGi life cycle. Depending upon your application, a stopped context may result in the need to restart its host bundle.

See also

- ► The *Listing routes in Karaf* recipe

Listing routes in Karaf

It is common to deploy dozens of Camel routes into an Apache Karaf container. To make administrating these routes easier, Apache Camel has provided a command to list all Camel-deployed routes by their ID.

Getting ready

Follow the instructions in the *Listing Camel Contexts in Karaf* recipe's *Getting ready* section for this recipe.

How to do it...

Use the `camel:route-list` command to list all routes deployed in Karaf as follows:

```
karaf@root()> camel:route-list

 Context               Route                 Status

 -------               -----                 ------

 CamelCommandContext   CamelRoute-timerToLog Started
```

The preceding invocation gathers and displays all the routes deployed in the container on Karaf's console.

How it works...

When the `route-list` command is executed, the route IDs of each route in each Camel Context are displayed along with their current status.

When developing routes, assign a descriptive ID to help make administration easier.

See also

► The *Displaying route information in Karaf* recipe

Displaying route information in Karaf

Apache Camel provides mechanisms to gather information surrounding the routes deployed inside a Camel Context. The `route-info` command has been provided to display route properties, statistics, and definitions to Karaf's console.

Getting ready

Follow the instructions in the *Listing Camel Contexts in Karaf* recipe's *Getting ready* section for this recipe.

How to do it...

Use the following `camel:route-info routeId` command to display information on a Camel route to Karaf's console; similar to the `camel:context-info` command, this command may generate a lot of output:

```
karaf@root()> camel:route-info CamelRoute-timerToLog
Camel Route CamelRoute-timerToLog
   Camel Context: CamelCommandContext

Properties
    id = CamelRoute-timerToLog
    parent = 20443040

Statistics
   Inflight Exchanges: 0
   Exchanges Total: 44
   Exchanges Completed: 44
   Exchanges Failed: 0
   Min Processing Time: 0 ms
   Max Processing Time: 2 ms
   Mean Processing Time: 0 ms
   Total Processing Time: 38 ms
   Last Processing Time: 1 ms
   Delta Processing Time: 0 ms
   Load Avg: 0.00, 0.00, 0.00
   Reset Statistics Date: 2014-02-27 17:59:46
   First Exchange Date: 2014-02-27 17:59:47
   Last Exchange Completed Date: 2014-02-27 18:03:22

Definition
<?xml version="1.0" encoding="UTF-8" standalone="yes"?>
```

```
<route customId="true" id="CamelRoute-timerToLog"
  xmlns="http://camel.apache.org/schema/spring">
    <from uri="timer:foo?period=5000"/>
    <setBody id="setBody8">
        <method ref="helloBean" method="hello"></method>
    </setBody>
    <log message="The message contains ${body}" id="log8"/>
    <to uri="mock:result" id="to8"/>
</route>
```

```
karaf@root() >
```

The preceding invocation shows the output generated when our sample Camel application's route is displayed.

How it works...

Apache Camel provides mechanisms to track route statistics; the `route-info` command connects to these facilities to provide route information. Note the appending of `8` to various IDs in the route definition—this is generated by Camel to help differentiate different components and avoid name collisions. The original route definitions will not carry this value.

See also

▸ The *Starting, stopping, suspending, and resuming routes in Karaf* recipe

Starting, stopping, suspending, and resuming routes in Karaf

Apache Camel provides users with fine-grained control of routes deployed inside a Camel Context, and as such, has provided Karaf with access to these controls. These management facilities are separate from OSGi's life cycle model, allowing users to select small portions of the Camel code that is currently being executed to start, stop, suspend, and resume operations.

Getting ready

Follow the instructions in the *Listing Camel Contexts in Karaf* recipe's *Getting ready* section for this recipe.

How to do it...

Managing Camel routes in Karaf is easy, and requires you to become familiar with four commands, which are as follows:

- ▶ `camel:route-start routeName`: This command is used to start a route
- ▶ `camel:route-stop routeName`: This command is used to stop a route
- ▶ `camel:route-suspend routeName`: This command is used to suspend a route
- ▶ `camel:route-resume routeName`: This command is used to resume a suspended route

To make these commands clear, let's review how to use them with the supplied sample Camel application from the *Listing Camel Contexts in Karaf* recipe.

In the following invocation, we list all the Camel routes deployed in Karaf and then issue a stop order upon `CamelRoute-timerToLog` (our sample Camel application). We can observe that it changes the status of the route from `Started` to `Stopped`. This can be done using the following commands:

```
karaf@root()> camel:route-list

  Context                Route                 Status

  -------                -----                 ------

  CamelCommandContext    CamelRoute-timerToLog Started
karaf@root()> camel:route-stop CamelRoute-timerToLog
karaf@root()> camel:route-list

  Context                Route                 Status

  -------                -----                 ------

  CamelCommandContext    CamelRoute-timerToLog Stopped
```

We can then issue the `route-start` command to return the route to the `Started` state, as shown in the following command snippet:

```
karaf@root()> camel:route-start CamelRoute-timerToLog
karaf@root()> camel:route-list

  Context                Route                 Status

  -------                -----                 ------

  CamelCommandContext    CamelRoute-timerToLog Started
```

We can now suspend the route via the `route-suspend` command and confirm that the named route enters the `Suspended` state, as shown in the following command snippet:

```
karaf@root()> camel:route-suspend CamelRoute-timerToLog
karaf@root()> camel:route-list
  Context              Route                  Status
  -------              -----                  ------

  CamelCommandContext  CamelRoute-timerToLog  Suspended
```

Finally, we can issue the `route-resume` command to return the suspended route to the `Started` state, as shown in the following command snippet:

```
karaf@root()> camel:route-resume CamelRoute-timerToLog
karaf@root()> camel:route-list
  Context              Route                  Status
  -------              -----                  ------

  CamelCommandContext  CamelRoute-timerToLog  Started
karaf@root()>
```

How it works...

The Camel route management commands are working from the point of view of the Camel Context, independently of the OSGi life cycle. During the execution of the commands, the host bundle's OSGi status is unaffected. This provides users with a fine-grained management approach, allowing a host bundle to remain running with its context(s), only manipulating one or more routes.

See also

▸   The *Starting and stopping Camel Contexts in Karaf* recipe

Listing endpoints in Karaf

Apache Camel users use endpoints to denote URIs from which events and information come from or go to. In Karaf, the `endpoint-list` command has been provided to help simplify tracking these URIs.

Getting ready

Follow the instructions in the *Listing Camel Contexts in Karaf* recipe's *Getting ready* section for this recipe.

How to do it...

Use the `camel:endpoint-list` command to list all endpoints in Karaf (use the `camel:endpoint-list context-name` command if you want to restrict output to one context's routes). This is shown in the following command:

```
karaf@root()> camel:endpoint-list
  Context              Uri                    Status
  -------              ---                    ------
  CamelCommandContext  mock://result          Started
  CamelCommandContext  timer://foo?period=5000  Started
```

In the preceding invocation, all endpoints found in Karaf are displayed (in this example, the endpoints were set in Blueprint—see the recipe's source code for details).

How it works...

When the endpoint list command is executed, all routes in every Camel Context are scanned and listed to Karaf's console.

See also

▶ The *Creating our own custom Karaf command using a Maven archetype* recipe of *Chapter 1, Apache Karaf for System Builders*

Making a pure Java-based Camel Router for deployment in Karaf

Developing our first Camel Router for deployment in Karaf doesn't necessarily require using a handful of frameworks and libraries. In this recipe, we'll make a Camel router using pure Java code with just a sprinkling of OSGi and Camel libraries.

Getting ready

The ingredients of this recipe include the Apache Karaf distribution kit, access to JDK, Maven, and a source code editor. The sample code for this recipe is available at `https://github.com/jgoodyear/ApacheKarafCookbook/tree/master/chapter2/chapter2-recipe3`. Follow the instructions in the *Installing Apache Camel modules into Apache Karaf* recipe to provide the base requirements to operate the sample code.

How to do it...

1. The first step is creating a Maven-based project. A `pom.xml` file containing the essential Maven coordinate information and bundle packaging directive will suffice.

2. The next step is adding Apache Camel and OSGi dependencies to the POM file. We need to add the `camel-core` and `org.osgi.core` artifacts' dependencies to the POM file. This is described in the following code:

```
<dependencies>
    <dependency>
        <groupId>org.apache.camel</groupId>
        <artifactId>camel-core</artifactId>
        <version>${camel.version}</version>
    </dependency>
    <dependency>
        <groupId>org.osgi</groupId>
        <artifactId>org.osgi.core</artifactId>
        <version>${osgi.version}</version>
        <scope>provided</scope>
    </dependency>
</dependencies>
```

For Apache Karaf 3.0.0, we use Camel Version 2.12.2 and OSGi Version 5.0.0.

3. Next, we add our build configuration, as shown in the following code:

```
<build>
    <plugins>
        <plugin>
            <groupId>org.apache.felix</groupId>
            <artifactId>maven-bundle-plugin</artifactId>
            <version>${maven-bundle-
              plugin.version}</version>
            <extensions>true</extensions>
            <configuration>
                <instructions>
                    <Bundle-SymbolicName>
                    ${project.artifactId}
                    </Bundle-SymbolicName>
                    <Bundle-Version>
                    ${project.version}
                    </Bundle-Version>
                    <Bundle-Activator>
                    com.packt.Activator
                    </Bundle-Activator>
```

```
            <Export-Package>
            com.packt*;version=${project.version}
            </Export-Package>
            <Import-Package>*</Import-Package>
        </instructions>
      </configuration>
    </plugin>
  </plugins>
</build>
```

We use `maven-bundle-plugin` to build our bundle, adding the `Bundle-Activator` instruction. When the bundle is deployed into Karaf, the OSGi container will call the start and stop methods contained within the `com.packt.Activator` class.

4. The next step is implementing OSGi BundleActivator. Now that we have established a base project structure, we can implement our Java code. We'll start by creating the `Activator.java` file in the `src/main/java/com/packt` folder.

The `Activator` class we write will implement the BundleActivator interface. The BundleActivator interface implements the methods the OSGi container calls when starting or stopping a bundle. We'll use the bundle's start and stop methods to control the creation of a Camel Context, the addition of a Camel route, and the actual start and stop of the router. For more details on Apache Camel, visit `http://camel.apache.org`. Consider the following code:

```
public void start(BundleContext context) {
    System.out.println("Starting the bundle");
    camelContext = new DefaultCamelContext();
    try {
        camelContext.addRoutes(new MyRouteBuilder());
        camelContext.start();
    }
    catch (Exception ex) {
        // Use logging subsystem in non-sample code.
        System.out.println("Exception occured! " +
          ex.getMessage());
    }
}
```

When our Activator interface is started, we will create a new `CamelContext` object, then attempt to add a `MyRouteBuilder` function (this creates a Camel route), and then start the context and the routes it contains. Consider the following code:

```
public void stop(BundleContext context) {
    System.out.println("Stopping the bundle");
```

```
        if (camelContext != null) {
            try {
                camelContext.stop();
            }
            catch (Exception ex) {
                System.out.println("Exception occurred during
                    stop context.");
            }
        }
    }
```

When our Activator interface is stopped, we first check whether our `CamelContext` object is null and then attempt to call the `stop` function upon it. When the context is stopped, all routes contained within it are also stopped.

5. Next, we implement our Camel Router. Our Camel router is defined in a custom router builder, which we extend from Camel's `RouteBuilder` class. This is shown in the following code:

```
public class MyRouteBuilder extends RouteBuilder {

    public void configure() {

        from("file:src/data?noop=true")
            .choice()
                .when(xpath("/recipe = 'cookie'"))
                    .log("Cookie  message")
                    .to("file:target/messages/cookies")
                .otherwise()
                    .log("Other message")
                    .to("file:target/messages/others");
    }

}
```

The `MyRouteBuilder` class extends the Camel `RouteBuilder` class, which provides the router configuration interface. We add a Camel route definition to the `configure` method using the Java-based DSL.

6. The next step is building and deploying our Camel Router into Karaf. Now that we have implemented our build configuration (POM file), tied it into the OSGi runtime (the `Activator` class), and implemented our Camel Router (the `MyRouteBuilder` class), we can proceed to compile and deploy the code into Karaf. Our first step is to invoke `mvn install`, and then we execute `install -s mvn:com.packt/osgi` (`mvn:groupId/artifactId`) on the Karaf console.

7. As the final step, we're ready to test out our Camel Router! Once our router bundle is installed and active in Karaf, you'll see a `src/data` folder created in the `KARAF_HOME` folder. Our sample router configuration processes XML-based recipe files. When it sees a cookie recipe (`<recipe>cookie</recipe>`), it places a copy of it in the `KARAF_HOME/target/messages/cookies` folder; otherwise, it places that copy in the `KARAF_HOME/target/message/other` folder.

How it works...

Our pure Java-based Camel Router works by taking advantage of OSGi's BundleActivator start and stop interfaces and direct use of the Apache Camel library. When deployed into Karaf, we can visualize the relevant components as shown in the following diagram:

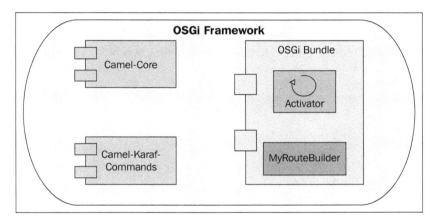

When a bundle is started in an OSGi container, it will have its `Bundle-Activator` class' `start` method called. Our sample project configures this to the `com.packt.Activator` class. We reuse the Activator's start and stop methods to control a Camel Context, which contains a Camel Router as built by our `RouteBuilder` class implementation.

See also

- ▸ The *Creating a Blueprint-based Camel Router for deployment in Karaf* recipe

Creating a Blueprint-based Camel Router for deployment in Karaf

Blueprint provides a dependency injection framework for OSGi. Many users will find that it has similarities with the Spring framework. However, Blueprint has been designed to deal with the dynamic runtime of OSGi where services come and go regularly.

The standard Apache Camel-Karaf feature contains the required Camel-Blueprint libraries for users to immediately start using Blueprint to wire together their routes. In this recipe, we'll build a Camel Router, taking advantage of the Blueprint Inversion of Control framework.

Getting ready

The ingredients of this recipe include the Apache Karaf distribution kit, access to JDK, Maven, and a source code editor. The sample code for this recipe is available at `https://github.com/jgoodyear/ApacheKarafCookbook/tree/master/chapter2/chapter2-recipe4`. Follow the instructions in the *Installing Apache Camel modules into Apache Karaf* recipe's *Getting ready* section to provide the base requirements to operate the sample code.

How to do it...

The Apache Camel community has provided its users with a Maven archetype to generate a Blueprint-based OSGi Camel Router:

1. The first step is generating a Camel Blueprint project with a Maven archetype. We can create our project by invoking the archetype as shown in the following command snippet:

```
mvn archetype:generate \
   -DarchetypeGroupId=org.apache.camel.archetypes \
   -DarchetypeArtifactId=camel-archetype-blueprint \
   -DarchetypeVersion=2.12.2 \
   -DarchetypeRepository=https://repository.apache.org/
      content/groups/snapshots-group
```

During the generation process, you will be asked to supply a `groupId`, `artifactId`, and project `version` value.

This archetype invocation will produce a POM file, Java source for a Hello interface and to implement HelloBean, a Blueprint descriptor XML file, and a sample unit test. The interface and the bean component are purely for sample purposes; in a real-world development scenario, you will delete these artifacts.

2. The next step is building and deploying the project into Karaf. To build the project, we invoke the `mvn install` command. This will populate your local `m2` repository with our bundle. To install the sample, execute the following command on the Karaf console:

```
karaf@root()> bundle:install -s mvn:com.packt/bp/1.0.0-SNAPSHOT
```

In the preceding command, we substitute your Maven coordinates in the format `mvn:{groupId}/{artifactID}/{version}`.

3. The last step is verifying the router function. Once installed and started (using the `start BundleID` command), you will observe the following entries in your Karaf logfile:

```
2014-02-06 10:00:49,074 | INFO  | Local user karaf |
   BlueprintCamelContext            | 85 - org.apache.camel.
   camel-core - 2.12.2 | Total 1 routes, of which 1 is
   started.
2014-02-06 10:00:49,075 | INFO  | Local user karaf |
   BlueprintCamelContext            | 85 -
   org.apache.camel.camel-core - 2.12.2 | Apache Camel
   2.12.2 (CamelContext: blueprintContext) started in 0.357
   seconds
2014-02-06 10:00:50,075 | INFO  | 12 - timer://foo |
   timerToLog       | 85 - org.apache.camel.camel-core -
   2.12.2 | The message
   contains Hi from Camel at 2014-02-06 10:00:50
```

How it works...

When our project bundle is deployed into Karaf, the project's dependencies are resolved, and upon start, the Blueprint descriptor file is processed and objects are instantiated and populated into the Blueprint container. The following diagram highlights the high-level view of the deployed components in Karaf:

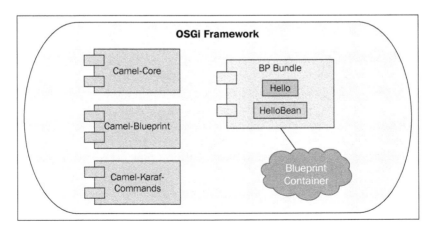

Given a successful instantiation of the services deployed into the Blueprint container, the `CamelContext` object embedded within the container is automatically started.

There's more...

The Apache Camel project also provides a Camel-Spring library in its standard feature deployment. The Spring framework can be made to work in a Karaf environment, but it's generally preferred to use Blueprint or Declarative Services.

See also

▸   The *Adding Configuration Admin to a Blueprint-based Camel Router* recipe

Adding Configuration Admin to a Blueprint-based Camel Router

Blueprint allows us to externalize some configuration elements from our code; we can take this to the next level by taking advantage of the OSGi configuration administration service (generally referred to as Configuration Admin).

The Configuration Admin service provides configuration properties to services in an OSGi container. In Apache Karaf, this functionality is improved by including the Apache Felix File Install directory-based management agent. File Install monitors a directory and can automatically install and start a bundle or make a configuration file update to Configuration Admin.

 Apache Felix File Install provides the magic behind Karaf's `deploy` and `etc` folders, automatically handling files as they are added, removed, or updated.

In this recipe, we'll integrate the Configuration Admin service into our Blueprint-based Camel project.

Getting ready

The ingredients of this recipe include the Apache Karaf distribution kit, access to JDK, Maven, and a source code editor. The sample code for this recipe is available at `https://github.com/jgoodyear/ApacheKarafCookbook/tree/master/chapter2/chapter2-recipe5`. Follow the instructions in the *Installing Apache Camel modules into Apache Karaf* recipe to provide the base requirements to operate the sample code.

How to do it...

The Apache Camel community has provided its users with a Maven archetype to generate a Blueprint-based OSGi Camel Router. We'll use this as a starting point to build our project, adding in the required bits for Configuration Admin support:

1. The first step is generating a Camel Blueprint project with a Maven archetype. We can create our project by invoking the archetype as follows:

```
mvn archetype:generate \
  -DarchetypeGroupId=org.apache.camel.archetypes \
  -DarchetypeArtifactId=camel-archetype-blueprint \
  -DarchetypeVersion=2.12.2 \
  -DarchetypeRepository=https://repository.apache.org/
    content/groups/snapshots-group
```

   During the generation process, you will be asked to supply a `groupId`, `artifactId`, and project `version` value.

   This will produce a POM file, Java source for a Hello interface and to implement HelloBean, a Blueprint descriptor XML file, and a sample unit test.

2. Now that we have a basic project structure, let's modify it to use Configuration Admin. As we're using Blueprint, we only need to modify the descriptor file found in the `src/main/resources/OSGI-INF/blueprint` folder.

   Our first modification is to add an additional namespace for Configuration Admin, as shown in the following code:

```
<blueprint xmlns="http://www.
  osgi.org/xmlns/blueprint/v1.0.0"
        xmlns:xsi="http://www.w3.org/2001/XMLSchema-
          instance"
        xmlns:camel="http://camel.apache.org/
          schema/blueprint"
        xmlns:cm="http://aries.apache.org/blueprint/xmlns/
          blueprint-cm/v1.1.0"
        xsi:schemaLocation="
        http://www.osgi.org/xmlns/blueprint/v1.0.0
        http://www.osgi.org/xmlns/blueprint/
          v1.0.0/blueprint.xsd
        http://aries.apache.org/blueprint/xmlns/blueprint-
          cm/v1.1.0
        http://camel.apache.org/schema/blueprint http:
          //camel.apache.org/schema/blueprint/camel-
          blueprint.xsd">
```

   We'll use the namespace `cm` to access configuration management.

3. The next step is modifying the bean wiring in the Blueprint file to use a Configuration Admin variable. We update the provided `HelloBean` bean to accept a configuration variable, as shown in the following code:

```
<bean id="helloBean" class="com.packt.HelloBean">
        <property name="say" value="${greeting}"/>
</bean>
```

Variables use the syntax `${variable-name}`.

4. Now, we can add our reference to Configuration Admin, as follows:

```
<!-- OSGI blueprint property placeholder -->
<!-- etc/recipe.cfg -->
<cm:property-placeholder persistent-id="recipe"
  update-strategy="reload">

    <!-- list some properties for this test -->
    <cm:default-properties>
        <cm:property name="greeting"
                    value="Hello World"/>
        <cm:property name="result"
                    value="mock:result"/>
    </cm:default-properties>
</cm:property-placeholder>
```

Here, we set the configuration management behavior to reload applications with configuration updates. Then, we provide default values to a pair of variables we'll use in the Blueprint file. We also set a `persistent-id` placeholder that we can use in conjunction with Karaf's `etc` folder to provide dynamic external configuration. In the preceding code, we can create a `recipe.cfg` file in the `etc` folder that contains the `greeting` and `result` properties.

> When writing an Apache Karaf feature descriptor, you can add a configuration file(s) to the list of resources the feature will install.

5. The next step is updating the Camel Context in Blueprint to use a Configuration Admin variable. This can be done as follows:

```
<camelContext id="blueprintContext" trace="false" xmlns="http://
camel.apache.org/schema/blueprint">
    <route id="timerToLog">
        <from uri="timer:foo?period=5000"/>
        <setBody>
```

```
        <method ref="helloBean" method="hello"/>
    </setBody>
    <log message="The message contains ${body}"/>
    <to uri="{{result}}"/>
</route>
</camelContext>
```

Our Camel route contains one direct modification: the introduction of a `{{result}}` variable. Camel uses double curly braces syntax for external variables. The `helloBean` reference remains unchanged. However, its runtime behavior is to now use a default variable from the Blueprint descriptor or a value provided by Configuration Admin.

6. The next step is building and deploying the project into Karaf. To build the project, we invoke the `mvn install` command. This will populate your local m2 repository with our bundle. To install the sample, execute the following command on the Karaf console:

   karaf@root()> bundle:install –s mvn:com.packt/bp-configadmin/1.0.0-SNAPSHOT

   In the preceding command, we substitute your Maven coordinates in the `mvn:{groupId}/{artifactID}/{version}` format.

7. The last step is verifying the router function. Once the router is installed and started, you will observe entries of the following form in your Karaf logfile:

```
2014-02-06 13:36:01,892 | INFO  | Local user karaf |
  BlueprintCamelContext | 85 - org.apache.
  camel.camel-core - 2.12.2 | Total 1 routes, of which
  1 is started.
2014-02-06 13:36:01,892 | INFO  | Local user karaf |
  BlueprintCamelContext | 85 - org.apache.camel.camel-core
  - 2.12.2 | Apache Camel 2.12.2 (CamelCon: blueprint
  Context) started in 0.272 seconds
2014-02-06 13:36:02,891 text| INFO  | 15 - timer://foo |
  timerToLog | 85 - org.apache.camel.camel-
  core - 2.12.2 |   The message contains Hello World at
  2014-02-06 13:36:02
```

Changing variable values requires editing the Blueprint file and refreshing the bundle in Karaf. However, changes to values in the configuration file will be picked up almost instantly.

How it works...

This recipe extends the *Creating a Blueprint-based Camel Router for deployment in Karaf* recipe by introducing Configuration Admin to the design. The following diagram highlights the high-level view of the deployed components in Karaf:

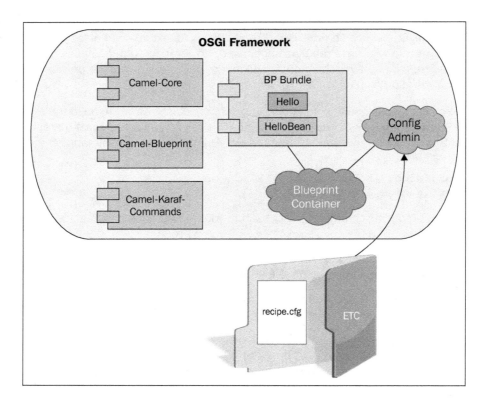

The addition of Configuration Admin to Blueprint exposes the Camel route to external configuration. This external configuration appears as Java properties files in Karaf's `etc` folder.

So, how do we associate the properties file to the Configuration Admin reference in our Blueprint specification? This is accomplished by setting the persistence ID in the Configuration Admin property placeholder's Blueprint definition. In our demo code, we use the persistence ID recipe—in our `etc` folder, we'd use a corresponding file named `recipe.cfg`.

How do we use the property name-value pairs? We include the default name-value pairs in the Blueprint definition. These are automatically overridden by Configuration Admin if values are available. We access their values using single curly braces in beans and double curly braces in Blueprint-defined Camel Contexts.

> ► The *Creating a managed service factory implementation of a Camel Router* recipe

Creating a managed service factory implementation of a Camel Router

In this recipe, we'll introduce the power of the OSGi pattern ManagedServiceFactory interface to Apache Camel smart routers. This pattern will allow us to manage multiple service instances, or in our case, Camel routes, via configuration. In fact, we'll produce a new router instance for each configuration we supply our service factory!

Getting ready

The ingredients of this recipe include the Apache Karaf distribution kit, access to JDK, Maven, and a source code editor. The sample code for this recipe is available at `https://github.com/jgoodyear/ApacheKarafCookbook/tree/master/chapter2/chapter2-recipe6`. Follow the instructions in the *Installing Apache Camel modules into Apache Karaf* recipe to provide the base requirements to operate the sample code.

How to do it...

This recipe will be somewhat more complex than our previous recipes. It is strongly urged that you follow along with the provided example code:

1. First, create a Blueprint-based Camel project using the handy Maven archetype we've used in the previous recipes (see the *Creating a Blueprint-based Camel Router for deployment in Karaf* recipe). We'll use this as a base to build our project, removing and/or modifying resources as required.

2. The next step is adding dependencies to the POM file. We'll edit the POM file, adding dependencies on the OSGi core and compendium, as shown in the following code:

```
<dependency>
    <groupId>org.osgi</groupId>
    <artifactId>org.osgi.core</artifactId>
    <version>${osgi-core-version}</version>
</dependency>
<dependency>
```

```
    <groupId>org.osgi</groupId>
    <artifactId>org.osgi.compendium</artifactId>
    <version>${osgi-compendium-version}</version>
</dependency>
```

For Apache Karaf 3.0.0, we use the OSGi core and compendium version 5.0.0.

3. Now, we prune the generated project structure. We'll remove the prepopulated `blueprint.xml` file, the `main` folder, and the `test` folder.

4. Now, we'll implement our ManagedServiceFactory interface in the `src/main/java` folder. To do this, we'll create a factory class that implements the ManagedServiceFactory interface and plug a dispatcher into this framework, which will handle building and executing of Camel routes. We'll cover the intricacies of these classes in the *How it works...* section of this recipe.

 The OSGi compendium rev 5 ManagedServiceFactory interface can be found at the OSGi Alliance website at `http://www.osgi.org/javadoc/r5/cmpn/org/osgi/service/cm/ManagedServiceFactory.html`.

5. Next, we create a Blueprint file in the `src/main/resources` folder that wires together Configuration Admin, a Camel Context, and our `Factory` class.

```xml
<blueprint xmlns="http://www.osgi.org/
  xmlns/blueprint/v1.0.0"
    xmlns:xsi="http://www.w3.org/2001/XMLSchema-instance"
    xmlns:cm="http://aries.apache.org/blueprint
      /xmlns/blueprint-cm/v1.1.0"
    xmlns:camel="http://camel.apache.org/schema/blueprint"
    xsi:schemaLocation="
    http://www.osgi.org/xmlns/blueprint/v1.0.0
    http://www.osgi.org/xmlns/blueprint/
      v1.0.0/blueprint.xsd
    http://camel.apache.org/schema/blueprint
    http://camel.apache.org/schema/blueprint/camel-
      blueprint.xsd">

  <!-- Setup process Id name for configuration file -->
  <cm:property-placeholder persistent-id="com.packt.
    hellofactory" update-strategy="reload">
    <cm:default-properties>
        <cm:property name="com.packt.hellofactory.pid"
          value="com.packt.hellofactory"/>
    </cm:default-properties>
  </cm:property-placeholder>
```

```
<!-- Create Camel Context -->
<camelContext id="helloContext" xmlns="http:
  //camel.apache.org/schema/blueprint
  " autoStartup="true">
</camelContext>

<!-- Setup Bean, wiring in contexts, and
  configuration data  -->
<bean id="apacheKarafCookbook" class="com.packt.
  HelloFactory" init-method="init" destroy-
  method="destroy">
  <property name="bundleContext" ref="blueprint
    BundleContext"/>
  <property name="configurationPid"        value="${com.
    packt.hellofactory.pid}"/>
  <property name="camelContext" ref="helloContext"/>
</bean>

</blueprint>
```

The Blueprint file in the preceding code contains the general structural elements required; we will cover the details of these entries in the *How it works...* section of this recipe.

6. The next step is building and deploying the router into Karaf. We build and deploy this assembly as a bundle into Karaf and provision it with configuration files in the `etc` folder. The configuration files each take the form of `PID-name.cfg`, with their contents being Java-style properties.

   To build our sample project, execute the `mvn install` command. Deployment will require the following two commands:

   karaf@root()> install -s mvn:commons-lang/commons-lang/2.6

   karaf@root()> install -s mvn:com.packt/msf/1.0.0-SNAPSHOT

7. Our managed service factory implementation of a Camel Router is now ready for use. The last step is creating a configuration for our router instances. Consider a sample configuration of the `etc/com.packt.hellofactory-test1.cfg` file with the following entries:

   ```
   HELLO_GREETING=hello
   HELLO_NAME=Jamie
   ```

   Also, consider the `etc/com.packt.hellofactory-test2.cfg` file with the following entries:

   ```
   HELLO_GREETING=hi
   HELLO_NAME=Laura
   ```

On running appropriate commands, these sample configurations will produce the following output:

```
karaf@root()> camel:route-list
  Context          Route            Status
  -------          -----            ------
  helloContext     Hello Jamie      Started
  helloContext     Hello Laura      Started
karaf@root()> log:display
hello Jamie
hi Laura
```

Now that we've reviewed a high-level process to build a managed service factory implementation of a Camel Router, let's dive deep into how and why this works.

How it works...

Bundles implementing the ManagedServiceFactory interface connect into the Configuration Admin service's capability to build and configure instances of the bundle. In our sample project, we use this functionality to create new route instances based upon the provided configurations.

Each service (route) instance is represented by a factory configuration called PID. When a given PID is updated, Configuration Admin will call the factory's updated method. If a new PID is passed in, then a new instance is created; if the PID exists, then its configuration is updated. The following diagram highlights the high-level view of the deployed components in Karaf:

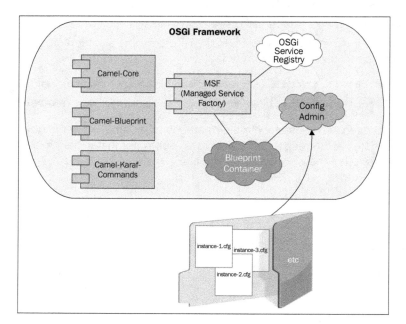

When we deploy the Camel components and the sample project into Karaf, we'll wire the MSF bundle and Configuration Admin via Blueprint. Under the hood, the MSF bundle is composed of three classes: `HelloConstants`, `HelloDispatcher`, and `HelloFactory`.

The `HelloFactory` class implements the ManagedServiceFactory interface. In our sample project, we override the `getName()`, `updated(String pid, Dictionary dict)`, and `deleted(String pid)` methods. We then provide the initialization and destruction methods to clean up after our routers. Finally, we provide setters to wire in our PID, `bundleContext`, and `camelContext` objects. Let's take a closer look at the core interface implementation in the `HelloFactory` class. Consider the following code:

```
@Override
public String getName() {
    return configurationPid;
}
```

We override the `getName()` method, returning our configuration PID, as shown in the preceding code. Consider the following code:

```
@Override
public void updated(String pid, Dictionary dict)
        throws ConfigurationException {
        log.info("updated " + pid + " with " + dict.toString());
        HelloDispatcher engine = null;

        if (dispatchEngines.containsKey(pid)) {
            engine = dispatchEngines.get(pid);

            if (engine != null) {
                destroyEngine(engine);
            }
            dispatchEngines.remove(pid);
        }
```

In the `updated` method in the preceding code, we begin by setting up our `HelloDispatcher` engine. A map of `<PID, HelloDispatcher>` is maintained, which we use to internally track our Camel Routers. If we have a PID entry for the dispatcher, then we safely destroy the existing engine so that a new one can be constructed. Now, consider the following code:

```
    //Verify dictionary contents before applying them to Hello
if (dict.get(HelloConstants.HELLO_GREETING) != null &&
  !StringUtils.isEmpty(dict.get(
  HelloConstants.HELLO_GREETING).toString())) {
  log.info("HELLO_GREETING set to " +
    dict.get(HelloConstants.HELLO_GREETING));
```

```
    } else {
        throw new IllegalArgumentException("Missing HELLO_GREETING");
    }

    if (dict.get(HelloConstants.HELLO_NAME) != null &&
        !StringUtils.isEmpty(dict.get(HelloConstants.HELLO_NAME).
        toString())) {
        log.info("HELLO_NAME set to " +
            dict.get(HelloConstants.HELLO_NAME));
    } else {
        throw new IllegalArgumentException("Missing HELLO_NAME");
    }
```

We then verify the presence of the required configuration entries in the properties dictionary provided by Configuration Admin. These dictionaries are constructed when configuration files are placed in Karaf's etc folder. Have a look at the following code:

```
    //Configuration was verified above, now create engine.
    engine = new HelloDispatcher();
    engine.setCamelContext(camelContext);
    engine.setGreeting(dict.get(HelloConstants.HELLO_GREETING).
        toString());
    engine.setName(dict.get(HelloConstants.HELLO_NAME).toString());

    dispatchEngines.put(pid, engine);
    log.debug("Start the engine...");
    if (engine == null) {
        log.debug("Engine was null, check configuration.");
    }
        engine.start();
    }
```

The updated method then creates and configures a new HelloDispatcher object and then starts operating it. Now, consider the following code:

```
    @Override
    public void deleted(String pid) {
        if (dispatchEngines.containsKey(pid)) {
            HelloDispatcher engine = dispatchEngines.get(pid);

            if (engine != null) {
                destroyEngine(engine);
            }

            dispatchEngines.remove(pid);
        }
        log.info("deleted " + pid);
    }
```

The `deleted` method safely cleans up all currently executing `HelloDispatcher` objects (our routers) when a PID is removed.

To integrate the `HelloFactory` object into the container, we included the `init` and `destroy` methods. The `init` call is used to register the ManagedServiceFactory interface with the register service and establish a ServiceTracker wiring (which is a utility class that simplifies working with service references from the service registry) between the ManagedServiceFactory interface bundle and the Configuration Admin service. The `destroy` call's main function is to clean up by unregistering the bundle safely from the registerService and close its `ServiceTracker` object.

The `HelloDispatcher` object implements our Camel Router. We provide start and stop methods that handle integration of our Camel route instance into an existing Camel Context. We also provide methods to set our parameters and specify the Camel Context we want to deploy our route into. Finally, we provide a mechanism from which our Camel route will be constructed. Let's take a closer look at the route builder in the `HelloDispatcher` object. This is shown in the following code:

```
protected RouteBuilder buildHelloRouter() throws Exception {

    return new RouteBuilder() {

        @Override
        public void configure() throws Exception {

        from("timer://helloTimer?fixedRate=true&period=10000").
    routeId("Hello " + name).
    log(greeting + " " + name);
        }
    };
```

The preceding route uses a timer component to generate an event every 10 seconds and then sends a message to a log. The configuration elements provide a `routeId` based on the name parameter, and the log message contains the `greeting` and `name` parameters.

Finally, `HelloConstants` is a utility class that provides our configuration parameter name constants.

The wiring of the ManagedServiceFactory bundle to Configuration Admin happens inside our Blueprint XML file. Let's take a closer look at the three important sections of this descriptor file, which are as follows:

```
<cm:property-placeholder
  persistent-id="com.packt.hellofactory"
  update-strategy="reload">
  <cm:default-properties>
```

```
    <cm:property
      name="com.packt.hellofactory.pid"
      value="com.packt.hellofactory"/>
  </cm:default-properties>
</cm:property-placeholder>
```

The `cm` namespace is used to set up configuration management. Consider the following code:

```
<camelContext id="helloContext"
  xmlns="http://camel.apache.org/schema/blueprint"
  autoStartup="true">
</camelContext>
```

Our Camel Context is created as our route container. This context will be shared by each route instance we introduce to the system. Consider the following code:

```
<bean id="apacheKarafCookbook" class="com.packt.HelloFactory"
  init-method="init" destroy-method="destroy">
  <property name="bundleContext"
    ref="blueprintBundleContext"/>
  <property name="configurationPid"
    value="${com.packt.hellofactory.pid}"/>
  <property name="camelContext" ref="helloContext"/>
</bean>
```

Finally, we wire together our `HelloFactory` object to the Blueprint context, Configuration Admin services, and to our shared Camel Context. We also wire in our factory's `init` and `destroy` methods. The following diagram illustrates the three instances of the Camel route, each producing a different message based upon their configuration:

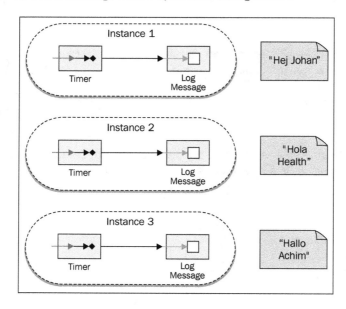

Once our ManagedServiceFactory bundle, Blueprint file, and Configuration Admin services are wired together and started, it will now accept configurations and instantiate routes. In Karaf, you can add configuration files of the `pid-name.cfg` format to the `etc` folder. For example, in our sample project, our configuration files are named `com.packt.hellofactory-test1.cfg`, `com.packt.hellofactory-test2.cfg`, and so on.

See also

 ▸ For more information on ActiveMQ and CXF, read *Chapter 3, Deploying a Message Broker with Apache ActiveMQ,* and *Chapter 4, Hosting a Web Server with Pax Web*

3
Deploying a Message Broker with Apache ActiveMQ

In this chapter, we will cover the following recipes:

- ► Installing Apache ActiveMQ modules into Apache Karaf
- ► Using the ActiveMQ query command
- ► Using the ActiveMQ list command
- ► Using the ActiveMQ dstat command
- ► Using the ActiveMQ purge command
- ► Using the JMS connection factory command
- ► Using the JMS send command
- ► Using the JMS browse command
- ► Configuring and deploying a master/slave broker with Apache Karaf
- ► Configuring and deploying a Network of Brokers with Apache Karaf

Introduction

ActiveMQ is a common framework used in enterprise software solutions to implement JMS messaging via TCP, SSL, HTTP(s), VM, and STOMP, which is one of the many ways to allow inter-bundle communications. ActiveMQ provides a lot of benefits, from handling data bursts to providing failover and scaling. In this chapter, we will cover the why and how of implementing the embedded ActiveMQ broker in a Karaf environment. We will also look at how to administer the broker under different deployment topologies.

Before we begin, we should discuss when to use the embedded broker deployment strategy versus standalone. This is just as important as learning how, since an embedded broker can bring the system to its knees just as fast as bad architecture. In many cases, the initial thought is embedding ActiveMQ is easier to deploy and will make messaging faster. While there is some truth to this, in most cases, the benefit does not outweigh the cost. Allowing ActiveMQ to share the JVM resources will cause contention in higher load systems. Also, if there is an issue with ActiveMQ that causes it to fail, it will more than likely have a direct impact on the Karaf instance, which will in turn cause the application to fail, or vice versa. Embedded ActiveMQ brings a lot of value to enterprise applications; just make sure it is used for the right purposes.

A common embedded solution is for geographically separated client/server applications. One example is the client application resides in a Karaf instance across a WAN and intermittent outages can occur. Then, it might be a good idea to have a local embedded ActiveMQ to allow the client to continue functioning while the broker re-establishes communications with the server. The following diagram demonstrates this:

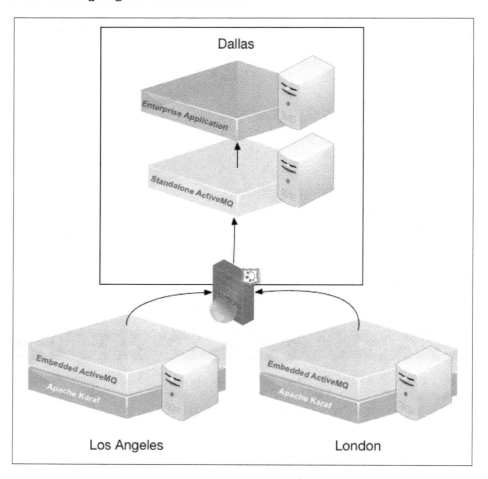

Give a lot of thought as to whether or not an embedded broker is needed.

Installing Apache ActiveMQ modules into Apache Karaf

Installing an ActiveMQ broker into a Karaf instance requires very little effort. This recipe will show you how easy it is to get ActiveMQ embedded and running. In order to install the ActiveMQ broker in Karaf, we first need to add the feature URL.

How to do it...

Out of the box, Karaf does not come with ActiveMQ installed. But do not fret, for Karaf makes it very easy to install it. The steps are as follows:

1. First we need to install the XML features by adding the repo for the version we expect to use. This can be done using the following command:

    ```
    feature:repo-add activemq <version>
    ```

    The following screenshot shows us how to start:

    ```
    Apache Karaf (3.0.0)

    Hit '<tab>' for a list of available commands
    and '[cmd] --help' for help on a specific command.
    Hit '<ctrl-d>' or type 'system:shutdown' or 'logout' to shutdown Karaf.

    karaf@root()> feature:repo-add activemq 5.9.0
    Adding feature url mvn:org.apache.activemq/activemq-karaf/5.9.0/xml/features
    karaf@root()>
    ```

2. Now that we have the features available, we can list them using the following command:

    ```
    feature:list | grep activemq
    ```

The screenshot should look like the following:

```
karaf@root()> feature:list | grep activemq
activemq-client              | 5.9.0        |            |  activemq-5.9.0
activemq                     | 5.9.0        |            |  activemq-5.9.0
activemq-broker-noweb        | 5.9.0        |            |  activemq-5.9.0
activemq-broker              | 5.9.0        |            |  activemq-5.9.0
activemq-camel               | 5.9.0        |            |  activemq-5.9.0
activemq-web-console         | 5.9.0        |            |  activemq-5.9.0
activemq-blueprint           | 5.9.0        |            |  activemq-5.9.0
```

There are several options for installing only what we need. If your application is connecting to any ActiveMQ instance, then all you need in the OSGi environment is the client APIs for connecting. Simply install the `activemq-client` feature; this provides the necessary classes for instantiating a connection and sending or receiving messages. You can do this using the following command:

`feature:install activemq-client`

But, since we are embedding a broker in the Karaf instance, we need to run the following command:

`feature:install activemq-broker`

Notice in the following screenshot that the `activemq-client`, `activemq`, `activemq-broker`, and `activemq-web-console` features have been installed. This is indicated by 'X' in the third column.

```
karaf@root()> feature:list | grep activemq
activemq-client              | 5.9.0        | x          |  activemq-5.9.0
activemq                     | 5.9.0        | x          |  activemq-5.9.0
activemq-broker-noweb        | 5.9.0        |            |  activemq-5.9.0
activemq-broker              | 5.9.0        | x          |  activemq-5.9.0
activemq-camel               | 5.9.0        |            |  activemq-5.9.0
activemq-web-console         | 5.9.0        | x          |  activemq-5.9.0
activemq-blueprint           | 5.9.0        |            |  activemq-5.9.0
```

How it works...

If we install the ActiveMQ broker, the instantiation is configured in the file `etc/org.apache.activemq.server-default.cfg`. This file is read at the time the embedded broker is started and will use the referenced `activemq.xml` file to define how the ActiveMQ broker will be initialized. Various other JVM parameters are also configured in this file. The default configuration file will look like the following code:

```
broker-name=amq-broker
data=${karaf.data}/${broker-name}
config=${karaf.base}/etc/activemq.xml
```

A big benefit to having the configuration settings in the `.cfg` file is that any changes to the values in the configuration file will cause the broker to stop and restart, thereby incorporating the changes. Changes to the `activemq.xml` file require a manual stop and start of the broker. A good update to the configuration file is to add memory settings such as the following:

```
jvmMemory=50
storage=100gb
tempStorage=10gb
```

Then, add the properties in the `activemq.xml` file using the following code:

```
<memoryUsage>
    <memoryUsage percentOfJvmHeap="${jvmMemory}"/>
</memoryUsage>
<storeUsage>
    <storeUsage limit="${storage}"/>
</storeUsage>
<tempUsage>
    <tempUsage limit="${tempStorage}"/>
</tempUsage>
```

The more configurations you can set as properties, the easier it is to administer the runtime.

Using the ActiveMQ query command

A convenient feature of an embedded ActiveMQ is the ability to run commands against the broker for monitoring broker activity. The `query` command provides basic information about the broker.

Getting ready

In order to get started, we need to get the `activemq-broker` feature installed as outlined in the previous recipe. Once that is installed, we can use the following command:

`activemq`

After typing the command, press the *Tab* key. This will list out all the available ActiveMQ commands as shown in the following screenshot:

```
karaf@root()> activemq:
activemq:browse     activemq:bstat      activemq:dstat      activemq:list
activemq:purge      activemq:query
```

Now, just running the command is pretty boring; there is not much to see in an empty broker.

Let's get some data loaded so that we can see what is happening.

How to do it...

Now, let's start sending some data through the broker in order to make this more entertaining and realistic. This recipe has some helper classes we can use to load the broker with data:

1. Run the `mvn clean install` command in the example code under the *Installing Apache ActiveMQ modules into Apache Karaf* recipe. Then, you can run the Publisher against the embedded ActiveMQ. If no defaults have been changed from the `activemq.xml` file, then the defaults in the publisher code will work. We can run the publisher using the following command:

   ```
   java -cp target/openwire-example-0.1-SNAPSHOT.jar
     example.Publisher
   ```

   This will send 10001 messages to the broker including the shutdown message.

2. Now that we can see we have 10001 messages waiting in the test queue, let's go ahead and consume them using our `Listener` as shown in the following command:

   ```
   java -cp target/openwire-example-0.1-SNAPSHOT.jar
     example.Listener
   ```

   This will create a consumer on the queue and pull the messages off.

3. It is nice to be able to see a queue at a glance, but what if we need to see more information about the queue? In many cases, we need to see how much memory a queue is consuming, or the consumer count, or any number of parameters. A good way is to use the query command as follows:

   ```
   activemq:query -QQueue=test
   ```

This will list out the properties of a queue much like you might find in JConsole, which is a JMX monitoring tool provided by Java. This is a nice way to be able to monitor queue properties using scripts, or for continuous integration tests to monitor results. We can look at a few of the properties that are often looked at in JConsole when debugging. We can see that the depth of the queue is 10001. This is found under the **QueueSize** parameter in JConsole. But if we want to see a parameter that tells us a little more about the health of the queue, let's look at the **MemoryPercentageUsage** parameter.

We can see in JConsole that the value is currently **3**, as shown in the following screenshot:

An easier way to see these parameters is to use the Karaf console command `activemq:query`. This saves us from having to open JConsole and enter the long remote process URL: `service:jmx:rmi://localhost:44444/jndi/rmi://localhost:1099/karaf-root`.

Then, we can type in the username and password. Alternatively, we can simply use the `activemq:query -QQueue=<queue_name>` command to query the queue statistics using JMX. The following screenshot shows what will be displayed in the console:

```
karaf@root()> activemq:query -QQueue=test
AverageMessageSize = 1296.973902609739
UseCache = true
MemoryPercentUsage = 3
Name = test
BlockedProducerWarningInterval = 30000
MaxMessageSize = 1297
MemoryUsagePortion = 1.0
CacheEnabled = true
destinationType = Queue
BlockedSends = 0
EnqueueCount = 10001
Options =
TotalBlockedTime = 0
MinMessageSize = 1036
PrioritizedMessages = false
Subscriptions = []
DLQ = false
CursorPercentUsage = 3
MessageGroupType = cached
CursorMemoryUsage = 12971036
AlwaysRetroactive = false
AverageEnqueueTime = 0.0
DispatchCount = 0
AverageBlockedTime = 0.0
destinationName = test
MemoryLimit = 333971456
MaxProducersToAudit = 1024
ProducerFlowControl = true
QueueSize = 10001
ConsumerCount = 0
MaxEnqueueTime = 0
MessageGroups = {}
CursorFull = false
MaxAuditDepth = 2048
InFlightCount = 0
MemoryUsageByteCount = 12971036
ExpiredCount = 0
brokerName = amq-broker
DequeueCount = 0
MaxPageSize = 200
MinEnqueueTime = 0
ProducerCount = 0
type = Broker
```

Since we are command-line gurus, we can use the | command to grep for information we are interested in. This is shown in the following screenshot:

```
karaf@root()> activemq:query -QQueue=test | grep Memory
MemoryPercentUsage = 3
MemoryUsagePortion = 1.0
CursorMemoryUsage = 12971036
MemoryLimit = 333971456
MemoryUsageByteCount = 12971036
```

Notice the statistics for **MemoryPercentUsage** (shown in the previous screenshot) are in there, along with all the other memory-based properties. Another useful filter is Count. This will show all the counts for enqueue, dequeue, inflight, producer, consumer, and so on.

The query command has many options. These can be seen by using the --help parameter as follows:

```
activemq:query --help
```

How it works...

The **QueueSize** column shows the number of messages that are currently in the queue waiting to be consumed. The **Dequeue** column is the total number of messages that have been consumed by a listener. If we were to run the publisher code again, we would see that the queue size increased again to 10001 but the **Dequeue** value has not moved, indicating we have 10001 messages in the queue.

Most of the ActiveMQ commands are provided via MBeans or JMX. Many of the same functions are available through JConsole.

See also

▶ The *Using the ActiveMQ list command* recipe
▶ The *Using the ActiveMQ dstat command* recipe

Using the ActiveMQ list command

The `list` command can be used to list out the brokers currently running inside the Karaf container.

Getting ready

In order to get started, we need to get the `activemq-broker` feature installed. Reference the `activemq:query` command, as shown in the following screenshot:

```
karaf@root()> activemq:
activemq:browse      activemq:bstat      activemq:dstat      activemq:list
activemq:purge       activemq:query
```

How to do it...

To list out all brokers currently running embedded inside this instance of Karaf, we can simply run the following command:

```
karaf@root()> activemq:list
```

This will list out the embedded broker names as follows:

```
brokerName = amq-broker
```

How it works...

This `activemq` command will invoke the `JmxMBeansUtil.getAllBrokers` class on the JMX connection and retrieve the name of any broker currently running.

See also

- ▸ The *Using the ActiveMQ query command* recipe
- ▸ The *Using the ActiveMQ dstat command* recipe

Using the ActiveMQ dstat command

The dstat command is a convenient way to see queue message statistics at a glance. It will list out the queues with queue size, the number of producers and consumers, the number of messages enqueued and dequeued, and the percentage of memory used.

Getting ready

In order to get started, we need to get the activemq-broker feature installed.

 If you have run any previous recipes, a good way to get a clean environment is to stop Karaf, delete the data directory, and restart. This will clean up any data from the previous runs. Remember to reinstall the activemq-broker feature after restarting.

As an example, let's run the activemq:dstat command, as shown in the following screenshot.

```
karaf@root()> activemq:dstat
Name                                Queue Size  Producer #  Consumer #  Enqueue #  Dequeue #  Memory %
ActiveMQ.Advisory.MasterBroker              0           0           0          1          0         0
karaf@root()> █
```

Not very impressive. Without data, these commands can be pretty boring. In the previous screenshot, we can see that we have one queue defined at this moment with no message, no producers, and no consumers. So, let's get some data loaded to see what is happening.

How to do it...

We need to start sending some data through the brokers in order to make this more entertaining and realistic. This recipe has some helper classes we can use to load the broker with data. This can be done as follows:

1. Run the mvn clean install command in the example code under the *Installing Apache ActiveMQ modules into Apache Karaf* recipe. Then, you can run the publisher against the embedded ActiveMQ.

2. If no defaults have been changed from the activemq.xml file, then the defaults in the publisher code will work. We can run the publisher using the following command:

   ```
   java -cp target/openwire-example-0.1-SNAPSHOT.jar
     example.Publisher
   ```

This will send 10001 messages to the broker. Now we can look at the `dstat` broker and see if there are any changes. The following screenshot shows the result from the `dstat` broker:

Name	Queue Size	Producer #	Consumer #	Enqueue #	Dequeue #	Memory %
ActiveMQ.Advisory.Producer.Queue.test	0	0	0	2	0	0
ActiveMQ.Advisory.MasterBroker	0	0	0	1	0	0
test	10001	0	0	10001	0	3
ActiveMQ.Advisory.Connection	0	0	0	2	0	0

Using the `dstat` command, we can see that the publisher has put 10001 messages on the test queue and that several advisory messages have been enqueued too.

> Advisory messages are specific ActiveMQ messages that are meant to inform you of an event.

3. Now that we can see we have 10001 messages waiting in the test queue, let's go ahead and consume them using our listener, using the following command:

```
java -cp target/openwire-example-0.1-SNAPSHOT.jar
    example.Listener
```

This will create a consumer on the queue and pull the messages off. We can see through the `dstat` command what is happening on our queue. This is displayed in the following screenshot:

Name	Queue Size	Producer #	Consumer #	Enqueue #	Dequeue #	Memory %
ActiveMQ.Advisory.Producer.Queue.test	0	0	0	2	0	0
ActiveMQ.Advisory.MasterBroker	0	0	0	1	0	0
ActiveMQ.Advisory.Consumer.Queue.test	0	0	0	2	0	0
test	0	0	0	10001	10001	0
ActiveMQ.Advisory.Connection	0	0	0	4	0	0

How it works...

The `dstat` command uses the ServerInvocationHandler interface to create an instance of the QueueViewMBean interface or the TopicViewMBean interface using the JMX connection. These provide statistics on the queues or topics. The stats are simply listed out to the console in order to provide a high level snapshot of the queues/topics.

See also

- ▸ The *Using the ActiveMQ purge command* recipe
- ▸ The *Using the ActiveMQ query command* recipe

Using the ActiveMQ purge command

A useful command for clearing data is the `purge` command. This can be used in conjunction with wildcards to clear out large numbers of queues.

Getting ready

Have the `activemq-broker` feature installed in a similar way as done in the *Using the ActiveMQ dstat command* recipe.

How to do it...

Before we can purge the data, we first need to load some data. We can load data using the example code provided in the earlier recipes. The steps are as follows:

1. We can run the publisher again using the following command:

   ```
   java -cp target/openwire-example-0.1-SNAPSHOT.jar
     example.Publisher
   ```

2. Using the `dstat` command from the earlier recipe, we can see in the following screenshot that we loaded 10001 messages into the test queue of our embedded broker:

Name	Queue Size	Producer #	Consumer #	Enqueue #	Dequeue #	Memory %
ActiveMQ.Advisory.Producer.Queue.test	0	0	0	2	0	0
ActiveMQ.Advisory.MasterBroker	0	0	0	1	0	0
test	10001	0	0	10001	0	3
ActiveMQ.Advisory.Connection	0	0	0	2	0	0

   The `purge` command will remove data from any number of queues using wildcards and SQL92 syntax.

3. Now, add messages to the queue using the publisher we saw in the *Installing Apache ActiveMQ modules into Apache Karaf* recipe. Run it a couple of times for fun. Now, query the queue using the following command to see how many messages we have:

   ```
   activemq:query -QQueue=* --view EnqueueCount
   ```

    Using the * character for the queue name will return the `EnqueueCount` value for all queues, but in this example, we only have the test queue anyway.

We can see that after two runs we have **20002** as the **EnqueueCount** value, as shown in the following screenshot:

```
karaf@root()> activemq:query -QQueue=* --view EnqueueCount
EnqueueCount = 20002
```

4. We can see thousands of messages now in the queue after running the publisher a couple of times. Now run the following `purge` command against the test queue:

```
activemq:purge test
```

```
karaf@root()> activemq:purge test
INFO: Purging all messages in queue: test
```

The `purge` command removes all messages in the given queue. Let's rerun the following `query` command to see if the queues were cleared out:

```
activemq:query -QQueue=* --view EnqueueCount
```

How it works...

The `PurgeCommand` class in the ActiveMQ code base is used to purge messages in the selected queue. If no queue is defined, as shown in the following command, it will purge all messages from all queues:

```
activemq:purge
```

We can use both an AMQ-specific language, which looks like `JMSPriority>2,MyHeader='Foo'`, or we can use the SQL-92 syntax `(JMSPriority>2) AND (MyHeader='Foo')` to select specific messages for deletion.

See also

▸ The *Using the ActiveMQ list command* recipe
▸ The *Using the ActiveMQ query command* recipe

Using the JMS connection factory commands

Now that we have an embedded broker and have looked at some of the commands for viewing the broker properties and statistics, let's look at how to interact with the broker using JMS commands. In this recipe, we will look at the command for creating and interacting with the broker by creating a connection factory.

Getting ready

In order for us to control the connection factory and send messages to the embedded broker, first we need to install the required commands using the following JMS feature command:

```
feature:install jms
```

Using the *Tab* key, we will see a list of the JMS commands available for creating, sending, and browsing messages as well as creating connection factories. These commands are listed in the following screenshot:

First, let's create a connection factory for our embedded broker. We do this using the `jms:create` command.

 Be sure to reference the `--help` command for required and optional parameters.

How to do it...

Let's create a connection factory first so that we can mess around with sending messages. All that is needed to create a connection factory is the following command:

```
jms:create [options] name
```

So, for this example, a command like the following will work to make a connection of type `-t activemq` to the URL `-u tcp://localhost:61616`:

```
jms:create -t activemq --url tcp://localhost:61616 cookbook
```

How it works...

This will create a connection factory using the ActiveMQConnectionFactory as defined by the `-t` option (the other option is WebsphereMQ). We can verify that our factory was indeed set up by performing a `la` command from the command line. Your last entry should look something like the following command-line output:

```
51 | Active   |  80 | 0.0.0 | connectionfactory-cookbook.xml
```

Notice that the pattern for the XML file naming is `connectionfactory-<name>.xml`. In the case of our example, we used the name 'cookbook'. If this is not the last entry, or you do not see it, try using the `la | grep cookbook` command.

A file called `connectionfactory-cookbook.xml` was created in the `deploy` directory of the Karaf instance, which is shown in the following code. This file is a Blueprint XML file that will instantiate the connection factory, pooled connection factory, the resource manager, and the transaction manager.

```xml
<?xml version="1.0" encoding="UTF-8"?>
<blueprint xmlns="http://www.osgi.org/xmlns/blueprint/v1.0.0">

    <bean id="activemqConnectionFactory"
      class="org.apache.activemq.ActiveMQConnectionFactory">
        <property name="brokerURL" value="tcp://localhost:61616"
          />
    </bean>

    <bean id="pooledConnectionFactory"
      class="org.apache.activemq.pool.PooledConnectionFactory">
        <property name="maxConnections" value="8" />
        <property name="connectionFactory"
          ref="activemqConnectionFactory" />
    </bean>

    <bean id="resourceManager" class="
      org.apache.activemq.pool.ActiveMQResourceManager" init-
      method="recoverResource">
        <property name="transactionManager"
          ref="transactionManager" />
        <property name="connectionFactory"
          ref="activemqConnectionFactory" />
        <property name="resourceName" value="activemq.localhost"
          />
    </bean>

    <reference id="transactionManager" interface="javax.transaction.
TransactionManager" />

    <service ref="pooledConnectionFactory"
      interface="javax.jms.ConnectionFactory">
        <service-properties>
```

```
            <entry key="name" value="cookbook" />
            <entry key="osgi.jndi.service.name"
              value="/jms/cookbook" />
        </service-properties>
      </service>

    </blueprint>
```

The pooled connection factory is added to the services with a JNDI name of `jms/cookbook`. The important piece of information to note here is the `-u` option that is used to define the URL for the connection based on which the connection pool is also created. This is an important input from a system resource management perspective.

See also

▸ The *Using the JMS send command* recipe

Using the JMS send command

When debugging or testing code, it is very handy to be able to send messages to a specific queue. This can be done from the command console in Karaf using the JMS subshell.

Getting ready

Make sure that the JMS feature is installed and available. In order to use most of the commands via JMS, we need to have a connection factory created (see the *Using the JMS connection factory commands* recipe).

How to do it...

First, let's make sure the service is in place using the `info` command. The connection factory can be referenced either from the specified name `cookbook` or by the JNDI service name `jms/cookbook`, as we can see in the following command:

```
karaf@root()> jms:info jms/cookbook


Property | Value
------------------
product  | ActiveMQ
version  | 5.9.0
```

Now that we have verified the JMS connection factory, we can use it to send messages to the broker. This can be done using the following command:

```
karaf@root()> jms:send jms/cookbook cookbookQueue "the recipes
  are sweet"
```

This will send a message, the recipes are sweet, to cookbookQueue using the JNDI name for our connection factory jms/cookbook.

How it works...

The send command will package up the string variable in the command line and put it in a JMS message, and then send the message to the specified queue. If you look at the command line, there are three parameters, which are as follows:

- ▶ The JNDI reference to the connection factory
- ▶ The name of the queue we are sending the message to
- ▶ The message body

See also

- ▶ Check out the browse command to see how to view the message you just sent to the broker. You can also see it at http://karaf.apache.org/manual/latest/users-guide/jms.html.

Using the JMS browse command

Now that we have an embedded broker and have looked at some of the commands for viewing the broker properties and statistics, let's look at how to interact with the broker using commands. In this recipe, we will look at the command for browsing messages.

Getting ready

In order for us to control the connection factory and send messages to the embedded broker, first we need to get the commands installed using the following JMS feature command, like we did in the previous recipe:

```
feature:install jms
```

First, let's create a connection factory for our embedded broker. We do this using the jms:create command.

Be sure to reference the `--help` command for required or optional parameters.

How to do it...

The real meat and potatoes of this command is the ability to browse the messages in the queue. An example `browse` command is as follows:

```
karaf@root()> jms:browse jms/cookbook cookbookQueue
```

This allows you to see the message content, persistence (delivery mode), expiration, ID, the replyTo value, destination, and so on. It is a quick way to monitor what is in the queue at any given time. The output of the preceding `browse` command is as follows:

```
ID:mbp.pk5001z-55253-1393261878969-4:2:1:1:1 | the recipes are sweet
   | UTF-8    |    | Persistent    | queue://cookbookQueue | Never
   | 4        | false    |           | Mon Feb 24 14:55:21 MST 2014
```

How it works...

Browsing messages in the queue is simple. The parameters on the command line tell the `browse` command what connection factory to use and what queue to browse.

Configuring and deploying a master/slave broker with Apache Karaf

In this recipe, we will set up and deploy two Karaf instances with embedded ActiveMQ in a master/slave configuration. This is used for high availability in messaging systems. This will allow systems to continue functioning in case of a failure of the active instance.

Getting ready

First we need to get two instances of Karaf started up with an embedded broker. If we are doing this on two different machines, it is actually easier since we will not have port conflicts when using the defaults on both machines. Keep in mind that if you decide to run this deployment on a single machine, one of the instances of Jetty and ActiveMQ embedded in Karaf needs to have its ports changed.

How to do it...

Since we can only assume that we have one machine to work with, we will go over how to get two instances of Karaf running on a single machine. We can create a second instance by unzipping the Karaf `.zip` or `.tar` file to a new directory or just copy and paste the current instance to a new directory. Now, we have to change the port setting on one of the instances. This can be done using the following steps:

1. Open the `org.apache.karaf.management.cfg` file and locate the following lines of code:

   ```
   #
   # Port number for RMI registry connection
   #
   rmiRegistryPort = 1099
   ```

2. Alter the port to something not in use, say `1096`. Then, alter the RMI server connection port as shown in the following code:

   ```
   #
   # Port number for RMI server connection
   #
   rmiServerPort = 44444
   ```

3. We can change this to something like `44446`. Now, we can start up the second instance without port conflicts. But we are not done yet. We still have to configure the ActiveMQ instances for failover.

Make the following changes to instance 1 and instance 2 of Karaf:

1. Open the `org.apache.activemq.server-default.cfg` file of the `<karaf-home>/etc/` folder and change the following code to a hardcoded location on the disk:

   ```
   data=${karaf.data}/${broker-name}
   ```

   An example might be something like the following code:

   ```
   data=/Users/default/data
   ```

2. Open the `jetty.xml` file of the `<karaf-home>/etc/` folder and change the value of `jetty.port` to something like `8186`, as shown in the following code:

   ```
   <Property name="jetty.port" default="8186" />
   ```

3. Open the `org.apache.karaf.shell.cfg` file of the `<karaf-home>/etc/` folder and change the value of `sshPort` to something like `8106`, as shown in the following code:

   ```
   sshPort = 8106
   sshHost = 0.0.0.0
   ```

4. Since we are running both ActiveMQ instances on the same machine, it would be more complete to change the port on the second ActiveMQ instance to a different port, although this is not required since the port is not allocated until ActiveMQ gets a lock on the file location (this step is optional in this configuration; however, it is more important in a Network of Brokers configuration on a single machine as both instances are active). This can be done as follows:

```
<transportConnector name="openwire"
  uri="tcp://0.0.0.0:61617?maximumConnections=1000&amp;
  wireFormat.maxFrameSize=104857600"/>
```

5. After changing the configuration files, save them and start both instances of Karaf. Install the `activemq-broker` feature on instance 1 as follows:

```
karaf> feature:repo-add activemq 5.9.0

karaf> feature:install activemq-broker
```

6. We will see that the embedded ActiveMQ instance starts up without issue. Now do the same on instance 2 and look at the log of instance 2 in the `karaf.log` file in the `data/log` folder.

7. Search the logfile of instance 2 for the phrase `could not be locked`. We will see the following output line:

```
2014-02-23 20:37:12,472 | INFO  | ctivemq.server]) |
  SharedFileLocker                 | 103 -
  org.apache.activemq.activemq-osgi - 5.9.0 | Database
  /Users/default/data/kahadb/lock is locked... waiting 10
  seconds for the database to be unlocked. Reason:
  java.io.IOException: File '/Users/default/data/kahadb
  /lock' could not be locked.
```

8. This indicates that the second embedded broker instance is in a wait state and not fully instantiated. To see instance 2 start up and initialize, press *Ctrl + D* on instance 1 (to shut down the instance). If you are tailing the logfile or you refresh the logfile in your viewer, you will see the following output:

```
2014-02-23 20:40:02,909 | INFO  | ctivemq.server]) |
  TransportServerThreadSupport     | 103 -
  org.apache.activemq.activemq-osgi - 5.9.0 | Listening for
  connections at: tcp://
  mbp.pk5001z:61616?maximumConnections=1000&wireFormat.
  maxFrameSize=104857600
2014-02-23 20:40:02,909 | INFO  | ctivemq.server]) |
  TransportConnector               | 103 -
  org.apache.activemq.activemq-osgi - 5.9.0 | Connector
  openwire started
```

```
2014-02-23 20:40:02,909 | INFO  | ctivemq.server]) |
   BrokerService                     | 103 -
   org.apache.activemq.activemq-osgi - 5.9.0 | Apache
   ActiveMQ 5.9.0 (cookbook-broker, ID: mbp.pk5001z-53046-
   1393213202778-0:1) started
```

This indicates that the slave broker on instance 2 has started up and initialized the connections.

How it works...

ActiveMQ gives us high availability via a couple of options. In the case of this recipe, we are using file-based persistence (kahadb). This allows us to point both instances at the same data file location to establish the master or the slave. The first instance to start up will get a lock on the file location and then finish initializing. The other instance will look at the same file location and see that a lock has already been established. Then, it will log the IOException and wait for the default 10 seconds before trying again.

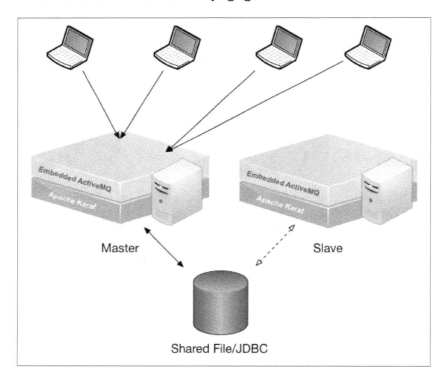

The previous diagram shows that the master ActiveMQ instance has established a lock from the file location. It has instantiated all the connections configured in the activemq.xml file under the etc folder as defined by the transport connection elements. This allows clients to now connect to the master instance. Once an instance is shut down, those connections are killed.

Consider that the clients are configured with a failover protocol to the slave instance as follows:

```
failover:(tcp://master:61616,tcp://slave:61617)?options
```

The client machines will automatically reconnect to the slave machine once the secondary broker finishes initializing. This is demonstrated in the following diagram:

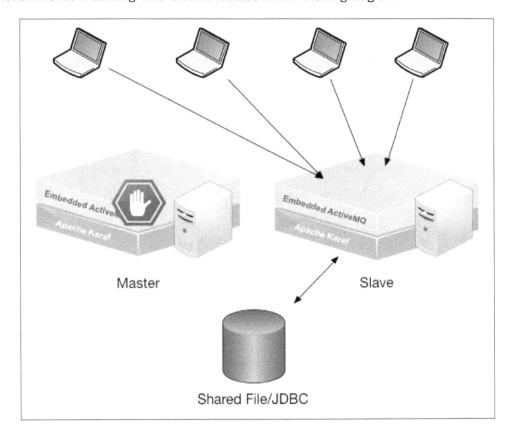

At this point, we can restart the original master (instance 1) and that will now wait to get a lock on the file. This gives us the master/slave setup without having to restart instances or restore data.

See also

▶ The *Configuring and deploying a Network of Brokers with Apache Karaf* recipe

Configuring and deploying a Network of Brokers with Apache Karaf

Many times, a single system may not be enough to handle the load of the applications. In this case, scaling is needed to balance load across multiple systems. We can scale applications using embedded ActiveMQ instances in a **Network of Brokers** (**NoB**) configuration.

This is different from a master/slave configuration because we will have two active instances rather than an active and passive pair.

Getting ready

By following the same initial setup in the previous recipe, we need to have two instances of Karaf running. We can prove this concept on a single machine or multiple machines. For this recipe, we will again be showing you how to set up two instances on the same machine, which requires different ports to be used for the different Karaf instances.

Ensure that the defaults for the two instances are in place.

How to do it...

Please follow these steps to configure and deploy a Network of Brokers configuration:

1. Open the `org.apache.activemq.server-defaults.cfg` file of the `<karaf-home>/etc/` folder and make sure the following data value is set:

   ```
   data=${karaf.data}/${broker-name}
   ```

   This will tell the embedded ActiveMQ instance to use a local data folder defined by the parameters mentioned earlier.

2. Change the instance 1 option for broker name to `recipe-3-broker-1` and change the instance 2 option for broker name to `recipe-3-broker-2`. So, the values in the file should look like the following code:

   ```
   Instance 1:
   broker-name=recipe-3-broker-1
   Instance 2:
   broker-name=recipe-3-broker-2
   ```

   That way, it is easy to differentiate between brokers when looking at them using JMX. The `karaf.data` property is a system property that is set based on the Karaf location.

3. For this recipe, let's work with instance 2. First, we have to alter the `etc/activemq.xml` file to have a network connector that links it with the instance. The following is the XML code that needs to be added:

```
<networkConnectors>
   <networkConnector   uri="static:(tcp://0.0.0.0:61616)"
                        duplex="true"
                        userName="karaf"
                        password="karaf"/>
</networkConnectors>
```

Note the URI has the static protocol with a TCP connection to the instance 1 port (in this case, the default port was left on instance 1 as `61616`). We turn on duplex to allow two-way communication through a single pipe and pass the username and password.

4. In order to avoid port conflicts, we need to change the transport connector port on instance 2 to something other than `61616`, as follows:

```
<transportConnector name="openwire"
   uri="tcp://0.0.0.0:61617?
maximumConnections=1000&wireFormat.maxFrameSize=
   104857600"/>
```

5. One more change and we are ready to test. We need to change the port in the `jetty.xml` file under the `etc` folder. By default, the port is `8181`, but since instance 1 is using that, we need to change instance 2 to something else. For this recipe, I have used `8182`, as shown in the following code:

```
<Set name="port">
   <Property name="jetty.port" default="8182" />
</Set>
```

6. We can start up both instances now. If we monitor the logs for instance 2, we will see the following output:

```
Establishing network connection from vm://recipe-3-broker-
   1?async=false&network=true to tcp://0.0.0.0:61616

vm:// recipe-3-broker-1 started

Network connection between vm:// recipe-3-broker-1#24 and
   tcp://mbp.pk5001z/192.168.0.97:61616@55254 (recipe-3-
   broker-2) has been established.
```

The log entries indicate that instance 2 has found instance 1 and established a connection between the two.

How it works...

The Network of Brokers configuration can be used for two different topologies: vertical or horizontal. First, let's look at horizontal, which is more for scaling purposes. This type of topology will often be used to provide great throughput for a system. The main idea is to NOT increase the number of brokers a message must pass through in order to be consumed by your application. Rather, it is designed to balance load across multiple servers. Notice in the following diagram that there are two client machines attached to each instance allowing each broker/Karaf pair to only have to process the messages for two clients.

 Each broker instance has its own message store and is not considered a highly available topology.

Even though clients can failover from one client to the other, persisted data is not shared between the instances. This means that if one instance of the broker dies, then the pending messages in that store are not processed until the broker is restarted, even though the clients move over to the one active broker instance. Have a look at the following diagram:

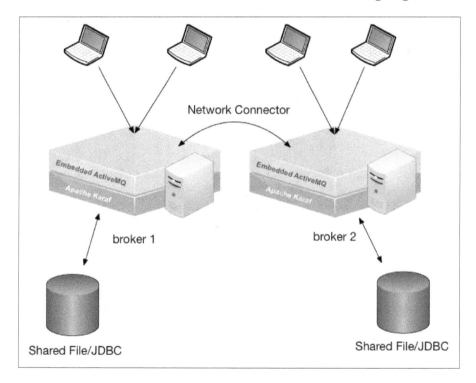

The benefit to having a network of brokers is the ability to forward messages to idle clients. If a message is produced to the local **broker 1** but all the clients are busy, then ActiveMQ will forward the message to any idle clients on **broker 2**. This is considered horizontal scaling.

There's more...

There is also the notion of vertical scaling. But this has an entirely different use case. When using vertical scaling, the obstacle is usually not performance. In most cases, vertical scaling is used for communication problems over a WAN. A good example of this is outlined in the following diagram:

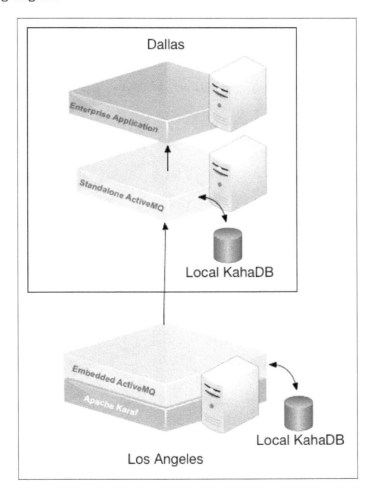

In the previous diagram, an embedded ActiveMQ is used locally to avoid application downtime if the connection between Los Angeles and Dallas is lost. So, the local application will communicate directly with the local instance without worrying if the WAN is up or down. Then, the local ActiveMQ will be in charge of establishing and maintaining the connection to the backend service.

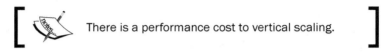 There is a performance cost to vertical scaling.

Vertical scaling is forcing a two-broker hop. So, you have to figure out which is more important from the requirements: performance or stability.

See also

> ▶   The *Configuring and deploying a master/slave broker with Apache Karaf* recipe

4
Hosting a Web Server
with Pax Web

In this chapter, we will cover the following topics:

- ▶ Installing Pax modules in Apache Karaf
- ▶ Installing extended Http Service in Apache Karaf
- ▶ Configuring Pax Web modules deployed in Apache Karaf
- ▶ Building a Http Service project to host in Apache Karaf
- ▶ Building a Http Service with the Whiteboard pattern in Apache Karaf
- ▶ Building an application with custom HttpContext with Apache Karaf
- ▶ Building a standard web project to host in Apache Karaf
- ▶ Configuring security for a web application in Apache Karaf
- ▶ Binding a web project to a specific host in Apache Karaf
- ▶ Building a Servlet 3.0 annotated web application with Apache Karaf
- ▶ Creating a CDI web application with Apache Karaf

Introduction

This chapter explains how to enhance your Apache Karaf with Pax Web to serve as a web container. The OPS4j Pax Web project is an OSGi R4 Http Service and Web Application (refer to *Chapter 128, OSGi Enterprise Release 4*) implementation. It extends the Http Service with better support for servlet, filters, listeners, error pages, JavaServer Pages (JSPs), and more in order to support the latest Java Servlet spec.

The standard features of Karaf contain a set of options to install Pax Web in different flavors. There are options for:

- A basic Http Service

- An enhanced Http Service with support for the Whiteboard pattern and JSPs

- A full-blown web container configuration with support for **Web Application Archive** (**WAR**) and **Web Application Bundle** (**WAB**) files

Readers interested in obtaining a deeper understanding of Apache Karaf in combination with Pax Web should consult the OPS4j community. You'll find a lot more samples concerning the usage of Pax Web in general and Apache Karaf specialties as a whole.

Installing Pax modules in Apache Karaf

To start with Http Service, you will need to install one of the features mentioned earlier. This recipe will guide you through the installation of the different extensions of Pax Web and how it works.

How to do it...

To install the basic Http Service, start your Apache Karaf server and install the Http Service feature via the console using the following command:

```
karaf@root()> feature:install http
```

How it works...

After installing this feature, list the bundles with an `la` command. This will show you the following additional bundles to your Karaf instance:

```
78 | Active   | 30 | 2.2.0    | Apache ServiceMix :: Specs :: Activation API 1.4
79 | Active   | 30 | 1.0      | Servlet 3.0
80 | Active   | 30 | 1.4.4    | JavaMail API (compat)
```

81	Active	30	1.1.1	geronimo-jta_1.1_spec
82	Active	30	1.0.1	Annotation 1.1
83	Active	30	1.1	Java Authentication SPI for Containers
84	Active	30	8.1.14	Jetty :: Aggregate :: All Server
85	Active	30	1.6.0	OPS4J Pax Swissbox :: OSGi Core
86	Active	30	1.6.0	OPS4J Pax Swissbox :: Optional JCL
87	Active	20	3.16.0	Apache XBean OSGI Bundle Utilities
88	Active	20	3.16.0	Apache XBean :: ASM 4 shaded (repackaged)
89	Active	20	3.16	Apache XBean :: Reflect
90	Active	20	3.16.0	Apache XBean :: Finder shaded (repackaged)
91	Active	30	3.1.0	OPS4J Pax Web - API
92	Active	30	3.1.0	OPS4J Pax Web - Service SPI
93	Active	30	3.1.0	OPS4J Pax Web - Runtime
94	Active	30	3.1.0	OPS4J Pax Web - Jetty
95	Active	30	3.0.1	Apache Karaf :: HTTP :: Core
96	Active	30	3.0.1	Apache Karaf :: HTTP :: Commands

Of course, it will install the needed Jetty server to serve the web content and the four basic Pax Web bundles needed to have a minimal Http Service. These four bundles contain the API, Services SPI, runtime, and the Jetty server wrapper, which takes care of starting the underlying Jetty instance. All of these bundles installed by the HTTP feature give you a few possible ways to use the Http Service, but nothing else. This scenario is usually good enough for running simple servlets and the Felix Web Console.

On top of this basic installation, Karaf already provides a simple command to inspect the currently installed servlets. It will give you an overview of the servlets and the registered aliases. The following is the command:

```
karaf@root()> http:list
ID | Servlet | Servlet-Name | State | Alias | Url
-------------------------------------------------
```

See also

▶ The *Building a Http Service project to host in Apache Karaf* recipe

Installing extended Http Service in Apache Karaf

Usually, just using the basic Http Service is not enough anymore these days, especially when it comes to serving JSP or complete web applications. So, a better usable container is needed.

How to do it...

1. To install the HTTP Whiteboard feature, start your Apache Karaf server and install the HTTP Whiteboard feature via the console using the following command:

   ```
   karaf@root()> feature:install http-whiteboard
   ```

2. Transform your Apache Karaf server into a full-featured web container using the following command:

   ```
   karaf@root()> feature:install war
   ```

How it works...

The Whiteboard feature installs another two Pax Web bundles. These bundles give you JSP and Whiteboard support. These two bundles are shown in the following command-line output:

```
97 | Active   | 30 | 3.1.0      | OPS4J Pax Web - Jsp Support
98 | Active   | 30 | 3.1.0      | OPS4J Pax Web - Extender - Whiteboard
```

This enables Pax Web to deploy and serve JSPs registered to the now available WebContainer interface. This interface is an extension to the standardized Http Service. The Whiteboard extender is another approach to register services in OSGi.

[More details about the Whiteboard pattern can be found at
http://www.osgi.org/wiki/uploads/Links/whiteboard.pdf.]

With the WAR feature, the installation of Pax Web is complete. This includes the WAR extender, which is used to install OSGi WAB files, and the Pax URL WAR handler, which takes care of transforming WAR archives into WAB files. These additional bundles are listed as follows:

```
99  | Active  | 30 | 3.1.0   | OPS4J Pax Web - Extender - WAR
100 | Active  | 30 | 3.1.0   | OPS4J Pax Web - FileInstall Deployer
101 | Active  | 30 | 1.4.2   | OPS4J Pax Url - war
102 | Active  | 30 | 1.4.2   | OPS4J Pax Url - Commons
103 | Active  | 30 | 1.6.0   | OPS4J Pax Swissbox :: Bnd Utils
104 | Active  | 30 | 1.6.0   | OPS4J Pax Swissbox :: Property
105 | Active  | 30 | 1.43.0  | aQute Bundle Tool Library
106 | Active  | 30 | 3.0.1   | Apache Karaf :: Web :: Core
107 | Active  | 30 | 3.0.1   | Apache Karaf :: Web :: Commands
```

With the Karaf WAR feature comes another command; the web:* commands help to analyze the state of the installed WARs. An example command is as follows:

```
karaf@root()> web:list
ID | State | Web-State | Level | Web-ContextPath | Name
----------------------------------------------------------
```

These commands also help to control the status of a web bundle. Consider the following command:

```
karaf@root()> web:
web:list       web:start       web:stop
```

The web:list command shows a list of the installed WAR files and gives a listing of the state and Web-ContextPath.

See also

- ▶ The *Building a Http Service with the Whiteboard pattern in Apache Karaf* recipe
- ▶ The *Building a standard web project to host in Apache Karaf* recipe
- ▶ For more details on how the WAR URL handler works, visit https://github.com/jgoodyear/ApacheKarafCookbook/tree/master/chapter4

Configuring Pax Web modules deployed in Apache Karaf

Pax Web uses Jetty as the underlying web container. The OSGi Http Service specification defines a set of parameters for configuration of the Http Service. In addition to these standard configuration parameters, the Pax Web-specific parameters are configurable. On top of those configuration parameters, it's also possible to configure Jetty itself for further needs.

How to do it...

The configuration of the Http Service is done through the Configuration Admin service. During the installation of the Http Service, the configuration is also set for the service PID `org.ops4j.pax.web`, as shown in the following code snippet:

```
javax.servlet.context.tempdir = ${karaf.data}/pax-web-jsp
org.ops4j.pax.web.config.file = ${karaf.home}/etc/jetty.xml
org.osgi.service.http.port = 8181
```

How it works...

This basic set of configuration defines the HTTP port the Jetty server is listening to, the servlet `temp` directory to create JSP servlet files, and the location of the optional `jetty.xml` file for enhanced Jetty configuration.

> Documentation on how to configure the `jetty.xml` file can be found at `http://wiki.eclipse.org/Jetty/Reference/jetty.xml`. Make sure that you also take a look at the specialties of running Jetty with Pax Web at `https://ops4j1.jira.com/wiki/display/paxweb/Advanced+Jetty+Configuration`.

There's more...

Additionally, a configuration file for all configuration parameters can be placed in the `etc` folder. It's named like the service PID appended by the `.cfg` suffix. The following is an excerpt from the `org.ops4j.pax.web.cfg` configuration file. This complete configuration file and also the `jetty.xml` file can be found at `https://github.com/jgoodyear/ApacheKarafCookbook/blob/master/chapter4/chapter4-recipe2`.

```
org.osgi.service.http.enabled = true
org.osgi.service.http.port = 8181
org.osgi.service.http.connector.name = default
org.osgi.service.http.useNIO = true
org.osgi.service.http.secure.enabled = true
```

```
org.osgi.service.http.port.secure = 8443
org.osgi.service.http.secure.connector.name = secureDefault
javax.servlet.context.tempdir = ${karaf.data}/pax-web-jsp
org.ops4j.pax.web.config.file=${karaf.base}/etc/jetty.xml
...
```

The following code configures extra JSP parameters:

```
org.ops4j.pax.web.jsp.scratch.dir =
org.ops4j.pax.web.jsp.check.interval = 300
...
org.ops4j.pax.web.jsp.precompilation = false
...
```

The following is the configuration for the NCSA log format:

```
org.ops4j.pax.web.log.ncsa.enabled = false
org.ops4j.pax.web.log.ncsa.format = yyyy_mm_dd.request.log
org.ops4j.pax.web.log.ncsa.retaindays = 90
org.ops4j.pax.web.log.ncsa.append = true
org.ops4j.pax.web.log.ncsa.extended = true
org.ops4j.pax.web.log.ncsa.dispatch = false
org.ops4j.pax.web.log.ncsa.logtimezone = GMT
org.ops4j.pax.web.log.ncsa.directory =
org.ops4j.pax.web.log.ncsa.latency = false
org.ops4j.pax.web.log.ncsa.cookies = false
org.ops4j.pax.web.log.ncsa.server = false
```

For details about the NCSA log format, refer to `http://en.wikipedia.org/wiki/Common_Log_Format`.

The following configuration is used to have different virtual hosts and connectors:

```
org.ops4j.pax.web.default.virtualhosts =
org.ops4j.pax.web.default.connectors =
```

For more details, see the *Binding a web project to a specific host in Apache Karaf* recipe.

How it works...

This configuration excerpt shows you the default configuration that is already internally used by Pax Web. If needed, some or all of these configuration parameters can be set either in the Karaf shell or be placed in the `org.ops4j.pax.web.cfg` file in the `etc` folder. A quick example of how to set the HTTP port via shell commands is as follows:

```
karaf@root()> config:edit org.ops4j.pax.web
karaf@root()> config:property-set org.osgi.service.http.port 8080
karaf@root()> config:update
```

More details on how to use the `config` commands can be found in *Learning Apache Karaf, Jamie Goodyear, Johan Edstrom, and Heath Kesler, Packt Publishing*.

It is best practice to use the `karaf.data` environment variable when referencing external directories, for example, when enabling the NCSA logger by switching the `org.ops4j.pax.web.log.ncsa.enabled` option to `true`. It is necessary to also configure the directory to a specific folder, as described in the following code line:

```
org.ops4j.pax.web.log.ncsa.directory = ${karaf.data}/ncsa-log/
```

The same is true for the `scratch` directory for JSP compilation—it is best to be configured as:

```
org.ops4j.pax.web.jsp.scratch.dir = ${karaf.data}/jsp-compile
```

Building a Http Service project to host in Apache Karaf

Building web applications only with the Http Service also means a reduction to servlet only services, as Http Service supports only servlets and no further web elements like filters and JSPs. With this reduced set, it is still possible to build modern web applications. For example, it just needs some JavaScript code and a servlet generating JSON to build a modern web application. Using these elements, along with OSGi, you get the perfect mixture for μ-services. The focus of this recipe, and the following ones, lies only on the usage of the Http Service; so, don't expect to create a fancy web application. After you're through, you will be able to build a single servlet application like the one in the following screenshot:

Getting ready

To precondition the Http Service installed in Apache Karaf, see the *Installing Pax modules in Apache Karaf* recipe. The sources can be found at `https://github.com/jgoodyear/ApacheKarafCookbook/tree/master/chapter4/chapter4-recipe3`.

It is best to always have a look at the complete sources, due to the limited amount of pages for this book and to spare you of the boilerplate code. This is why only the critical section is referenced here in this recipe. The example application used in this recipe can be installed and started with the following command:

```
install -s mvn:com.packt/chapter4-recipe3/1.0.0-SNAPSHOT/jar
```

How to do it...

As we are using Http Service with this recipe, we need to get hold of the `HttpService` service. For this, it is very common to use a ServiceTracker mechanism. The steps are as follows:

1. The first step is referencing the Http Service. In the activator of our sample application, a `ServiceTracker` object is created with a reference to the bundle creating this tracker and declaring the class of the service to be tracked. The third parameter is an implementation of the ServiceTrackerCustomizer interface. A default implementation is provided by the ServiceTracker itself, and therefore we use it as is. All of this takes place in the bundle activator code as follows:

```
public void start(BundleContext bc) throws Exception {
  bundleContext = bc;
  tracker = new ServiceTracker
    <HttpService, HttpService>(bc, HttpService.class
    , this);
  tracker.open();
}
```

2. The second step is registering the servlet as a service. The moment the service is available, the ServiceTracker will kick in and the `addingService` method of the bundle activator will be called. Here, the `HttpContext` function for the servlet is created together with the `init` parameter for the servlet to register, as shown in the following code:

```
HttpContext httpContext = httpService.
    createDefaultHttpContext();
Dictionary<String, Object> initParams = new Hashtable
    <String, Object>();
```

3. After this, we are ready to register the servlet as a service with the Http Service. This is done by the following simple API call:

```
httpService.registerServlet("/hello",
    new HelloServlet(), initParams, httpContext);
```

The Http Service also supports registering of resources, for example, images and CSS files. The Felix Web Console is based on these two mechanisms.

To register resources, the Http Service API provides another method for registration, as shown in the following code:

```
httpService.registerResources("/images", "/images", httpContext);
```

The image should be contained within a JAR file in the `images` folder (as shown in the following screenshot), which is used when registering the image's alias:

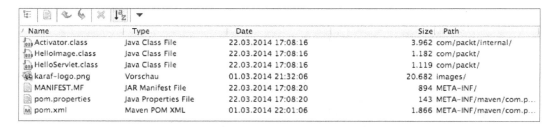

Name	Type	Date	Size	Path
Activator.class	Java Class File	22.03.2014 17:08:16	3.962	com/packt/internal/
HelloImage.class	Java Class File	22.03.2014 17:08:16	1.182	com/packt/
HelloServlet.class	Java Class File	22.03.2014 17:08:16	1.119	com/packt/
karaf-logo.png	Vorschau	01.03.2014 21:32:06	20.682	images/
MANIFEST.MF	JAR Manifest File	22.03.2014 17:08:20	894	META-INF/
pom.properties	Java Properties File	22.03.2014 17:08:20	143	META-INF/maven/com.p...
pom.xml	Maven POM XML	01.03.2014 22:01:06	1.866	META-INF/maven/com.p...

 The corresponding API can be found at `http://www.osgi.org/javadoc/r4v42/org/osgi/service/http/HttpService.html`.

To use this image, create a second servlet that uses this image and register it with a different alias, as shown in the following code:

```
httpService.registerServlet("/hello/logo", new HelloImage()
    , initParams, httpContext);
```

The servlet refers to the image as a resource from the root context, as shown in the following code:

```
out.println("<img src='/images/karaf-logo.png' border='0'/>");
```

How it works...

The Http Service configures and registers the HelloServlet with the underlying Jetty server. From this point on, it is regarded as a classic servlet and handled accordingly. The resources take some extra handling, as the ResourceServlet needs to be aware of the OSGi class loading, and thus needs to know where to look for the resources in the bundle's class path.

▸ The Http Service only provides basic HTTP services, such as to serve servlets and resources. If you want to serve dynamic content like JSPs, you'll need the Pax Web extension to the OSGi Http Service—the Pax Web web container. This is available together with the Whiteboard extender and is used in the *Building a Http Service with the Whiteboard pattern in Apache Karaf* recipe.

Building a Http Service with the Whiteboard pattern in Apache Karaf

The Whiteboard pattern is a much easier approach to registering servlets, resources, JSPs, or filters. With the Whiteboard extender, the registration of services works in the opposite way to the last recipe. The bundle activator doesn't wait for the Http Service to show up; it just registers the servlets and the other resources as services while the Whiteboard extender picks up those services and makes sure that everything is ready to be served. With the Whiteboard feature, it is possible to use all web technologies available to the underlying Jetty server, as we are not bound to the restricted Http Service interface anymore. This recipe will guide you through this by using two different technologies; first, the standard way, which is via a bundle activator, and second, via Blueprint.

How to do it...

1. The first step is registering a servlet as a service. First, register your servlet via the activator using the bundle context. As the servlet is registered as an OSGi service, the alias needs to be placed in the service properties. These properties are interpreted and partially used for a servlet's `init` parameters.

```
Hashtable<String, String> props = new Hashtable
  <String, String>();
props.put("alias", "/whiteboard");
```

The servlet itself is registered as any usual OSGi service, as shown in the following code:

```
servletReg = bundleContext.registerService(Servlet
  .class, new HelloServlet(), props);
```

2. The second step is registering resources. As this is not a standardized OSGi Http Service, a special Pax Web `ResourceMapping` class is needed to register a resource as a service, as shown in the following code:

```
DefaultResourceMapping resourceMapping = new Default
  ResourceMapping();
resourceMapping.setAlias("/whiteboardresources");
resourceMapping.setPath("/images");
resourcesReg = bundleContext.register
  Service(ResourceMapping.class, resourceMapping, null);
```

After the registration, it is possible to use these resources by the servlet, as follows:

```
out.println("<img src='/whiteboardresources/karaf-logo.png'
  border='0'/>");
```

This pattern to register web components as services will repeat itself.

3. The next step is registering a servlet with Blueprint. Instead of using an activator for registration, the Whiteboard pattern also gives you the freedom to use other means of registering services, like Blueprint or DS. With a Blueprint XML file, it is now only a configuration for the wiring of services, instead of creating the boilerplate code contained in the activator:

```
<service id="filteredServletService" ref="filteredServlet"
  interface="javax.servlet.Servlet">
  <service-properties>
    <entry key="alias" value="/filtered"/>
  </service-properties>
  <bean class="com.packt.HelloServlet"/>
</service>
```

This registers the servlet with the alias `/filtered`, which is used as the URL pattern for the matching filter.

4. The last step is registering the filter with Blueprint. Registering a filter is just as easy as registering a servlet. Using Blueprint for this kind of registration uses less boilerplate code. This can be done using the following code:

```
<service id="servletFilterService" interface="javax.servlet.
Filter">
  <service-properties>
    <entry key="urlPatterns" value="/filtered/*"/>
  </service-properties>
  <bean class="com.packt.ServletFilter"/>
</service>
```

As a result, the filtered call of Hello Servlet can be seen when navigating to /filtered, as shown in the following screenshot:

There is more to the Whiteboard approach. It is possible to configure a complete web application just by registering services.

Registering error pages

Registering `DefaultErrorPageMapping`, for example, easily configures an error page. The corresponding class is provided by Pax Web and is available through the Apache Karaf Http Whiteboard feature. Consider the following code:

```
<service interface=" org.ops4j.pax.web.extender.
  whiteboard.ErrorPageMapping">
  <bean class=" org.ops4j.pax.web.extender.whiteboard.
  runtime.DefaultErrorPageMapping">
    <property name="error" value="java.lang.Exception"/>
    <property name="location" value="/uncaughtException.html"/>
  </bean>
</service>
```

This error page mapping defines that any exception thrown in the container will result in serving the `uncaughtException.html` page, as shown here in the following screenshot:

Defining error page mapping

While at it, a custom 404 error code handling page can be registered with extra mapping, which again is registered as a service, as shown in the following code:

```
<!-- 404 mapping -->
<service id="errorPageMapping" interface="org.ops4j.pax.
  web.extender.whiteboard.ErrorPageMapping">
  <bean class="org.ops4j.pax.web.extender.
    whiteboard.runtime.DefaultErrorPageMapping">
    <property name="error" value="404"/>
    <property name="location" value="/404.html"/>
  </bean>
</service>
```

`DefaultErrorPageMapping` provided by Pax Web just needs the HTTP error code and the location of the custom error code page.

Registering a welcome page

The configuration and registration of a service for welcome pages is as easy as the previous registrations have been. Consider the following code:

```
<service id="welcomeFileService" interface="org.ops4j.pax.web.
  extender.whiteboard.WelcomeFileMapping">
  <bean class="org.ops4j.pax.web.extender.whiteboard.
    runtime.DefaultWelcomeFileMapping">
```

```
      <property name="redirect" value="true" />
      <property name="welcomeFiles">
        <array>
          <value>index.html</value>
          <value>welcome.html</value>
        </array>
      </property>
    </bean>
  </service>
```

The Whiteboard extender bundle provides a default implementation of `WelcomeFileMapping`. The following screenshot shows the welcome page:

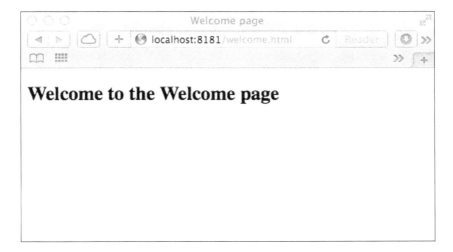

Register JSPs

The registration of a JSP is as simple as all the previous recipes. You just need to register `DefaultJspMapping` with the corresponding URL patterns. After this is done, you are set to serve JSPs right away. Consider the following code:

```
<service id="jspMapping" interface="org.ops4j.pax.web.
  extender.whiteboard.JspMapping">
  <bean class="org.ops4j.pax.web.extender.whiteboard.
    runtime.DefaultJspMapping">
    <property name="urlPatterns">
      <array>
        <value type="java.lang.String">/jsp</value>
      </array>
    </property>
  </bean>
</service>
```

Once you are set to serve the JSP, the following screen will appear:

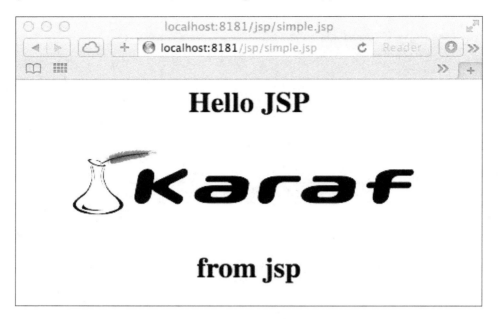

How it works...

The now available Whiteboard extender starts a ServiceListener that registers any incoming new service such as a servlet, filter, and JSP and hands them over to either the standard Http Service or the extended Http Service (the WebContainer interface).

Using the direct service approach has only one downside—all of the registered servlet services use the same `ServletContextPath`. This is due to the fact that the Http Service registered servlets neglect a way to register the servlet with a specialized ServletContextPath, and therefore are bound to/with an extra URL path for the servlet. For example, the first two servlets of this recipe register with `/whiteboard` and `/whiteboard/logo`, where the ServletContextPath is `/`. To distinguish between different ServletContextPaths, a WAB is needed.

All of the previous samples have one thing in common: all of them are registered within the same bundle. To separate servlets from filters, you need to make sure that you have the same HttpContext in use; this is handled in a later recipe.

Building an application with custom HttpContext with Apache Karaf

All previous recipes have covered how to register servlets and filters, and all from within the same bundle bound to a default HttpContext. If no other HttpContext is defined, DefaultHttpContext is created while registering a servlet or resource. With this recipe, we will work with a custom HttpContext.

Getting ready

As this recipe is a specialization of the previous recipes, you'll find the source code for it in the *Building a Http Service with the Whiteboard pattern in Apache Karaf* recipe. As usual, the recipe demands the successful installation of the `http-whiteboard` feature; how this can be achieved is explained in the *Installing extended Http Service in Apache Karaf* recipe. The source code in this recipe is reduced to the important sections. The full sources can be found at `https://github.com/jgoodyear/ApacheKarafCookbook/tree/master/chapter4/chapter4-recipe4`.

How to do it...

1. The first step is defining properties. As with servlets, registering an HttpContext requires configuring a name for the HttpContext, as shown in the following code:

   ```
   props = new Hashtable<String, String>();
   props.put(ExtenderConstants.PROPERTY_HTTP_CONTEXT_ID,
     "forbidden");
   ```

2. The next step is registering, HttpContext. This will register the custom WhiteboardContext as HttpContext with a specialized ID `forbidden`. This way, other services are able to select this HttpContext. This is shown in the following code:

   ```
   httpContextReg = bundleContext.registerService(
     HttpContext.class, new WhiteboardContext(), props);
   ```

3. The next step is registering the servlet. The servlet using this HttpContext is referencing the HttpContext by just being registered using the same HttpContext ID. Consider the following code:

   ```
   props = new Hashtable<String, String>();
   props.put(ExtenderConstants.PROPERTY_ALIAS, "/forbidden");
   props.put(ExtenderConstants.PROPERTY_HTTP_CONTEXT_ID, "
     forbidden");
   forbiddenServletReg = bundleContext.registerService
     (Servlet.class, new HelloServlet(), props);
   ```

The custom HttpContext returns `false` for the `handleSecurity` method. Therefore, the request will return a 401 error as HTTP return code. Consider the following code:

```
public boolean handleSecurity(final HttpServletRequest
  request,final HttpServletResponse response)
  throws IOException {
  // Forbidden access!
  return false;
}
```

The following screenshot shows the HTTP error window:

There's more...

Till now, the registration of servlets, filters, and other resources always took place from the same bundle. How does this fit into the OSGi world? Doesn't it make sense to split this apart? It actually does, but it isn't easy and the OSGi spec doesn't require it to be possible. With Pax Web 3, it is possible to have this working but requires some specialties. First of all, it needs a shared HttpContext (its description and how to work with it you will find in the next set of steps). The following is a component diagram to give you an idea of the setup:

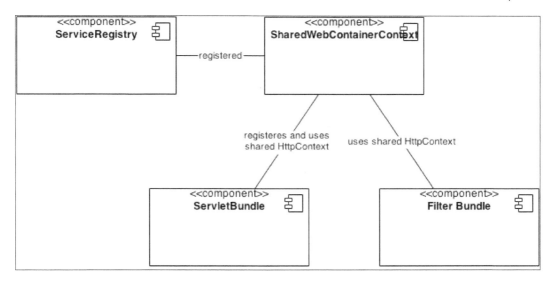

This can be done as follows:

1. The first step is registering the SharedWebContainerContext. For the shared HttpContext, it is essential to have the SharedWebContainerContext, which is a specialized HttpContext. At this point, the WebContainer interface is our friend and helps us by providing a method for the creation of the SharedWebContainerContext, which is the `getDefaultSharedHttpContext` method. This is described in the following code:

```
WebContainer service = (WebContainer) context.
  getService(serviceReference);
HttpContext httpContext = service.
  getDefaultSharedHttpContext();
```

    This freshly created SharedWebContainerContext needs to be registered as a service, as the filter from the other bundle needs to refer to it. Consider the following code:

```
props = new Hashtable<String, String>();
props.put(ExtenderConstants.PROPERTY_HTTP_CONTEXT_ID
  , "shared");
httpContextReg = context.registerService(HttpContext.class,
  httpContext, props);
```

2. The next step is registering the servlet with the shared context. As we want to add a filter from a different bundle, we need to add a servlet first. We will do this using the following code:

```
props = new Hashtable<String, String>();
props.put( ExtenderConstants.PROPERTY_ALIAS, "/
  extfilter" );
props.put("servlet-name", "FilteredServlet");
props.put(ExtenderConstants.PROPERTY_HTTP_CONTEXT_ID
  , "shared");
registerService = context.registerService( Servlet.class
  , new HelloServlet(), props );
```

At this point, the first bundle is set in our recipe, and we need to take care of the second bundle that only contains the filter.

3. The next step is referencing the shared HttpContext. We need to get the *shared* HttpContext first, though this time we don't create a new one; we just need to reference the one that the first bundle registered.

Find the service reference for the HttpContext service that matches the given LDAP filter (`httpContext.id=shared`). Also, see step 1, where we registered the service with this property. Consider the following code:

```
Collection<ServiceReference<HttpContext>> service
  References = context.getServiceReferences(HttpContext.
  class, "(httpContext.id=shared)");

if (serviceReferences.size() > 1) {
  throw new RuntimeException("should only be one http
    shared context");
}

HttpContext httpContext = context.getService(service
  References.iterator().next());
```

From this service reference, we acquire the HttpContext instance, which in our case is the SharedWebContainerContext at this point.

4. The next step is registering the filter for the shared context. From here on, it's quite simple. The registration of the servlet filter is done in the usual way.

```
Dictionary<String, String> props;
props = new Hashtable<String, String>();
props.put("pattern", ".*");
props.put(ExtenderConstants.PROPERTY_HTTP_CONTEXT_ID
  , "shared");
```

```
service.registerFilter(new ServletFilter(), new String[]
  { "/*" }, null, props, httpContext);
```

Create the properties needed for registration and register the filter with the WebContainer service. It is important that the properties contain the reference to the right HttpContext, `shared` at this point. The most important part is that it needs to actually register the filter with the preregistered HttpContext.

Can't this be done easier?

The not-yet-released version of Pax Web 4 helps with the sharing of contexts. It will especially help in working with the Whiteboard pattern. Since the release of Karaf 3 (which uses Pax Web 3), the `features.xml` file of Pax Web is maintained and released in the Pax Web release cycle. This will help to upgrade just this feature while Karaf itself might stay on another version.

Building a standard web project to host in Apache Karaf

As building a standard web application and WAR isn't really in the scope of this book, the focus of this recipe lies on the *transformation* of a standard WAR into a WAB.

Getting ready

The sample code for this recipe is available at `https://github.com/jgoodyear/ApacheKarafCookbook/tree/master/chapter4/chapter4-recipe6`.

How to do it...

Transforming a standard WAR project into a WAB is simple. So, let's take a look at the specialties around WAR and WAB files. For simplicity, let's call this project web project from here on.

Contrasting with a standard bundle project, where the classes reside directly in the JAR file, the classes of a web project should be contained in the `classes` folder under the `WEB-INF` folder. The same is true for embedded libraries; in a web project, these libraries are required to be placed in the `lib` folder under the `WEB-INF` folder.

Beware—embedding other JAR files should be done only if the JAR file is needed internally. Referencing other bundles should be your first choice.

The good news is that `maven-bundle-plugin` is capable of taking care of this special placement of classes and libraries. The `<_wab>` section takes care of this. Here, you define the base path of your web application folder. As this is a Maven project, the web application path resides in the `webapp` folder in the `src/main` folder. Consider the following code:

```
<plugin>
  <groupId>org.apache.felix</groupId>
  <artifactId>maven-bundle-plugin</artifactId>
  <version>2.4.0</version>
  <extensions>true</extensions>
  <configuration>
    <instructions>
      <_wab>src/main/webapp</_wab>
      <Web-ContextPath>packt-sample</Web-ContextPath>
    </instructions>
  </configuration>
</plugin>
```

As it is required for a web application bundle to have a `Web-ContextPath` manifest entry, this is set to `packt-sample` in this recipe.

How it works...

The WAR feature installs the Pax Web War extender. The WAR extender waits for bundles containing the `Web-ContextPath` header and will scan this bundle for the `web.xml` and `jetty-web.xml` configuration files. It also takes care of the annotated servlet's classes. For each WAR file, there will be a unique servlet context with the path defined in the `Web-ContextPath` manifest header. This is different from registering servlets via the Http Service (with or without the Whiteboard extender), where it is all about the alias.

There's more...

The only downside of the previously created WAB file is that it is not a WAR file anymore. As the POM file declares the resulting package to be of type bundle, the artifact is packaged as a JAR file. This surely will cause issues in the case of a WAR file that is supposed to be run on Apache Karaf or a non-OSGi container.

To make this work, the Maven POM file of the project needs to be adapted. First, set the packaging to WAR. This will use `maven-war-plugin` to package this bundle, and in turn, the WAR file is not a WAB file anymore, as it lacks a valid OSGi manifest.

It's necessary to combine the two plugins to create a valid OSGi WAB file. For this, we need to configure `maven-bundle-plugin` in the following manner:

```
...
<executions>
  <execution>
    <id>bundle-manifest</id>
    <phase>process-classes</phase>
    <goals>
      <goal>manifest</goal>
    </goals>
  </execution>
</executions>
<configuration>
  <supportedProjectTypes>
    <supportedProjectType>jar</supportedProjectType>
    <supportedProjectType>bundle</supportedProjectType>
    <supportedProjectType>war</supportedProjectType>
  </supportedProjectTypes>
...
```

The plugin is configured just to produce a manifest file, and as the packaging is of the type WAR, `maven-bundle-plugin` needs to be configured to support the WAR format as valid packaging.

The manifest file generated from the preceding code will be merged into the WAR bundle explicitly using the `manifestFile` attribute, as shown in the following code:

```
<configuration>
  <archive>
    <manifestFile>${project.build.outputDirectory}/META-
      INF/MANIFEST.MF</manifestFile>
  </archive>
</configuration>
```

With these configurations, you'll generate a web application that can run in Apache Karaf and outside of OSGi.

For a complete sample, take a look at the source code at `https://github.com/jgoodyear/ApacheKarafCookbook/tree/master/chapter4/chapter4-recipe6`. Here, you will find a special POM file, `pom.war_xml`.

Configuring security for a web application in Apache Karaf

This recipe will handle how to build a web application with authentication enabled. As we are running within Apache Karaf and Karaf supports **Java Authentication and Authorization Service (JAAS)** out of the box, we will show you everything that is needed to run a basic authentication with JAAS on Karaf.

Getting ready

The prerequisite is to install the WAR feature. The source code for this recipe is available at `https://github.com/jgoodyear/ApacheKarafCookbook/tree/master/chapter4/chapter4-recipe7`.

How to do it...

1. The first step is configuring the user/password combination in Karaf. Let's start with the user configuration. Let's make sure that the `users.properties` file in the `/etc` folder contains the following setup (it's the default configuration):

   ```
   karaf = karaf,_g_:admingroup
   _g_\:admingroup = group,admin,manager,viewer
   ```

   The `users.properties` file follows the following syntax:

   ```
   USER=PASSWORD, ROLE1, ROLE2, …
   ```

   It can also have the following syntax:

   ```
   USER=PASSWORD, _g_:GROUP, …
   _g_\:GROUP=ROLE1,ROLE2, …
   ```

2. The next step is configuring JAAS in Jetty. The `jetty.xml` file used by Pax Web needs to contain a valid authentication realm. This realm needs to be configured for the usage of JAAS. Configuration of the `JAASLoginService` class will look like the following:

   ```
   <Call name="addBean">
     <Arg>
       <New class="org.eclipse.jetty.plus.
       jaas.JAASLoginService">
         <Set name="name">default</Set>
         <Set name="loginModuleName">karaf</Set>
         <Set name="roleClassNames">
   ```

```
          <Array type="java.lang.String">
            <Item>org.apache.karaf.jaas.
              boot.principal.RolePrincipal
            </Item>
          </Array>
        </Set>
      </New>
    </Arg>
```

The key to accessing the realm of Karaf is to define the `loginModuleName` value to `karaf` and define the right principal. As we are running within Karaf, we need as configure the `roleClassNames` value to be `org.apache.karaf.jaas.boot.principal.RolePrincipal`. With this, the security handshake configuration between Jetty and Karaf is complete.

3. The last step is configuring the web application to use JAAS. To use it from within the web application, the `web.xml` file needs to have security enabled and configured, as shown in the following code:

```
<security-constraint>
  <web-resource-collection>
    <web-resource-name>Protected Area</web-resource-name>
    <description>Protect the Example Servlet</description>
    <url-pattern>/secured/*</url-pattern>
    <http-method>GET</http-method>
    <http-method>POST</http-method>
  </web-resource-collection>
  <auth-constraint>
    <description>Authorized Users Group</description>
    <role-name>admin</role-name>
  </auth-constraint>
</security-constraint>
```

The security for this application is set to secure the secured URL for both the `GET` and `POST` methods. The required role has to be of the name `admin`, as was configured in step 1. Consider the following code:

```
<login-config>
  <auth-method>BASIC</auth-method>
  <realm-name>default</realm-name>
</login-config>
```

The login configuration is set to be of the type `BASIC`, so the container takes care of the authentication and it's configured to use the default realm. This configuration points to the defined `JAASLoginService` class with the name `default` (configured in step 2).

How it works...

The key for authentication in a web application is the JAAS security mechanism provided by Karaf. It's just a matter of configuration to make sure all parts are connected appropriately.

When working with Karaf and JAAS security realms, it might be of interest to know which realms are currently available. There is a shell command available to list all realms—the `jaas:realm-list` command.

This command will show us the available realms, as shown in the following screenshot:

```
karaf@root()> jaas:realm-list
Index | Realm Name | Login Module Class Name
--------------------------------------------------------------------------
1      | karaf      | org.apache.karaf.jaas.modules.properties.PropertiesLoginModule
2      | karaf      | org.apache.karaf.jaas.modules.publickey.PublickeyLoginModule
karaf@root()> []
```

There's more...

Now that we have configured security in the web application, the only thing missing is a way of addressing the application in a secure way. To enable SSL, we need to take parts of the configuration from the *Configuring Pax Web modules deployed in Apache Karaf* recipe and enable certain values that are off by default. All this is done to the `org.ops4j.pax.web.cfg` configuration file, as shown in the following code snippet:

```
org.osgi.service.http.secure.enabled = true
org.osgi.service.http.port.secure = 8443
org.osgi.service.http.secure.connector.name = secureDefault

org.ops4j.pax.web.ssl.keystore = ${karaf.base}/etc
   /keystore/.keystore
org.ops4j.pax.web.ssl.password = password
org.ops4j.pax.web.ssl.keypassword = password
org.ops4j.pax.web.ssl.clientauthwanted = false
org.ops4j.pax.web.ssl.clientauthneeded = false
```

With this configuration, we enable listening on the secure port, which is 8443 in our case. The `keystore` value is stored at a location relative to the Karaf base directory.

The `clientauthwanted` and `clientauthneeded` properties are set to `true` if the client should send a certificate for authentication instead of login credentials.

Once the configurations have been saved, they will be picked up by the FileInstaller bundle and applied to running Jetty server through Pax Web.

For a fully working SSL, you'll need a certificate, and so we need to create one. The following steps will work on the Linux and Mac environments and most likely on Windows:

1. The first step is the `keystore` setup. First of all, create the directory to contain the keystore that will be used with Karaf. It has to match the `org.ops4j.pax.web.ssl.keystore` property configured in the `org.ops4j.pax.web.cfg` file. This is shown in the following screenshot:

```
anierbeck@achims-macbook-pro:~/apache-karaf-3.0.1 \ $ mkdir etc/keystore
```

   On the system shell, not the Karaf shell, you will need to use a tool to create SSH keys. We will be using the Java tool named **keytool** to create keys and certificates. First, create the key to sign the certificate. Make sure that you're doing this in the `keystore` directory (`etc/keystore`). This can be done as follows:

   ```
   keytool -genkey -keyalg RSA -validity 1024 -alias serverkey -
     keypass password -storepass password -keystore server.jks
   ```

   We use a simple password as the password, as this is an example, but you shouldn't actually do this in production. As password, we use server. Have a look at the following screenshot:

```
                               keystore — bash — 104×22
anierbeck@achims-macbook-pro:~/apache-karaf-3.0.1/etc/keystore \ $ keytool -genkey -keyalg RSA -validity
1024 -alias serverkey -keypass password -storepass password -keystore server.jks
Wie lautet Ihr Vor- und Nachname?
  [Unknown]:
Wie lautet der Name Ihrer organisatorischen Einheit?
  [Unknown]:
Wie lautet der Name Ihrer Organisation?
  [Unknown]:
Wie lautet der Name Ihrer Stadt oder Gemeinde?
  [Unknown]:
Wie lautet der Name Ihres Bundeslands?
  [Unknown]:
Wie lautet der Ländercode (zwei Buchstaben) für diese Einheit?
  [Unknown]:
Ist CN=Unknown, OU=Unknown, O=Unknown, L=Unknown, ST=Unknown, C=Unknown richtig?
  [Nein]:  JA

anierbeck@achims-macbook-pro:~/apache-karaf-3.0.1/etc/keystore \ $
```

Once you see the previous screenshot, you are already set to use SSL in your application. You will need to navigate your browser to the application with the SSL port configured previously; in our example, it is 8443. Your browser will complain about an unsigned certificate of an unknown source. After accepting it, you'll have the login prompt from your authentication WAR file.

2. The next step is importing the client certificate. It is also possible to connect to the server with a signed client certificate. The client needs to do the same as has been done for the server—create a self-signed certificate. This certificate needs to be imported to the keystore of the server so that the server knows which certificate to accept. This can be done as follows:

```
keytool -import -trustcacerts -keystore server.jks -storepass
    password -alias clientkey -file client.cer
```

This client certificate needs to be transmitted by the HTTP client software, which may be a browser or some other means of communicating software.

Binding a web project to a specific host in Apache Karaf

With Karaf 3 and Pax Web 3, it is possible to bind a web application to a specific HTTP connector. This is a feasible solution to separate internal and external applications on the same server.

Getting ready

The sample code for this recipe is available at https://github.com/jgoodyear/ApacheKarafCookbook/tree/master/chapter4/chapter4-recipe8. Here, you will find a jetty.xml file at the src/main/etc location. It can be used to add an extra connector. Two extra recipes are available to show how to use this with a standard WAB file or the Whiteboard extender.

How to do it...

First of all, the server needs to be configured to support different HTTP connectors. Therefore, it is necessary to configure the Jetty server by editing the jetty.xml file found in the etc folder, as shown in the following code:

```
<Call name="addConnector">
  <Arg>
    <New class="org.eclipse.jetty.server.nio.
      SelectChannelConnector">
```

```
        <Set name="host"><Property name="jetty.host" /></Set>
        <Set name="port"><Property name="jetty.port"
          default="8282"/></Set>
        <Set name="maxIdleTime">300000</Set>
        <Set name="Acceptors">2</Set>
        <Set name="statsOn">false</Set>
        <Set name="confidentialPort">8443</Set>
        <Set name="name">alternateConnector</Set>
        <Set name="lowResourcesConnections">20000</Set>
        <Set name="lowResourcesMaxIdleTime">5000</Set>
      </New>
    </Arg>
```

Changes to the `jetty.xml` file will take effect only on the restart of the server and will not be picked up by FileInstaller and applied at runtime.

The second connector is bound to port `8282` and named `alternateConnector`. This will be referenced by the application to be bound to this connector.

To do so, the WAB file needs two additional manifest entries, which are as follows:

```
<plugin>
  <groupId>org.apache.felix</groupId>
  <artifactId>maven-bundle-plugin</artifactId>
  <version>2.4.0</version>
  <extensions>true</extensions>
  <configuration>
    <instructions>
      <_wab>src/main/webapp</_wab>
      <Web-ContextPath>packt-sample</Web-ContextPath>
      <Web-Connectors>alternateConnector</Web-Connectors>
      <Web-VirtualHosts>localhost</Web-VirtualHosts>
    </instructions>
  </configuration>
</plugin>
```

How it works...

The extra connector configured in the `jetty.xml` file is interpreted by Pax Web and is added to Jetty. With the special manifest entries, the web application bundle is bound to the configured HTTP connector. The number of connectors and applications bound to them are not limited.

There's more...

With Pax Web 3, and therefore with Apache Karaf 3, it is not only possible to bind the WAB file to the web connector, but also to a normal bundle. This needs some special handling, as there is no `Web-ContextPath` manifest header to define the context path.

The best way to achieve this is to use the Whiteboard extender. For this, we need to register a specialized HttpContext, as shown in the following code:

```
//preparing special HTTP Context with HTTP Connector
Hashtable<String, String> props = new Hashtable<String, String>();
props.put( ExtenderConstants.PROPERTY_HTTP_CONTEXT_ID,
  "httpConnector" );
HashMap<String,String> contextMappingParams = new HashMap
  <String,String>();
contextMappingParams.put(ExtenderConstants.PROPERTY_HTTP_VIRTUAL_
  HOSTS, "localhost");
contextMappingParams.put(ExtenderConstants.PROPERTY_HTTP_
  CONNECTORS, "alternateConnector");
contextMappingReg = bundleContext.registerService
  ( HttpContextMapping.class, new WhiteboardHttp
  ContextMapping("httpConnector", "whiteboard"
  , contextMappingParams), props );
```

The registered servlet just needs to use the following HttpContext:

```
props.put(ExtenderConstants.PROPERTY_ALIAS, "/connector");
props.put( ExtenderConstants.PROPERTY_HTTP_CONTEXT_ID
  , "httpConnector" );
servletReg = bundleContext.registerService(Servlet.class
  , new HelloServlet(), props);
```

That's it. Now you need to call the servlet with the `http://localhost:8282/whiteboard/connector` URL.

The servlet is registered with the alias/connector, but the HttpContext takes care of the Whiteboard context path.

Building a Servlet 3.0 annotated web application with Apache Karaf

With the Servlet 3.0 API, it's possible to have web archives only with annotated servlets and omit a `web.xml` file, or at least omit the configuration of the application within a `web.xml` file.

Getting ready

As usual, you will find the code for this recipe at the GitHub location at `https://github.com/jgoodyear/ApacheKarafCookbook/tree/master/chapter4/chapter4-recipe9`.

How to do it...

As with the *Building a standard web project to host in Apache Karaf* recipe, we just build another WAB bundle. Only this time, we have a `web.xml` file containing only the definition for the `welcome-file-list` method and annotated servlets:

1. The first step is defining the `web.xml` file. This can be done as follows:

```
<web-app xmlns="http://java.sun.com/xml/ns/
  javaee" xmlns:xsi="http://www.w3.org/2001/XMLSchema-
  instance"
    xsi:schemaLocation="http://java.sun.com/xml/ns/
      javaee http://java.sun.com/xml/ns/javaee/web-
      app_3_0.xsd"
    version="3.0">

    <welcome-file-list>
      <welcome-file>welcome.html</welcome-file>
    </welcome-file-list>

</web-app>
```

2. The next step is annotating the servlet. The servlet is simple and consists only of the usual servlet code and annotation. Consider the following code:

```
@WebServlet (value="/test", name="test")
public class HelloServlet extends HttpServlet {
```

3. The next step is annotating the filter. The filter also consists of the annotation to declare it to be a filter together with the `init` parameters, as shown in the following code:

```
@WebFilter(urlPatterns={"/*"}, servletNames = {"test"})
public class ServletFilter implements Filter {
```

With this assembly, you are all set to run Servlet 3.0 API applications in Apache Karaf.

There's more...

Pax Web does go a step further. As long as the bundle contains a `Web-ContextPath` in its `MANIFEST.MF` file, it's considered as a WAB file, and therefore, the Pax Web WAR extender handles it as such.

Make sure that you have a `Web-ContextPath` in your manifest, as shown in the following line of code:

```
<Web-ContextPath>packt-sample</Web-ContextPath>
```

Next, make sure that you have an annotated servlet contained in your bundle, as shown in the following line of code:

```
@WebServlet (value="/test", name="test")
public class HelloServlet extends HttpServlet {
```

Pointing the browser to `http://localhost:8181/packt-sample/test` will return the desired web content.

How it works...

The Pax Web WAR extender usually looks for bundles containing a `Web-ContextPath` in the manifest and for a `web.xml` file to publish the web archive. From Pax Web 3.0 on, the WAR extender also accepts bundles containing a `Web-ContextPath` in their manifest only.

Creating a CDI web application with Apache Karaf

Nowadays, modern web applications use **Contexts and Dependency Injection** (**CDI**) to wire the application. In the context of OSGi, it would be nice to have this working together with OSGi services. Pax Web, together with Pax CDI, takes care of this scenario.

Getting ready

Besides the installation of the WAR feature, it is required to install Pax CDI. Use the following commands to install them:

```
feature:install war
feature:install pax-cdi-web-openwebbeans
```

Alternatively, you can use the `weld` command as follows:

```
feature:install pax-cdi-web-weld
```

The source code for this recipe can be found at `https://github.com/jgoodyear/ApacheKarafCookbook/tree/master/chapter4/chapter4-recipe10`.

This recipe needs the bundle and web submodules. The bundle submodule contains the OSGi service, and the web submodule contains the CDI web application.

How to do it...

Let's start with the web application. The `web.xml` file can either be empty or can contain the entry for a `welcome-file-list` method, as the application is a Servlet 3.0 application. For a CDI application, it is required to have a `beans.xml` definition in the class path. As this is a web application, the `beans.xml` file is expected to be in the `WEB-INF` folder. For our use, it is sufficient to keep an empty `beans.xml` file in this directory.

The servlet needs to be annotated with the `@WebServlet` annotation to be picked up by Pax Web. This is shown in the following code:

```
@WebServlet(urlPatterns = "/sample")
public class OsgiServiceServlet  extends HttpServlet {
```

The servlet uses an OSGi service to retrieve simple quotes. This service is referenced via an injection, as shown in the following code:

```
@Inject
@OsgiService (dynamic = true)
private MessageService messageService;
```

The specialty of Pax CDI is the `@OsgiService` annotation. This annotation will wire the corresponding OSGi service to this servlet. The `dynamic = true` property makes sure that the dynamism of OSGi services is used.

For a smooth interaction between Pax Web and Pax CDI, a few more configurations are required. These are handled in the POM file, as shown in the following code:

```
<instructions>
  <_wab>src/main/webapp/</_wab>
  <Bundle-SymbolicName>${project.artifactId}</Bundle-SymbolicName>
  <Bundle-Version>${project.version}</Bundle-Version>
  <Web-ContextPath>cdi-sample</Web-ContextPath>
  <Pax-ManagedBeans>WEB-INF/beans.xml</Pax-ManagedBeans>
  <Require-Capability>
    org.ops4j.pax.cdi.extension;
  </Require-Capability>
</instructions>
```

Other than the already-known instructions such as `<_wab>` and `<Web-ContextPath>`, a CDI bundle requires the `<Require-Capability>` instruction. With this instruction, the resolver is informed of the fact that the web bundle requires the capability of the CDI bundle.

How it works...

Pax Web registers all of the servlets of a CDI web application. These servlets wait for the initialization of the context through Pax CDI. The service is provided by another bundle. As long as this service isn't available, the servlet will not start. The other important part is the `<Require-Capability>` manifest entry. It helps the resolver to wire the WAR bundle to the Pax CDI extension bundle. This way, the Pax CDI extender is capable of taking care of the injections.

This `<Require-Capability>` header can also be bound to a specific version. To do so, the following needs to be configured instead:

```
<Require-Capability>
  org.ops4j.pax.cdi.extension;
  filter:="(&amp;(extension=pax-cdi-extension)(version&gt
    ;=${version;==;${pax.cdi.osgi.version.clean}})(!(
    version&gt;=${version;=+;${pax.cdi.osgi.version.clean}})))",
  osgi.extender; filter:="(osgi.extender=pax.cdi)"
</Require-Capability>
```

See also

- ▶ Although this recipe gave you a brief overview of how to use CDI to wire services in OSGi, a lot more is possible. You can use CDI not only to wire an application within the same bundle but also to provide services through CDI and use it in another bundle. For more details about Pax CDI and the possibilities, refer to the Pax CDI project page at `https://ops4j1.jira.com/wiki/display/PAXCDI/Documentation`.

- ▶ Some more samples can be found at `https://github.com/ops4j/org.ops4j.pax.cdi/tree/master/pax-cdi-samples`.

5
Hosting Web Services with Apache CXF

In this chapter, we will cover the following recipes:

- ▸ Installing Apache CXF modules in Apache Karaf
- ▸ Using the CXF list endpoints command
- ▸ Using the CXF stop/start endpoints command
- ▸ Building and deploying a RESTful service in Karaf
- ▸ Building and deploying a Camel CXF web service in Karaf

Introduction

In *Chapter 3, Deploying a Message Broker with Apache ActiveMQ*, we discussed how and when to set up JMS systems. Another way to communicate between systems or applications is to provide web service or RESTful endpoints. Apache CXF provides a way to easily set up and publish web service endpoints. Publishing web services in Apache Karaf provides commands to control the endpoint lifecycle and monitor what is deployed.

Installing Apache CXF modules in Apache Karaf

Before we can deploy any web service or RESTful services, we need to get CXF installed in the Karaf container. Just like other frameworks, we need to get the features that support the required services installed.

How to do it...

To install the CXF framework, just install the CXF feature from the default Karaf instance. If no version is specified, it will use the latest version. For this example, we are using `version 3.0.0-milestone2`. We can do this using the following command:

```
karaf@root()> feature:repo-add cxf <version>
```

Once the feature URL is added, we can see all the CXF features that are provided. This can be done using the following command:

```
karaf@root()> feature:list | grep cxf
```

The list of CXF features is extensive, but for all of our recipes, we can simply install the CXF feature using the following command. This will install all the required features that will be used in this book.

```
karaf@root()> feature:install cxf
```

We can see that a large number of the required features have been installed at this point. The following list is a subset from a `feature:list` command:

```
cxf-specs                  | 3.0.0-milestone2 | x
cxf-jaxb                   | 3.0.0-milestone2 | x
wss4j                      | 2.0.0-rc1        | x
cxf-core                   | 3.0.0-milestone2 | x
cxf-wsdl                   | 3.0.0-milestone2 | x
cxf-ws-policy              | 3.0.0-milestone2 | x
cxf-ws-addr                | 3.0.0-milestone2 | x
cxf-ws-rm                  | 3.0.0-milestone2 | x
cxf-ws-mex                 | 3.0.0-milestone2 | x
cxf-ws-security            | 3.0.0-milestone2 | x
cxf-http                   | 3.0.0-milestone2 | x
cxf-http-jetty             | 3.0.0-milestone2 | x
cxf-bindings-soap          | 3.0.0-milestone2 | x
cxf-jaxws                  | 3.0.0-milestone2 | x
cxf-jaxrs                  | 3.0.0-milestone2 | x
cxf-databinding-aegis      | 3.0.0-milestone2 | x
cxf-databinding-jaxb       | 3.0.0-milestone2 | x
cxf-databinding-xmlbeans   | 3.0.0-milestone2 | x
cxf-features-clustering    | 3.0.0-milestone2 | x
```

cxf-bindings-corba	3.0.0-milestone2	x
cxf-bindings-coloc	3.0.0-milestone2	x
cxf-bindings-object	3.0.0-milestone2	x
cxf-transports-local	3.0.0-milestone2	x
cxf-transports-jms	3.0.0-milestone2	x
cxf-transports-udp	3.0.0-milestone2	x
cxf-javascript	3.0.0-milestone2	x
cxf-frontend-javascript	3.0.0-milestone2	x
cxf-xjc-runtime	3.0.0-milestone2	x
cxf	3.0.0-milestone2	x

How it works...

If we look at the features.xml file from the CXF code base, we can see that the cxf
feature is just a feature that installs all the required features for CXF deployment in Karaf.
This is shown in the following code:

```
<feature name="cxf" version="${version}" resolver='(obr)'>
  <feature version="[3,4)">spring</feature>
  <feature version="[1.2,2)">spring-dm</feature>
  <feature version="${version}">cxf-core</feature>
  <feature version="${version}">cxf-jaxws</feature>
  <feature version="${version}">cxf-jaxrs</feature>

  <feature version="${version}">cxf-databinding-jaxb</feature>
  <feature version="${version}">cxf-databinding-aegis</feature>
  <feature version="${version}">cxf-databinding-xmlbeans</feature>
  <feature version="${version}">cxf-bindings-corba</feature>
  <feature version="${version}">cxf-bindings-coloc</feature>
  <feature version="${version}">cxf-bindings-object</feature>

  <feature version="${version}">cxf-http-jetty</feature>

  <feature version="${version}">cxf-transports-local</feature>
  <feature version="${version}">cxf-transports-jms</feature>
  <feature version="${version}">cxf-transports-udp</feature>


  <feature version="${version}">cxf-xjc-runtime</feature>
  <feature version="${version}">cxf-ws-security</feature>
  <feature version="${version}">cxf-ws-rm</feature>
  <feature version="${version}">cxf-ws-mex</feature>
```

```
<feature version="${version}">cxf-javascript</feature>
<feature version="${version}">cxf-frontend-javascript</feature>
<feature version="${version}">cxf-features-clustering</feature>

<bundle start-level='50'>mvn:org.apache.cxf/cxf-bundle-
compatible/${version}</bundle>
</feature>
```

The `cxf` feature adds a compatibility bundle for the required bundle, as stated in the `features.xml` file.

See also

▶ The *Using the CXF list-endpoints command* recipe
▶ The *Using the CXF stop and start commands* recipe

Using the CXF list-endpoints command

In order to view what is deployed into an instance of CXF, we can use the `list-endpoints` command. This will list out all the buses currently deployed in the Karaf runtime.

 This recipe is only to demonstrate the use of the commands; we will cover how to create different CXF bundles in later recipes.

Getting ready

After completing the *Installing Apache CXF modules in Apache Karaf* recipe, we now need to build and deploy a sample CXF application into Karaf.

Go to the code bundle of this chapter and run the Maven build using the following command:

mvn clean install

This will build and install the sample applications for this chapter in the Maven repository so we can easily install them in the Karaf instance.

From the command line in the Karaf instance, install this recipe's CXF module using the following command:

Install -s mvn:com.packt/chapter5-recipe2/1.0.0-SNAPSHOT

How to do it...

We can run the following command to list CXF endpoints published in this instance of Karaf:

```
karaf@root()> cxf:list-endpoints
```

This will provide us with a list of CXF buses that have been started from our sample bundle. This is shown in the following command-line output:

```
Name            State       Address    BusID
[StringRestSe…] [Started] [/chapter5]  [chapter5-recipe2-cxf1752581114 ]
```

We can see from the result that our endpoint is published and available. The name of the implementation class name is `StringRestServiceImpl`. Also note that it is in the `Started` state and the address where we can locate the REST service.

 Use the `-f` parameter on the `list-endpoints` command to get the full address to the endpoint.

So let's give this a try. When you go to `http://localhost:8181/cxf/chapter5/recipeTwo`, it will display the message returned from the recipe code.

The type of browser might impact what you see; we are using Chrome in this example.

The following screenshot displays what will be seen in the browser:

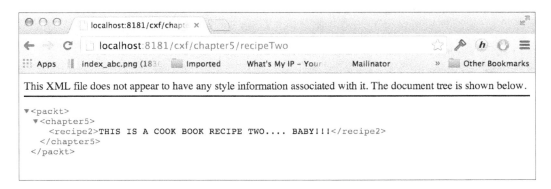

As you can see, we are able to hit the endpoint and see our message from the implementation class.

How it works...

Just like the list-busses command, this command uses the CXF controller to get the information needed for display in the console. The code for this is in the ListEndpointsCommand class. This will get the buses using the CXF controller, and then loop through the list and pull the ServiceRegistry in order to get a list of servers. From the server, we can get the rest of the details of the list, including the name, state, and address.

See also

► The *Using the CXF stop and start commands* recipe

Using the CXF stop and start commands

In some instances, there might be a need to control the state of the endpoint manually. Using the stop-endpoint or start-endpoint commands, we can shut down and start up a published endpoint from the command line. This is useful when testing client code to make sure that you are handling unavailable endpoints correctly.

Getting ready

Follow the steps from the *Using the CXF list-endpoints command* recipe.

How to do it...

Let's look at how to use the stop-endpoint and start-endpoint commands. Both commands require parameters for the bus and endpoint in order to know what to start or stop. The syntax for these commands looks like the following:

```
cxf:stop-endpoint <bus> <endpoint name>
cxf:start-endpoint <bus> <endpoint name>
```

To stop an endpoint, follow these steps:

1. Use the list-endpoints command to get the bus ID and the name of our published endpoint. The following will be the output:

   ```
   Name            State       Address       BusID

   [StringRestSe...] [Started] [/chapter5]  [chapter5-recipe2-
      cxf1752581114   ].
   ```

2. The information in the output of the preceding step can now be used to start and stop endpoints published in this instance of Karaf. Consider the following command:

```
cxf:stop-endpoint chapter5-recipe2-<cxf identifier>
   StringRestServiceImpl
```

3. The preceding command will stop the endpoint we published in the *Getting ready* section. Rerun the `list-endpoints` command in order to see the state change as follows:

```
Name            State       Address     BusID
[StringRestSe...] [Stopped] [/string] [chapter5-recipe2-
   <cxf identifier>   ].
```

Notice that the state has been changed to `Stopped`. This indicates that our REST service endpoint is no longer available from our browser. Use a browser to hit this endpoint address: `http://localhost:8181/cxf/chapter5/recipeTwo`.

The browser cannot find the address specified, which is exactly what we expect to happen. The following screenshot is what you should see:

Now, perform the following steps to start the endpoint again:

1. Use the endpoint listed in the `list-endpoints` command as follows:

```
cxf:start-endpoint chapter5-recipe2-<cxf identifier>
   StringRestServiceImpl
```

2. This will start the endpoint we published in the *Getting ready* section. Rerun the `list-endpoints` command in order to see the state change as follows:

```
Name            State       Address     BusID
[StringRestSe...] [Started  ] [/chapter5] [chapter5-recipe2-
   <cxf identifier> ].
```

How it works...

The command is made available from the `cxf` feature implemented by the
`StopEndpointCommand` class (the `start-endpoint` command is very similar).
This is shown in the following code line:

```
@Command(scope = "cxf", name = "stop-endpoint", description = "
    Stops a CXF Endpoint on a Bus.")
```

The command annotation shows you that the CXF defines the subshell and the command
name is `stop-endpoint`. This command also has several required parameters defined by
the following code:

```
@Argument(index = 0, name = "bus", description = "The CXF bus
    name where to look for the Endpoint", required = true
    , multiValued = false)
String busName;

@Argument(index = 1, name = "endpoint", description = "The
    Endpoint name to stop", required = true, multiValued = false)
String endpoint;
```

There are two parameters that are required (as noted by the `required=true` parameter in
the `Argument` annotation).

See also

▶ The *Using the CXF list-endpoints command* recipe

Building and deploying a RESTful service in Karaf

Now, let's look at how the code is assembled in order to publish a CXF endpoint in Karaf
using just CXF.

Getting ready

In this recipe, we will work with the `chapter5-recipe3` example from the code bundle.
Uninstall the `recipe2` code before going ahead with this recipe

First, install CXF as shown in the *Installing Apache CXF modules in Apache Karaf* recipe,
and then build and deploy a sample CXF application as `recipe3` in Karaf.

Go to the `chapter5-recipe3` example from the code bundle and run the Maven build using the following command:

```
mvn clean install
```

This will build and install the sample applications for the `chapter5-recipe3` example into the Maven repository, so we can easily install them in the Karaf instance.

How to do it...

Once the bundle is deployed, we can look at deploying and starting the CXF endpoint.

From the command line in the Karaf instance, install the `chapter5-recipe3` example's CXF module, start the bundle, and publish the endpoint with the following command:

```
install -s mvn:com.packt/chapter5-recipe3/1.0.0-SNAPSHOT
```

The `list-endpoints` command will show us that our endpoint has been started and is available, as shown in the following command-line snippet:

```
karaf@root()> cxf:list-endpoints

Name            State      Address       BusID

[StringRes...] [Started] [/chapter5] [chapter5-recipe3-<cxf identifier>
```

Now that we have verified that our endpoint is published, let's test it by hitting this endpoint address: `http://localhost:8181/cxf/chapter5/recipeThree`. The output is as shown in the following screenshot:

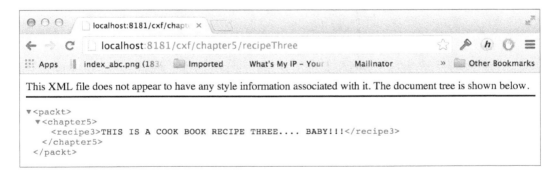

How it works...

Let's examine the different pieces of this puzzle to find out how we got the endpoint published.

First, we need to define the endpoint using an interface. In the sample code, look at the `StringRestService` interface class shown as follows:

```
@Path("/")
public interface StringRestService {
    @GET
    @Path("/recipeThree")
    @Produces("application/xml")
    public String getRecipeThree() throws Exception;
}
```

The `@Path("/")` annotation is set to null. This means that there is no address location that has been defined to access this RESTful endpoint.

This interface only defines the `@GET` value (not the `@POST` value) of the RESTful endpoint. In order to access this endpoint, we only need to use the `/recipeThree` location after the default in order to access the `getRecipeThree()` method.

The `@Produces` annotation defines the type of data that will be returned to the caller. In this case, we are defining XML via `application/xml`.

Then, we have to implement the interface in order to process the request to the endpoint. In our simple example, we are just returning a string value with XML. The implementation class looks like the following code:

```
public class StringRestServiceImpl implements StringRestService {
  @Override
  public String getRecipeThree() throws Exception {
    System.out.println("RECIPE 3 :: restful endpoint hit.");
    return "<packt>
      <chapter5>
        <recipe3>THIS IS A COOK BOOK RECIPE THREE....BABY!!!
          </recipe3>
      </chapter5>
    </packt>";
  }
}
```

The implementation class is simple—we are creating the `getRecipeThree` method and returning an XML string.

Now that we have the interface and implementation class defined, we need to configure the endpoint. Consider the following code:

```
<cxf:bus>
  <cxf:features>
    <cxf:logging/>
  </cxf:features>
</cxf:bus>

<jaxrs:server id="stringRestService" address="/chapter5">
  <jaxrs:serviceBeans>
    <ref component-id="stringRestServiceBean"/>
  </jaxrs:serviceBeans>
</jaxrs:server>

<bean id="stringRestServiceBean" class=
  "com.example.test.cxf.StringRestServiceImpl"/>
```

When working in the OSGi environment, it is suggested that you use Blueprint. The preceding XML code is from a Blueprint XML file.

In this configuration, we are defining the `cxf` bus and adding the `logging` feature. There is no reason to specify the implementation class for the bus since all of the logging information is embedded in the underlying schema definition.

Then, we need to instantiate the implementation class as a bean. Here, we give this an ID of `stringRestServiceBean`.

This bean ID is used in the server configuration to define ServiceBean. This will use the interface class implemented by the implementation class to publish the endpoint at the `/chapter5` location. Since we did not define a class with a base location, the address will look like `http://localhost:8181/cxf/chapter5/recipeThree` once it is deployed.

Notice that in the previous URL, the `/chapter5` location comes first, which is the address for the JAX-RS server, followed by the path defined in the interface class.

See also

▸   The *Building and deploying a Camel CXF web service in Karaf* recipe.

Building and deploying a Camel CXF web service in Karaf

In the previous recipe, we saw how easy it can be to deploy a RESTful service using CXF and Karaf. Now, we will explore how to deploy a WSDL first CXF endpoint using Camel. This is a good way to implement integration routes that expose web services. Uninstall the `recipe2` code before going ahead with this recipe

Getting ready

The example code for this recipe is in the `chapter5-recipe4` example of the code bundle. More than likely, you have already built the code, but just in case, go ahead and run the `mvn clean install` command against the `chapter5` folder. This will build and move the bundle to the Maven repository for deployment in Karaf.

Notice that there is the following line in the console for the build:

```
[INFO] --- cxf-codegen-plugin:2.7.4:wsdl2java (generate-sources
  ) @ chapter5-recipe4 ---
```

The preceding line indicates that the codegen plugin for CXF has been run and has generated the code from the WSDL defined in the `pom.xml` file. The following is the plugin definition that instructs Maven to build code from the WSDL:

```
<plugin>
  <groupId>org.apache.cxf</groupId>
  <artifactId>cxf-codegen-plugin</artifactId>
  <version>2.7.4</version>
  <executions>
    <execution>
      <id>generate-sources</id>
      <phase>generate-sources</phase>
      <configuration>
        <sourceRoot>
          ${basedir}/target/generated/src/main/java
        </sourceRoot>
        <wsdlOptions>
          <wsdlOption>
            <wsdl>
              ${basedir}/src/main/resources/META-
                INF/wsdl/report_domain.wsdl
            </wsdl>
```

```
        </wsdlOption>
      </wsdlOptions>
    </configuration>
    <goals>
      <goal>wsdl2java</goal>
    </goals>
  </execution>
</executions>
</plugin>
```

The WSDL is identified by the `<wsdl>` tags, so we can see that the `report_domain.wsdl` file is found in the `${basedir}/src/main/resources/META-INF/wsdl/` directory.

The `wsdl2java` goal indicates that we want the plugin to generate the necessary files from the WSDL.

How to do it...

First, we need to get the environment set up to run our Camel CXF endpoint. This can be done as follows:

1. We need to get Apache Camel installed using the following Camel feature command:

   feature:repo-add camel 2.12.3

   This will add the feature definitions for Camel into the Karaf instance.

2. Now, we need to actually install the `camel` and `camel-cxf` features using the following commands:

   feature:install camel

   feature:install camel-cxf

3. Once the `camel` and `camel-cxf` features are installed, we can install the bundle for this recipe using the following command:

   install -s mvn:com.packt/chapter5-recipe4/1.0.0-SNAPSHOT

We can list the bundles in order to make sure that the bundle was successfully installed using the `bundle:list` command. The output will be as follows:

```
START LEVEL 100 , List Threshold: 50
 ID | State  | Lvl | Version  | Name
---------------------------------------------------------
```

```
 85 | Active |  50 | 2.12.3    | camel-core
 86 | Active |  50 | 2.12.3    | camel-karaf-commands
101 | Active |  50 | 1.1.1     | geronimo-jta_1.1_spec
102 | Active |  50 | 2.12.3    | camel-spring
103 | Active |  50 | 2.12.3    | camel-blueprint
179 | Active |  50 | 2.7.10    | Apache CXF Compatibility Bundle Jar
180 | Active |  50 | 2.12.3    | camel-cxf-transport
181 | Active |  50 | 2.12.3    | camel-cxf
182 | Active |  80 | 1.0.0.SNA | Chapter 5 :: Recipe 4 ::
```

We can see that the last bundle is our recipe bundle. It has been started and is active, which indicates that the endpoint has been published.

To verify this, we can use CXF commands. When we use the `karaf@root()> cxf:list-busses` command, the output will be as follows:

```
Name                              State

[chapter5-recipe4-<id>          ] [RUNNING            ]
```

When we use the `karaf@root()> cxf:list-endpoints -f` command, the output will be as follows:

```
Name                    State

[ReportDomainService   ] [Started ]

Address

[http://localhost:9080/webservices/domain   ]

BusID

[chapter5-recipe4-<id>          ]
```

This indicates that our Camel CXF web service is deployed and available at `http://localhost:9080/webservices/domain`.

You can also look at the WSDL code available from the endpoint at
`http://localhost:9080/webservices/domain?wsdl`.

Put the preceding address in your favorite web browser and we will see the WSDL code.
This should look like the following screenshot:

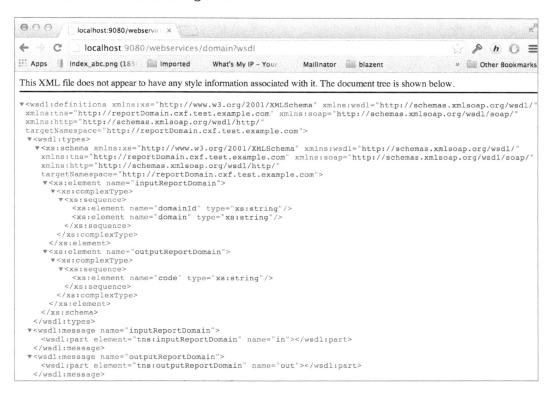

We see that the endpoint is published and available through several avenues. Let's go ahead and test it using SoapUI, which is a free web service testing tool that is available at `http://www.soapui.org/`. The steps are as follows:

1. Load the WSDL code as a project in SoapUI, and it will automatically set up a request for us based on the WSDL definition. The following screenshot shows us what the request should look like:

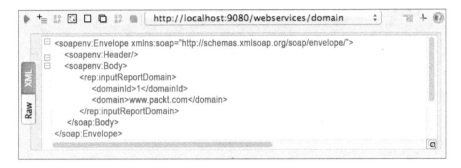

   This will also autoload the address for the request.

2. We can hit the play button to submit the request to the endpoint. It will respond with a simple `OK`, as shown in the following screenshot:

```
<soap:Envelope xmlns:soap="http://schemas.xmlsoap.org/soap/envelope/">
   <soap:Body>
      <ns2:outputReportDomain xmlns:ns2="http://reportDomain.cxf.test.example">
         <code>ok</code>
      </ns2:outputReportDomain>
   </soap:Body>
</soap:Envelope>
```

This shows that we were able to submit a request to the endpoint and retrieve the response. The response is a simple hardcoded `OK` but demonstrates the availability of the endpoint.

How it works...

First, let's look at the endpoint configuration for the Camel component. In the Blueprint file, we define the service endpoint as shown in the following code:

```
<blueprint
        xmlns="http://www.osgi.org/xmlns/blueprint/v1.0.0"
        xmlns:xsi="http://www.w3.org/2001/XMLSchema-instance"
```

```
    xmlns:camelcxf="http://camel.apache.org/schema/
      blueprint/cxf"
    xsi:schemaLocation="http://www.osgi.org/xmlns
      /blueprint/v1.0.0 http://www.osgi.org/xmlns/blueprint/
      v1.0.0/blueprint.xsd
    ">

  <camelcxf:cxfEndpoint id="reportDomain"
        address="http://localhost:9080/webservices/domain"
        wsdlURL="META-INF/wsdl/report_domain.wsdl"
        serviceClass="com.example.test.cxf.reportdomain.
          ReportDomainEndpoint"/>

  <bean id="domainRoutes" class="com.example.test.cxf.
    routes.DomainRoutes"/>

  <camelContext id="camel">
    <routeBuilder ref="domainRoutes"/>
  </camelContext>

</blueprint>
```

The preceding code is the CXF endpoint configuration; notice that we are specifying the address and port for our published web service as well as the location of the WSDL file.

The route is instantiated via a Blueprint with a `domainRoutes` bean ID. This will allow us to reference it from the CamelContext configuration.

The CamelContext defines all the Camel routes to be used in this bundle.

Now, let's look at the actual code for the route:

```
public class DomainRoutes extends RouteBuilder {
    OutputReportDomain ok = new OutputReportDomain();

    public void configure() throws Exception {
        // webservice response for OK
        ok.setCode("OK");

        from("cxf:bean:reportDomain").id("domainService")
          .choice().when().simple("${in.header.
          operationName} == 'ReportDomain'")
          .convertBodyTo(InputReportDomain.class)
          .to("log:dummy").process(new Processor() {
```

```
                        public void process(Exchange exchange)
                          throws Exception {
                            exchange.getIn().setBody(ok);
                        }
                })
                .end();
        }
    }
```

The `from("cxf:bean:reportDomain")` code line is the start of the route. We need to be able to configure it so that it can handle any calls to our web service. The `reportDomain` part in the URI is a reference to the `cxfEndpoint` object configured in the `blueprint.xml` file.

 Note that no implementation code is needed when using the Camel CXF endpoint, as all requests are intercepted and processed by the route.

The rest of the route is just for show. We convert the body to the defined data type in the WSDL. In this case, it is converted to `InputReportDomain.class`. Then, we log it to the `karaf.log` file using `.to("log:dummy")`. Finally, we return `OutputReportDomain.class` with an `OK` code.

See also

▶ The *Building and deploying a RESTful service in Karaf* recipe

6

Distributing a Clustered Container with Apache Karaf Cellar

In this chapter, we will cover the following topics:

- ▸ Installing Apache Karaf Cellar modules in Apache Karaf
- ▸ Using Apache Karaf Cellar commands
- ▸ Building and deploying a distributed architecture with Cellar

Introduction

This chapter shows how to install and use Apache Karaf Cellar with Apache Karaf. Apache Karaf Cellar's main aim is to enable a cluster-wide provisioning for Apache Karaf. This provisioning can be controlled with white and black lists for bundles, features, and configurations. Besides these core features, it is also possible to use Cellar to cluster in or with a cloud and send events through the cluster. It is also possible to have distributed OSGi services with Cellar.

 If you are looking for more insight on how Apache Karaf Cellar works, take a look at *Learning Karaf Cellar*, *Jean-Baptiste Onofré*, *Packt Publishing*.

Installing Apache Karaf Cellar modules in Apache Karaf

First of all, we will need to add the ability to cluster multiple Karaf instances. For this, Cellar needs to be installed on Apache Karaf first. For this, the required feature repository URL needs to be added, which can be done using the following convenient method:

```
karaf@root()> feature:repo-add cellar
```

After this, all the possible Cellar features of the latest version are available for installation. In our case, this is Cellar 3.0.0. Besides installing Cellar, it is required to have multiple Karaf instances running for verification of the recipes.

How to do it...

Follow these steps to set up Cellar and create multiple Karaf instances on the same machine:

1. Install the required `cellar` feature with the following command:

    ```
    karaf@root()> feature:install cellar
    ```

    This will install all the required Cellar bundles so that we have the basic setup to run a Karaf cluster.

2. Next, it's important to have another node for clustering. For this, we will set up a second Karaf instance on the same machine. For this, you'll find the following commands useful. So, create another Karaf instance using the following command:

    ```
    karaf@root()> instance:create second
    ```

    This will create a new Karaf instance that looks like a freshly extracted Apache Karaf ZIP archive.

3. The second instance is created; now, we need to start this second instance. There is a command in Karaf to do so, which is as follows:

    ```
    karaf@root()> instance:start second
    ```

4. This just started the second instance, which can now be connected to, by either an external SSH client or through Karaf. This can be done using the following command:

    ```
    karaf@root()> instance:connect second
    ```

5. With this, you are connected to the second instance of Karaf. We need to add the `cellar` repository to this instance too. This can be done using the following command:

    ```
    karaf@second()> feature:repo-add cellar
    ```

6. After the `cellar` feature repository becomes available to the second instance, the `cellar` feature is ready to be installed.

   karaf@second()> feature:install cellar

This installs the required bundles; therefore, we have two nodes ready to be clustered. As the Cellar cluster works with auto discovery through multicast, both nodes should be able to find each other.

 As Cellar uses Hazelcast as its underlying cluster technology, the multicast is handled by Hazelcast. More information about Hazelcast is available at `http://www.hazelcast.org/docs/3.0/manual/html/ch12s02.html`.

These nodes can be checked by listing the available groups using the following command:

karaf@second()> cluster:group-list

This will list the available groups together with the nodes contained in each group. As there has been no configuration for any group yet, the default group contains both nodes—the root Karaf instance and the second instance. The following screenshot shows the execution of the `group-list` command, which is an alias of the `cluster:group-list` command:

```
karaf@second()> cluster:group-list
   Group                  Members
* [default               ] [achims-macbook-pro.fritz.box:5701 achims-macbook-pro.fritz.box:5702* ]
```

How it works...

After the installation of Cellar on both nodes, Cellar created a default group on both the nodes, and therefore, both these nodes are automatically added to this default group. The basis of Cellar is a Hazelcast-based memory cluster configuration, which replicates itself to all known nodes in the cluster. Hazelcast itself scans the network via multicast for other instances of itself. Hazelcast can be configured to use other means of network connection technologies. Apache Karaf Cellar uses this behavior to synchronize the cluster configuration over the running nodes.

A Cellar cluster is defined by a group, where each group consists of a list of nodes. For each cluster group, there is a Hazelcast topic, which is the communication backend. With this topic, all nodes within the same group communicate changes in bundles, features, or configuration. Additionally, services and events are also communicated through this topic.

Due to this topic, the configuration of all nodes is combined to a shared cluster configuration, as shown in the following screenshot:

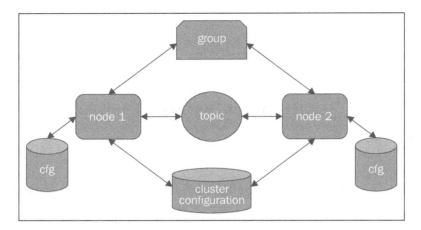

Using Apache Karaf Cellar commands

As with a lot of other features of Apache Karaf, Cellar provides a couple of commands to administer an Apache Karaf Cellar cluster.

Getting ready

Make sure that you follow the basic setup of the *Installing Apache Karaf Cellar modules in Apache Karaf* recipe to run a simple Apache Karaf cluster.

How to do it...

We have two different kinds of commands to work with the Apache Karaf Cellar cluster: basic commands to manage and configure the cluster and some more enhanced commands for extra management.

Group commands

After installing Cellar, there is already a default group available that contains all the future available nodes per default. Different tasks can be performed using the following commands:

1. Now, let's create a new group and add both nodes to it using the following command:

    ```
    karaf@root()> cluster:group-create main-cluster
    ```

The previous command creates a new cluster group called `main-cluster`. This group contains no nodes in it. Check using the `group-list` command to see how the cluster looks right now. The result of this command can be seen in the following screenshot:

```
karaf@root()> cluster:group-list
    Group                    Members
* [default                 ] [achims-macbook-pro.fritz.box:5701* achims-macbook-pro.fritz.box:5702 ]
  [main-cluster            ] []
```

2. The newly created group is still empty. Therefore, we need to add some nodes. Adding nodes to a cluster can be done in different ways. The following command is an example:

   karaf@root()> cluster:group-pick default main-cluster

   The following is the complete syntax for the preceding command:

   cluster:group-pick source-group destination-group number-of-nodes

   It picks a number of nodes from the given source group and transfers these nodes to the target group. If no number is given, one is picked from the source group. The execution and what it looks like is shown in the following screenshot:

```
karaf@root()> cluster:group-pick default main-cluster
    Group                    Members
  [default                 ] [achims-macbook-pro.fritz.box:5702 ]
* [main-cluster            ] [achims-macbook-pro.fritz.box:5701* ]
```

3. Another way of adding a node to a cluster group is to use the `join` command. With this command, you also have the possibility to add a node to more than one group.

   karaf@root()> cluster:group-join main-cluster achims-macbook-pro.fritz.box:5702

   The syntax of the preceding command is as follows:

   cluster:group-join group-destination node-id

   The command, including its output, is shown in the following screenshot:

```
karaf@root()> cluster:group-join main-cluster achims-macbook-pro.fritz.box:5702
    Group                    Members
  [default                 ] [achims-macbook-pro.fritz.box:5702 ]
* [main-cluster            ] [achims-macbook-pro.fritz.box:5701* achims-macbook-pro.fritz.box:5702 ]
```

4. As you can tell, the second node is now contained in both cluster groups, though we don't want to have this node in the default group anymore. For this, we need to remove it from this group by using the following command:

```
karaf@root()> cluster:group-quit default achims-macbook-
    pro.fritz.box:5702
```

The syntax for the preceding command is as follows:

```
cluster:group-quit group-id node-id
```

The command returns a list of the current state of the groups, as shown in the following screenshot:

```
karaf@root()> cluster:group-quit default achims-macbook-pro.fritz.box:5702
    Group                    Members
    [default                 ] []
* [main-cluster             ] [achims-macbook-pro.fritz.box:5701* achims-macbook-pro.fritz.box:5702 ]
karaf@root()>
```

5. This empty group can be deleted using the following command:

```
karaf@root()> cluster:group-delete default
```

When checking with the `cluster:group-list` command, you'll see that the default group can't be deleted. This is because of its default character. So, if you create a new test group and delete it right away, you will see that the test group has been created and deleted with the commands.

The node commands

The following is a brief introduction of the node commands.

1. Similar to the `group-list` command, the `node-list` command will list all available nodes:

```
karaf@root()> cluster:node-list
```

The output of the preceding command is shown in the following screenshot:

```
karaf@root()> cluster:node-list
    ID                                          Host Name                    Port
* [achims-macbook-pro.fritz.box:5701] [achims-macbook-pro.fritz.box] [ 5701]
  [achims-macbook-pro.fritz.box:5702] [achims-macbook-pro.fritz.box] [ 5702]
```

2. Similar to a network ping, it is possible to ping a cluster node to test the network accessibility of this node. This can be done using the following command:

```
karaf@root()> cluster:node-ping achims-macbook-pro:5702
```

The output will be as shown in the following screenshot:

```
karaf@root()> cluster:node-ping achims-macbook-pro.fritz.box:5702
PING achims-macbook-pro.fritz.box:5702
from 1: req=achims-macbook-pro.fritz.box:5702 time=14 ms
from 2: req=achims-macbook-pro.fritz.box:5702 time=6 ms
from 3: req=achims-macbook-pro.fritz.box:5702 time=5 ms
from 4: req=achims-macbook-pro.fritz.box:5702 time=5 ms
from 5: req=achims-macbook-pro.fritz.box:5702 time=4 ms
from 6: req=achims-macbook-pro.fritz.box:5702 time=5 ms
from 7: req=achims-macbook-pro.fritz.box:5702 time=6 ms
from 8: req=achims-macbook-pro.fritz.box:5702 time=5 ms
from 9: req=achims-macbook-pro.fritz.box:5702 time=5 ms
from 10: req=achims-macbook-pro.fritz.box:5702 time=7 ms
```

Cluster configuration commands

So far, the previous commands have been used for administration of the cluster itself, by either adding or removing cluster groups and configuring the nodes of one cluster group.

1. The last administrational command is the `cluster:sync` command:

   ```
   karaf@root()> cluster:sync
   ```

   This will force a synchronization of all nodes in the cluster, as shown in the following screenshot:

   ```
   karaf@root()> cluster:sync
   Synchronizing cluster group main-cluster
       sync class Proxy4e32cf2c_4bad_4a2d_8fd0_0fc7717d5175 ...OK
       sync class Proxy5b8922f5_7836_47a8_9b46_c209561188db ...OK
       sync class Proxy38062597_a4a0_4910_9417_621aaf61be48 ...OK
   ```

2. Now, the following commands are used to configure the content of the cluster. For example, it is possible to install features and bundles across the cluster. To list the currently available features for one cluster group, just issue the following command:

   ```
   karaf@root()> cluster:feature-list main-cluster
   ```

   ```
   karaf@root()> cluster:feature-list main-cluster
   Features in cluster group main-cluster
     Status          Version               Name
     [uninstalled]   [2.2.2             ]  openjpa
     [uninstalled]   [3.0.1-SNAPSHOT    ]  http-whiteboard
     [uninstalled]   [1.4.0             ]  jclouds-cloudfiles-uk
     [uninstalled]   [1.4.0             ]  jclouds-elastichosts-lon-b
     [uninstalled]   [1.4.0             ]  jclouds-cloudonestorage
     [uninstalled]   [3.0.1-SNAPSHOT    ]  http
     [uninstalled]   [3.2.4.RELEASE     ]  spring-tx
     [uninstalled]   [0.6.0             ]  pax-cdi-web-openwebbeans
     [installed   ]  [3.0.1-SNAPSHOT    ]  region
     [uninstalled]   [1.4.0             ]  jclouds-driver-slf4j
     [uninstalled]   [1.4.0             ]  jclouds-elastichosts-tor-p
     [uninstalled]   [1.4.0             ]  jclouds-rimuhosting
     [uninstalled]   [3.1.4.RELEASE     ]  spring-struts
     [uninstalled]   [3.0.7-SNAPSHOT    ]  pax-war
     [uninstalled]   [1.4.0             ]  jclouds-elastichosts-lax-p
     [uninstalled]   [0.6.0             ]  pax-cdi-1.1-web
     [uninstalled]   [4.0.2.RELEASE_1]     spring-web-portlet
     [uninstalled]   [3.1.4.RELEASE     ]  spring
     [uninstalled]   [1.4.0             ]  jclouds-api-filesystem
   ```

3. The preceding command also works for listing the bundles installed across the cluster:

```
karaf@root()> cluster:bundle-list main-cluster
```

This results in a list of bundles available to the cluster group. The output will be as follows:

```
karaf@root()> cluster:bundle-list main-cluster
Bundles in cluster group main-cluster
  ID      State           Name
 [0    ] [Active       ] OPS4J Base - Lang (1.4.0)
 [1    ] [Active       ] Apache Karaf :: Cellar :: Hazelcast
    (3.0.0.SNAPSHOT)
 [2    ] [Active       ] Apache Karaf :: Cellar :: Features
    (3.0.0.SNAPSHOT)
 [3    ] [Active       ] Apache Karaf :: Cellar :: Core
    (3.0.0.SNAPSHOT)
 [4    ] [Active       ] JLEdit :: Core (0.2.1)
 [5    ] [Active       ] Apache Karaf :: JAAS :: Command (3.0.1)
 [6    ] [Active       ] Apache Mina SSHD :: Core (0.9.0)
 [7    ] [Active       ] Apache Karaf :: Cellar :: Management
    (3.0.0.SNAPSHOT)
 [8    ] [Active       ] jansi (1.11.0)
```

4. For further bundle interaction in the cluster, use the following special bundle commands for clusters:

```
cluster:bundle-* <groupId>
```

These bundle commands are similar to the standard Apache Karaf bundle commands. The scope of these commands is to distribute the command within the cluster.

5. For features, the commands are similar to the `cluster:bundle` commands. Commands that are possible for features are also available to be run in the cluster scope:

```
cluster:feature-* <groupId>
```

The `cluster:feature` commands will work on the cluster as for a standalone Karaf instance.

6. Similar to the bundle and feature commands, the configuration commands can also alter, set, or unset configurations which are valid throughout the cluster. Consider the following command:

```
karaf@root()> cluster:config-list main-cluster
```

The output of the preceding command is the same as that of the `config:list` command, restricted only to the configurations that are valid for the cluster group, as can be seen in the following screenshot:

```
karaf@root()> cluster:config-list main-cluster
----------------------------------------------------------------------
Pid:            org.apache.karaf.service.acl.command.bundle.start
Properties:
   start[/.*[-][f].*/] = admin
   start = manager
   execute[/.*/,/.*[-][f].*/] = admin
   service.pid = org.apache.karaf.service.acl.command.bundle.start
   service.guard = (&(osgi.command.scope=bundle)(osgi.command.function=start))
   execute = manager
   * = *
----------------------------------------------------------------------
Pid:            org.apache.karaf.command.acl.kar
Properties:
   service.pid = org.apache.karaf.command.acl.kar
   uninstall = admin
   install = admin
----------------------------------------------------------------------
```

7. In general, the cluster configuration commands have the following pattern:

```
cluster:config-* <groupId>
```

The preceding commands give the possibility to edit, delete, or add a configuration, which is then automatically shared throughout the cluster.

How it works...

As seen, Apache Karaf Cellar provides a couple of specialized cluster commands. This functionality is based on the fact that all of the configurations, installed bundles, and installed features are shared throughout the cluster. To have a dedicated control over this information, it is possible to whitelist or blacklist certain information. This information is defined in two configuration files, `org.apache.karaf.cellar.node.cfg` for node configurations and `org.apache.karaf.cellar.groups.cfg` containing the group configuration information.

In general, it is better to work with features instead of bundles when deploying applications throughout the cluster. This makes it easier to filter whitelisted and blacklisted bundles or features for certain cluster nodes.

See also

▶ *Learning Karaf Cellar, Jean-Baptiste Onofré, Packt Publishing*, covers the insights of Cellar in greater detail compared to what can be done with this Cookbook.

Building and deploying a distributed architecture with Cellar

This recipe describes how to build a clustered application and the transparent usage of services throughout the cluster. We will show you how to create a Cellar-based **Distributed OSGi** (**DOSGi**) application and how you can profit from Apache Karaf Cellar.

Getting ready

It is essential that you finish at least the *Installing Apache Karaf Cellar modules in Apache Karaf* recipe to have a clustered environment for testing. You should also be familiar with the cluster commands presented to you in the *Using Apache Karaf Cellar commands* recipe. The sources used in this recipe can be found at `https://github.com/jgoodyear/ApacheKarafCookbook/tree/master/chapter6/chapter6-recipe3`.

How to do it...

First of all, we will need an additional cluster group with an extra node. For this, we will create an additional instance first, using the following command:

```
karaf@root()> instance:create sender
```

Start this instance and install the `cellar` feature in it as described in the *Installing Apache Karaf Cellar modules in Apache Karaf* recipe. This instance will be added to a new group. First, create a new cluster group using the following command:

```
karaf@root()> cluster:group-create second-cluster
```

Now, add the new instance to the newly created cluster group using the following command:

```
karaf@root()> cluster:group-pick default second-cluster
```

After this setup is done, we need to take care of the distributed OSGi service. For this, you will create three different bundles, where the first will contain the service interface, the second will contain the service implementation that is located on one node, and the third will contain the consuming bundle.

The following diagram shows this setup:

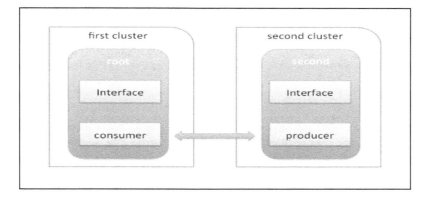

First, we need to install the required feature. For this, we will install the `cellar-dosgi` feature on each node using the following command. By default, all Cellar features are blacklisted.

`karaf@root()> feature:install cellar-dosgi`

After this feature is installed in the cluster, you will have a new command to use. The `cluster:service-list` command will list all services that are distributed throughout the cluster. The command when called right after installing the feature will give you the following output:

```
karaf@root()> cluster:service-list
No service available on the cluster
karaf@root()>
```

Producing a service bundle

After this setup, we will need a bundle that provides a service that is available to remote clients. For this, we create a simple service that returns a random message. This can be done as follows:

1. To register this service, we will use the following `blueprint.xml` file:

```xml
<!-- Service Implementation -->
<bean id="messageService"
  class="com.packt.impl.MessageServiceImpl"/>

<!-- Registering the Service -->
<service ref="messageService"
  interface="com.packt.MessageService">
  <service-properties>
    <entry key="service.exported.interfaces" value="*"/>
  </service-properties>
</service>
```

2. Install the `chapter6-recipe3-interface` bundle from the code bundle on both cluster groups using the following commands:

```
karaf@root()> cluster:bundle-install master
  mvn:com.packt/chapter6-recipe3-interface/1.0.0-SNAPSHOT
karaf@root()> cluster:bundle-install second-cluster
  mvn:com.packt/chapter6-recipe3-interface/1.0.0-SNAPSHOT
```

3. After this, install the `chapter6-recipe3-producer` bundle from the code bundle on the second group, `second-cluster`, using the following command:

```
karaf@root()> cluster:bundle-install second-cluster
  mvn:com.packt/chapter6-recipe3-producer/1.0.0-SNAPSHOT
```

4. The freshly-installed bundles need to be started. For easy finding of these installed bundles, issue a `bundle-list` command with the `grep` command, as shown in the following command:

```
karaf@root()> cluster:bundle-list main-cluster | grep -i
  chapter
```

This results in the following output:

```
karaf@root()> cluster:bundle-list main-cluster | grep chapter6

[36  ] [Installed  ] chapter6-recipe3-interface
  (1.0.0.SNAPSHOT)
```

5. Now that you have found the corresponding bundle ID, just issue a start command for it:

```
karaf@root()> cluster:bundle-start main-cluster <bundle id>
```

A quick use of the `list` command will give you the bundle listing of the node, showing the freshly-installed and running bundle `chapter6-recipe3-interface`. This is shown in the following screenshot:

```
karaf@root()> list
START LEVEL 100 , List Threshold: 50
ID | State   | Lvl | Version         | Name
-----------------------------------------------------------
88 | Active  | 80  | 1.0.0.SNAPSHOT | chapter6-recipe3-interface
karaf@root()> []
```

Now that we have checked the consuming side, we need to make sure the sending side is running. We need to look for the bundle that we just installed. This can be done using the following command:

```
karaf@root()> cluster:bundle-list second-cluster | grep -i chapter
```

This results in the following output:

```
karaf@root()> cluster:bundle-list second-cluster | grep chapter6
[38  ] [Installed  ] chapter6-recipe3-interface (1.0.0.SNAPSHOT)
[39  ] [Installed  ] chapter6-recipe3-producer (1.0.0.SNAPSHOT)
```

We can start the bundle with the following command:

```
karaf@root()> cluster:bundle-start main-cluster <bundle id>
```

After this bundle is started, we can check with the `cluster:service-list` command, called from the root bundle, for services available to the cluster. The result of this is as shown in the following screenshot:

```
karaf@root()> cluster:service-list
Service Class                                      Provider Node
org.apache.aries.proxy.weaving.WovenProxy          achims-macbook-pro.fritz.box:5702
com.packt.MessageService                           achims-macbook-pro.fritz.box:5702
karaf@root()> []
```

Service consuming bundle

As the service is now available throughout the cluster, the consuming bundle can be installed on the main cluster and will consume this service. Consider the following code:

```
<!-- reference service -->
<reference id="messageService" interface=
  "com.packt.MessageService" />

<!-- Service Implementation -->
<bean class="com.packt.consumer.MessageConsumer" init-
  method="doRun">
  <property name="messageService" ref="messageService"/>
</bean>
```

The consuming bundle retrieves the service reference from the registry and uses it. The consuming class is started with the `init-method` call.

The interface bundle is already installed because we have already issued the `cluster:bundle-install` command for it. Now, just install the `consumer` bundle on the root node, using the following command:

```
karaf@root()>cluster:bundle-install main-cluster mvn:com.packt/chapter6-
recipe3-consumer/1.0.0-SNAPSHOT
```

Now, start the `consumer` bundle by issuing the following command; you might be required to change the bundle ID:

```
karaf@root()> cluster:bundle-list master | grep -i chapter
[36  ] [Active     ] chapter6-recipe3-interface (1.0.0.SNAPSHOT)
[52  ] [Installed  ] chapter6-recipe3-consumer (1.0.0.SNAPSHOT)
```

You can start the bundle using the following command:

```
karaf@root()> cluster:bundle-start <bundle-id>
```

 Note that if you started the second node in a separate terminal, you will gain the most from this, as you'll see both nodes receiving the messages from the sender.

How it works...

By default, Cellar DOSGi doesn't share any service throughout the cluster. A service meant to be used in a cluster environment and to be bound to a dedicated cluster node will require special handling on the service. You might have noticed the extra service property on the `MessageService` registration. The property entry, `service.exported.interfaces`, marks this service to be exported throughout the cluster. Cellar will create a proxy for the remote service on the nodes not containing the actual service.

Why did we need the extra node and group? As Apache Karaf Cellar is for provisioning bundles across a cluster group, this will result in spreading all bundles across the same group. While running services across a cluster actually needs the separation of bundles across the cluster, this results in actually separating nodes with explicit groups again.

Take a look at the following screenshot; it sums up the communication ways within one cluster group. Installation of one bundle throughout the cluster is either achieved through the commands mentioned previously or by just installing this bundle on **node 1**. This *state* of a new bundle will be synchronized throughout the cluster group unless this explicit bundle is blacklisted. Another way of disabling this automatic synchronization throughout the cluster is by using a management node. A management node requires one *master* node within the cluster group that manages the installation of the features across the cluster. This works contrary to the default setup and idea behind the *all-knowing* cluster *brain*. For more details, check out *Learning Karaf Cellar, Jean-Baptiste Onofré, Packt Publishing*.

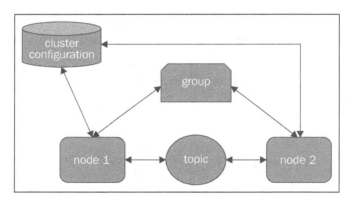

7
Providing a Persistence Layer with Apache Aries and OpenJPA

In this chapter, we will cover the following recipes:

- ▶ Installing OpenJPA modules in Apache Karaf
- ▶ Installing Apache Aries JTA modules in Apache Karaf
- ▶ Building a project with a persistence layer for deployment in Karaf
- ▶ Building a project with a persistence layer and transaction support for deployment in Karaf

Introduction

Your applications will commonly need to safely persist data and make use of transactional behaviors. A preferred way to accomplish this for Java developers is to use the **Java Persistence API** (**JPA**) and **Java Transaction API** (**JTA**). In the context of Apache Karaf, developers will use an OSGi-ready JPA implementation, such as **Apache OpenJPA**, **EclipseLink**, or **Hibernate** and the **Apache Aries JTA**.

This book will use OpenJPA as an implementation of the JPA specification for the transparent persistence of Java objects. In relation to OSGi containers, it provides container-managed persistence for the Blueprint container.

The Apache Aries JTA provides a transaction management service to the container. Using this service, developers can build applications requiring the following transactional flow:

```
getTransaction()
begin()  // demark beginning of transaction
doWork() // your business logic
if (rollback) then rollback() else commit()
```

The previous pseudo code outlines the general form of a transaction; the developer obtains from the container a transaction session, demarks the beginning of the transaction, performs their business logic and, then must decide if they can commit the transaction or rollback resources.

The recipes in this chapter will aid you in deploying JPA and JTA resources into Karaf, and guide you by example to use these APIs in your bundles.

Installing OpenJPA modules in Apache Karaf

Before we can begin to explore how to build OpenJPA-backed applications, we must first install all the required JPA modules into the Karaf container.

Getting ready

The ingredients of this recipe include the Apache Karaf distribution kit, access to JDK, and Internet connectivity.

How to do it...

Thanks to Apache Karaf's feature system, installing OpenJPA is a very simple two-step process: install the JPA and OpenJPA feature in Karaf. The steps are as follows:

 Why do we not have to add the feature URL? This is because Apache Karaf's standard distribution includes the JPA and OpenJPA feature URLs by default.

1. We can install a feature by executing the `feature:install` command with the feature's name as follows:

   karaf@root()> feature:install jpa

   We can verify the installation by executing the `list -t 0 | grep -i JPA` command, which will list all installed OpenJPA components and dependencies in Karaf (Geronimo-jta_1.1_spec, Geronimo-jpa_2.0_spec, Aries JPA API, Aries JPA Blueprint, Aries JPA Container, and Aries JPA Container Context).

2. Similar to the installation of the JPA, we use the feature's name to install the OpenJPA engine, as follows.

```
karaf@root()> feature:install openjpa/2.2.2
```

We can verify the installation by executing the `list -t 0 | grep -i OpenJPA` command, which will list all installed OpenJPA components and dependencies in Karaf (core among them is the OpenJPA Aggregate JAR).

How it works...

The Apache Karaf community maintains an Apache Karaf feature descriptor for JPA and OpenJPA. These feature descriptor files contain all of the essential bundles and dependencies required to install these APIs and providers, which are shown in the following diagram:

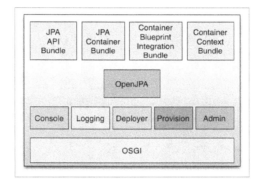

When the JPA or OpenJPA feature is installed (using the `feature:install` command), Karaf will use the appropriate URL handlers to obtain the required resources and install them into the container. Next, it attempts to bring them to a started state. If you execute the `list -t 0` command on the Karaf console, you will see the JPA and all other artifacts deployed into the container. We can depict the integration of OpenJPA components into Karaf more simply by illustrating the key artifacts being deployed atop a standard Karaf installation.

See also

▸ The *Deploying applications as a feature* recipe of *Chapter 1, Apache Karaf for System Builders*.

Installing Apache Aries JTA modules in Apache Karaf

Applications often require transaction management alongside the JPA. This is accomplished by including the JTA into the Karaf container.

Getting ready

The ingredients of this recipe include the Apache Karaf distribution kit, access to JDK, and Internet connectivity. Generally, you'll also need to perform the steps outlined in the *Installing OpenJPA modules in Apache Karaf* recipe.

How to do it...

Thanks to Apache Karaf's feature system, installing JTA is a very simple one-step process.

 Why do we not have to add the feature URL? This is because Apache Karaf's standard distribution includes the JTA feature URL by default.

Installing the JTA feature into Karaf

We install a feature by executing the `feature:install` command with the feature's name as follows:

```
karaf@root()>  feature:install transaction
```

We can verify the installation by executing the `list -t 0 | grep -i transaction` command, which will list all installed transaction components and dependencies in Karaf (such as Apache Aries Transaction Blueprint and Apache Aries Transaction Manager). In addition, we can verify that `geronimo_jta_1.1_spec` has been installed by grepping on `jta`.

How it works...

The Apache Karaf community maintains an Apache Karaf features descriptor for JTA. The features descriptor file contains all of the essential bundles and dependencies required to install the transaction manager, which are shown in the following diagram:

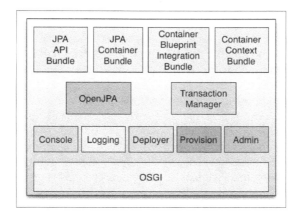

When the JTA feature is installed (using the `feature:install` command), Karaf will use the appropriate URL handlers to obtain the required resources and install them in the container. Next, it attempts to bring them to a started state. If you execute the `list -t 0` command on the Karaf console, you will see the JTA and all other artifacts deployed into the container. We can depict the integration of JTA components into Karaf more simply by illustrating the key artifacts being deployed atop a standard Karaf installation. In this deployment, we see the Transaction Manager (JTA) deployed among the various JPA modules from the *Installing OpenJPA modules in Apache Karaf* recipe.

See also

▸ The *Deploying applications as a feature* recipe of *Chapter 1, Apache Karaf for System Builders*

▸ The *Installing OpenJPA modules in Apache Karaf* recipe

Building a project with a persistence layer for deployment in Karaf

Application developers often need to make use of a persistence layer in their projects; one of the preferred methodologies to perform this in Karaf is to make use of the Java Persistence API and OpenJPA.

In the *Installing OpenJPA modules in Apache Karaf* recipe, we learned how to install OpenJPA in Karaf; in this recipe, we'll make use of the JPA and OpenJPA to build a simple application that persists recipes to a database using a `RecipeBookService` class, which will hide the complexities of data storage and retrieval from its users.

Getting ready

The ingredients of this recipe include the Apache Karaf distribution kit, access to JDK, and Internet connectivity. Sample code for this recipe is available at `https://github.com/jgoodyear/ApacheKarafCookbook/tree/master/chapter7/chapter7-recipe3`. Generally, you'll also need to perform the steps outlined in the *Installing OpenJPA modules in Apache Karaf* recipe.

 Please uninstall contents of the *Building a project with a persistence layer and transaction support for deployment in Karaf* recipe before attempting this recipe as conflicts may occur. This recipe comes later in the chapter.

How to do it...

Building a project with a JPA persistence layer will require the following nine steps:

1. The first step is generating a Maven-based bundle project. Create an empty Maven-based project. A `pom.xml` file containing the essential Maven coordinate information and a bundle packaging directive will suffice.

2. The next step is adding dependencies to the POM file as shown in the following code:

```
<dependencies>
  <dependency>
    <groupId>org.apache.servicemix.bundles</groupId>
    <artifactId>
      org.apache.servicemix.bundles.commons-dbcp
    </artifactId>
    <version>1.4_3</version>
  </dependency>
  <dependency>
    <groupId>org.osgi</groupId>
    <artifactId>org.osgi.core</artifactId>
    <version>5.0.0</version>
  </dependency>
  <dependency>
    <groupId>org.osgi</groupId>
    <artifactId>org.osgi.compendium</artifactId>
    <version>5.0.0</version>
  </dependency>
  <dependency>
    <groupId>org.osgi</groupId>
    <artifactId>org.osgi.enterprise</artifactId>
    <version>5.0.0</version>
```

```
    </dependency>
    <dependency>
      <groupId>org.apache.geronimo.specs</groupId>
      <artifactId>geronimo-jpa_2.0_spec</artifactId>
      <version>1.1</version>
    </dependency>
    <dependency>
      <groupId>org.apache.openjpa</groupId>
      <artifactId>openjpa</artifactId>
      <version>2.2.2</version>
      <scope>test</scope>
    </dependency>
    <dependency>
      <groupId>org.apache.derby</groupId>
      <artifactId>derby</artifactId>
      <version>10.8.1.2</version>
      <scope>provided</scope>
    </dependency>
<!-- custom felix gogo command -->
    <dependency>
      <groupId>org.apache.karaf.shell</groupId>
      <artifactId>
        org.apache.karaf.shell.console
      </artifactId>
      <version>3.0.0</version>
    </dependency>
</dependencies>
```

For Karaf 3.0.0, we use OpenJPA 2.2.2 and OSGi version 5.0.0.

3. The next step is adding build plugins. Our recipe requires two build plugins to be configured: OpenJPA and bundle.

    1. First, we configure the `openjpa-maven-plugin`. The `openjpa-maven-plugin` provides tasks for building and maintaining an OpenJPA-based project. We add to our POM file the following plugin configuration:

        ```
        <plugin>
          <groupId>org.codehaus.mojo</groupId>
          <artifactId>openjpa-maven-plugin</artifactId>
          <configuration>
            <addDefaultConstructor>
              true
            </addDefaultConstructor>
            <enforcePropertyRestriction>
              true
        ```

```
            </enforcePropertyRestriction>
        </configuration>
        <executions>
          <execution>
            <id>enhancer</id>
            <phase>process-classes</phase>
            <goals>
              <goal>enhance</goal>
            </goals>
          </execution>
        </executions>
        <dependencies>
          <dependency>
            <groupId>org.apache.openjpa</groupId>
            <artifactId>openjpa</artifactId>
            <version>2.2.2</version>
          </dependency>
          <dependency>
            <groupId>org.slf4j</groupId>
            <artifactId>slf4j-api</artifactId>
            <version>1.6.1</version>
          </dependency>
        </dependencies>
    </plugin>
```

In `openjpa-maven-plugin`, given in the previous block of code, we instruct the plugin to perform an enhance process upon our entity classes to provide the persistence functionality. As stated by the OpenJPA project: "Build time enhancement is the recommended method to use with OpenJPA, as it is the fastest and most reliable method".

2. Next, we configure the `maven-bundle-plugin`. We configure the `maven-bundle-plugin` to assemble our project code into an OSGi bundle. We add the following plugin configuration to our POM file:

```
<plugin>
    <groupId>org.apache.felix</groupId>
    <artifactId>maven-bundle-plugin</artifactId>
    <version>2.4.0</version>
    <extensions>true</extensions>
    <configuration>
      <instructions>
        <Bundle-SymbolicName>
          ${project.artifactId}
        </Bundle-SymbolicName>
```

```
        <Meta-Persistence>
          META-INF/persistence.xml
        </Meta-Persistence>
        <Bundle-Activator>
          com.packt.jpa.demo.Activator
        </Bundle-Activator>
        <Export-Package>
          com.packt.jpa.demo.api.*
        </Export-Package>
        <Import-Package>
          org.osgi.service.blueprint;resolution
            :=optional,
          javax.persistence;version="[1.1,2)",
          javax.persistence.criteria;version="[1.1,2)",
          javax.sql,
          org.apache.commons.dbcp;version="[1.4,2)",
          org.apache.derby.jdbc,
          org.apache.felix.service.command,
          org.apache.felix.gogo.commands,
          org.apache.karaf.shell.console,
          *
        </Import-Package>
      </instructions>
    </configuration>
  </plugin>
```

As highlighted in the previous code snippet, the `Meta-Persistence` tag will add an entry to our bundle's manifest file pointing to our `persistence.xml` file location (we'll create this resource in our next step). The import statements for the `javax.persistence`, `dbcp`, and `derby` packages are of greatest importance for our example project. The Felix and Karaf imports are required by the optional Karaf commands.

4. The next step is creating the persistence descriptor file. Create a directory tree as `src/main/resources/META-INF` in your project. We'll then create a file named `persistence.xml` in this folder. This file is shown in the following code snippet:

```
<persistence xmlns="http://java.sun.com/xml/ns/persistence"
             xmlns:xsi="http://www.w3.org/2001/XMLSchema-
               instance"
             version="1.0">

  <persistence-unit name="recipe" transaction-
    type="RESOURCE_LOCAL">
    <provider>
```

```
            org.apache.openjpa.persistence.Persistence
              ProviderImpl
          </provider>

          <non-jta-data-source>
            osgi:service/javax.sql.DataSource/ (osgi.
              jndi.service.name=jdbc/demo)
          </non-jta-data-source>

          <class>com.packt.jpa.demo.entity.Recipe</class>
          <exclude-unlisted-classes>
            true
          </exclude-unlisted-classes>

          <properties>

            <!-- OpenJPA Properties -->
            <property name="openjpa.ConnectionDriverName"
              value="org.apache.derby.jdbc.ClientDriver.class"/>
            <property name="openjpa.ConnectionURL"
              value="jdbc:derby://localhost:1527/demo;
              create=true"/>
            <property name="openjpa.Multithreaded" value="true"/>
            <property name="openjpa.TransactionMode"
              value="managed"/>
            <property name="openjpa.ConnectionFactoryMode"
              value="managed"/>
            <property name="openjpa.LockManager" value="
              pessimistic(VersionCheckOnReadLock=true,
              VersionUpdateOnWriteLock=true)"/>
            <property name="openjpa.LockTimeout" value="30000"/>
            <property name="openjpa.jdbc.MappingDefaults"
              value="ForeignKeyDeleteAction=restrict, Join
              ForeignKeyDeleteAction=restrict"/>
            <property name="openjpa.LockManager" value="
            pessimistic(VersionCheckOnReadLock=true,
            VersionUpdateOnWriteLock=true)"/>
            <property name="openjpa.Log" value="
              DefaultLevel=INFO, Runtime=INFO, Tool=
              INFO, SQL=INFO"/>
            <property name="openjpa.jdbc.SynchronizeMappings"
              value="buildSchema"/>
            <property name="openjpa.jdbc.DBDictionary"
              value="derby"/>
          </properties>
        </persistence-unit>
      </persistence>
```

The persistence descriptor file contains a multitude of configuration entries required by our application. The most important among them being the definition of the `persistence-unit` and `non-jta-data-source` objects; the former sets the data persistence to `RESOURCE_LOCAL`, and the latter sets the use of a JDBC service for non-transactional data storage. The various OpenJPA properties are beyond the scope of this book, but they are included here to provide a sample configuration. The more interesting part of the previous example is the reference of the datasource. Since the `persistence.xml` file only knows of JNDI lookup syntax for resources, the OSGi service of the datasource needs to be referenced in a JNDI way. This results in `osgi:service` being the JNDI lookup for an OSGi service that provides a `javax.sql.DataSource` interface where the filter matches the `osgi.jndi.service.name` value as equivalent to `jdbc/demo`.

5. The next step is creating the Blueprint descriptor file. In your project, create the `src/main/resources/OSGI-INF` directory tree. We'll then create a file named `blueprint.xml` in this folder as follows:

```xml
<blueprint default-activation="eager"
      xmlns="http://www.osgi.org/xmlns/blueprint/v1.0.0"
      xmlns:xsi="http://www.w3.org/2001/XMLSchema-instance"
      xmlns:tx="http://aries.apache.org/xmlns/
         transactions/v1.0.0"
      xmlns:jpa="http://aries.apache.org/xmlns/jpa/v1.1.0">

  <!-- Define RecipeBookService Services,
     and expose them. -->
  <bean id="recipeBookService" class="com.packt.jpa.demo.
    dao.RecipeBookServiceDAOImpl">
    <jpa:unit property="entityManagerFactory"
      unitname="recipe" />
  </bean>

  <service ref="recipeBookService" interface="com.packt.
    jpa.demo.api.RecipeBookService" />

  <bean id="dataSource" class="org.apache.derby.
    jdbc.ClientDataSource" >
    <property name="databaseName" value="demo"/>
    <property name="createDatabase" value="create"/>
  </bean>

  <service id="demoDataSource" ref="dataSource"
    interface="javax.sql.DataSource">
    <service-properties>
      <entry key="osgi.jndi.service.name"
        value="jdbc/demo"/>
```

```
        <entry key="transactional" value="false"/>
    </service-properties>
  </service>
</blueprint>
```

You should note the inclusion of the `DataSource` service as an OSGi service in this `blueprint.xml` file. It contains the service property `osgi.jndi.service.name` with the value `jdbc/demo`. This is the `DataSource` service that is referenced by the `persistence.xml` file.

6. The next step is developing the OSGi service with the JPA backend. We've created the basic project structure and plumbed in configurations for the persistence and Blueprint descriptors; now we'll focus on the underlying Java code of our JPA-backed application. We break down this process into the following three steps:

   1. The first step is defining a service interface. The service interface will define the user API for our project. In our sample code, we implement a `RecipeBookService` class, which provides the methods required to interact with a collection of recipes. This is shown in the following code:

      ```
      package com.packt.jpa.demo.api;

      import java.util.Collection;
      import com.packt.jpa.demo.entity.Recipe;

      public interface RecipeBookService {

          public Collection<Recipe> getRecipes();

          public void addRecipe(String title, String ingredients);

          public void deleteRecipe(String title);

      }
      ```

      The interface's implementation follows the standard Java conventions, requiring no special OSGi packages.

   2. The next step is implementing a service DAO. Now that we have defined our service interface, we'll provide an implementation as a DAO. Consider the following code:

      ```
      public class RecipeBookServiceDAOImpl implements
      RecipeBookService {

          @PersistenceUnit(unitName="recipe")
          private EntityManagerFactory factory;

          public void setEntityManagerFactory(EntityManager
            Factory factory) {
            this.factory = factory;
      ```

```
      }

      @Override
      public List<Recipe> getRecipes() {
        List<Recipe> result = new ArrayList<Recipe>();
        EntityManager entityManager = factory.
          createEntityManager();
        EntityTransaction entityTransaction = entityManager
          .getTransaction();
        entityTransaction.begin();
        result = entityManager.createQuery("select r from
          RECIPE r", Recipe.class).getResultList();
        entityTransaction.commit();
        return result;
      }

      @Override
      public void addRecipe(String title, String ingredients) {
        EntityManager entityManager = factory.
          createEntityManager();
        EntityTransaction entityTransaction = entityManager
          .getTransaction();
        entityTransaction.begin();
        entityManager.persist(new Recipe(title, ingredients));
        entityTransaction.commit();
  }

      @Override
      public void deleteRecipe(String title) {
        EntityManager entityManager = factory.
          createEntityManager();
        EntityTransaction entityTransaction = entityManager
          .getTransaction();
        entityTransaction.begin();
        entityManager.remove(entityManager.
          getReference(Recipe.class, title));
        entityTransaction.commit();
      }
}
```

The `EntityManagerFactory` function will be wired into our DAO using Blueprint. Each service method implemented in our DAO service implementation will require management of the JPA-style transaction elements.

3. The next step is implementing entities. Finally, we implement our entities as shown in the following code:

```java
package com.packt.jpa.demo.entity;

import javax.persistence.Column;
import javax.persistence.Entity;
import javax.persistence.Id;
import javax.persistence.Table;

@Entity( name = "RECIPE" )
@Table( name = "RECIPES" )
public class Recipe {

  @Id
  @Column(nullable = false)
  private String title;

  @Column(length=10000)
  private String ingredients;

  public Recipe() {
  }

  public Recipe(String title, String ingredients) {
    super();
    this.title = title;
    this.ingredients = ingredients;
  }

  public String getTitle() {
    return title;
  }
  public void setTitle(String title) {
    this.title = title;
  }
  public String getIngredients() {
    return ingredients;
  }
  public void setIngredients(String ingredients) {
    this.ingredients = ingredients;
  }

  public String toString() {
    return "" + this.title + " " + this.ingredients;
  }
}
```

Our `Entity` class is where our objects meet their persistent storage definition requirement. To store an object into a database, we must describe their storage in terms of tables, columns, and so on, and override the `equals` and `hashCode` methods.

7. The next step is the optional creation of Karaf commands to directly test the persistence service. To simplify manual testing of our `RecipeBookService` class, we can create a set of custom Karaf commands, which will exercise our JPA-backed data storage and retrieval operations. Sample implementations of these commands are available from the book's website. Of particular interest is how they obtain a reference to the `RecipeBookService` class and make calls to the service. Now, we must wire the command implementation into Karaf via Blueprint as follows:

```xml
<!-- Apache Karaf Commands -->
<command-bundle
  xmlns="http://karaf.apache.org/xmlns/shell/v1.1.0">
  <command>
    <action class="com.packt.jpa.demo.commands
      .AddRecipe">
      <property name="recipeBookService"
        ref="recipeBookService"/>
    </action>
  </command>
  <command>
    <action class="com.packt.jpa.demo.commands.
      RemoveRecipe">
      <property name="recipeBookService"
        ref="recipeBookService"/>
    </action>
  </command>
  <command>
    <action class="com.packt.jpa.demo.commands.
      ListRecipes">
      <property name="recipeBookService"
        ref="recipeBookService"/>
    </action>
  </command>
</command-bundle>
```

Each of our custom command's implementation classes are wired to our `recipeBookService` instance.

8. The next step is deploying the project into Karaf. Deploying our application in Karaf will require the following three steps: installing a JDBC driver for a backing database, installing JNDI, and adding our project bundle to the container. For our example project, we'll use Apache Derby as our JDBC provider.

    1. We can install the JDBC driver using the following command:

        ```
        karaf@root()> install -s mvn:org.apache.derby/
        derbyclient/10.8.1.2
        ```

        Once installed, you can check whether the client driver is available by executing the classes command and grepping upon the `ClientDataSource` implementation.

        This demo will require a running instance of the Derby database. See `http://db.apache.org/derby/papers/DerbyTut/install_software.html` for a short tutorial on installing Apache Derby.

    2. We need to install the `jndi` feature using the following command:

        ```
        karaf@root()> feature:install jndi
        ```

        Once the `jndi` feature is installed in Karaf, we'll be able to use the `jndi:names` command to view the configured datasources in the container.

    3. We install our project bundle by executing the `install` command on its Maven coordinates as follows:

        ```
        karaf@root()> install -s mvn:com.packt/jpa-only/1.0.0-
        SNAPSHOT
        ```

        We can verify the installation by executing the `list -t 0 | grep -i JPA-only` command, which will list the bundle state of our project.

9. The last step is testing the project. We've now deployed a large collection of bundles into the Karaf container; we can test our integration using the supplied Karaf test commands as follows:

    ```
    karaf@root()> test:addrecipe "Simple Chocolate Chip Cookies"
    "2/3 cup butter, 1 cup brown sugar, 2 eggs, 2 tbsp milk, 2 cups
    flour, 1 tsp baking powder, 1/4 tsp baking soda, 1/2 tsp vanilla,
    1 cup chocolate chips. Whip the butter and sugar together, then
    add in the eggs and beat well. In a second bowl combine the dry
    ingredients. Make sure to thoroughly mix together the flour,
    baking soda and powder. Add the dry ingredients, milk, and vanilla
    into the butter , sugar, and egg mixture. Beat until dough is
    consistent. You may now preheat your oven to 375F. Drop teaspoon
    full amounts of dough onto greased or lined cookie sheets. Bake
    for 10 to 12 minutes. This recipe should yield between three to
    four dozen cookies."
    ```

```
Executing command addrecipe

Recipe added!

karaf@root()>
```

Using the supplied custom Karaf commands, we can add recipe entries to our database. In the previous example, we added a recipe for chocolate chip cookies. Consider the following command line snippet:

```
karaf@root()> test:listrecipes

Executing command list recipes

 Simple Chocolate Chip Cookies 2/3 cup butter, 1 cup brown sugar,
2 eggs, 2 tbsp milk, 2 cups flour, 1 tsp baking powder, 1/4 tsp
baking soda, 1/2 tsp vanilla, 1 cup chocolate chips. Whip the
butter and sugar together, then add in the eggs and beat well. In
a second bowl combine the dry ingredients. Make sure to thoroughly
mix together the flour, baking soda and powder. Add the dry
ingredients, milk, and vanilla into the butter , sugar, and egg
mixture. Beat until dough is consistent. You may now preheat your
oven to 375F. Drop teaspoon full amounts of dough onto greased or
lined cookie sheets. Bake for 10 to 12 minutes. This recipe should
yield between three to four dozen cookies.

karaf@root()>
```

The `listrecipes` custom command performs a select all function upon our recipe data store, displaying all entries on the console. Alternatively, you could use any JDBC tool of your choice to verify that your recipe entries are persisted to disk.

Simplifying datasource administration with the JDBC feature

Apache Karaf 3.0 contains a JDBC feature that provides many useful commands for interacting with datasources. Try installing the `jdbc` feature and then executing the following commands:

- ▶ `karaf@root()> feature:install jdbc`
- ▶ `karaf@root()> jdbc:datasources`
- ▶ `karaf@root()> jdbc:tables jdbc/demo`
- ▶ `karaf@root()> jdbc:query jdbc/demo "select * from RECIPES"`

Output from these commands are not formatted to small consoles, so you may need to expand your terminal to comfortably display results.

Finally, even after restarting Karaf, all of your recipe entries will be available.

How it works...

Observing from a high-level point of view, our persistence layer works by integrating several Apache Aries libraries and OpenJPA together in the Karaf container. The following diagram shows this high-level view:

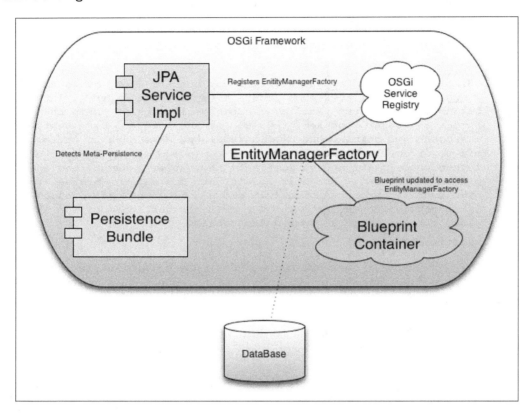

The key interactions in this design are the discovery and wiring of the persistence unit and Blueprint descriptor and wiring the entity and data access objects. This results in having our persistence bundle interacting with the JPA service implementation (OpenJPA), which in turn interacts with the EntityManagerFactory interface (from the persistence unit) wired into our DAO service implementation in the Blueprint descriptor file. These key deployment artifacts are illustrated in the following diagram:

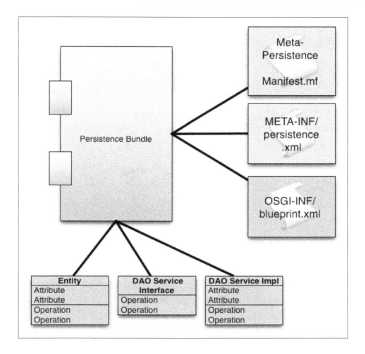

From the point of view of the architecture of our persistence-enabled bundle, its operation depends upon the interaction of the bundle manifest, persistent configuration, and Blueprint wiring.

The `Meta-Persistence` manifest header triggers the processing of the bundles' persistence configuration, which in turn configures JNDI data source declaration, entity discovery, and JDBC integration.

The Blueprint descriptor wires together our DAO service interface and implementation, as well as further defining datasources. A key feature of this service wiring is linking the persistence unit to the DAO service implementation. The DAO service uses the persistence unit's `EntityManagerFactory` function to enable entity access, manipulation, and transactions.

See also

> ▶ The *Building a project with a persistence layer and transaction support for deployment in Karaf* recipe

Building a project with a persistence layer and transaction support for deployment in Karaf

Transaction support for your JPA-persisted data can be simply added by introducing Apache Aries JTA modules to your project. The JTA components provide a transaction manager that coordinates data storage and retrieval.

In the *Building a project with a persistence layer for deployment in Karaf* recipe, we learned how to use JPA and OpenJPA to build a simple application that persists recipes to a database using a `RecipeBookService` class. In this recipe, we'll add container-based transaction management via JTA.

Getting ready

The ingredients of this recipe include the Apache Karaf distribution kit, access to JDK, and Internet connectivity. Sample code for this recipe is available at `https://github.com/jgoodyear/ApacheKarafCookbook/tree/master/chapter7/chapter7-recipe4`. Generally, you'll also need to perform the steps outlined in the *Building a project with a persistence layer for deployment in Karaf* recipe and the *Installing Apache Aries JTA modules in Apache Karaf* recipe.

 Please uninstall contents of the *Building a project with a persistence layer for deployment in Karaf* recipe before attempting this recipe as conflicts may occur.

How to do it...

Given a JPA-based project as outlined in the *Building a project with a persistence layer for deployment in Karaf* recipe, we can add Java transaction support using the following five steps:

1. The first step is updating the persistence to JTA. First, we switch the transaction type from `RESOURCE_LOCAL` to `JTA`; this switches the project from self-managed persistence to container-managed. This is shown in the following code:

   ```
   <persistence-unit name="recipe" transaction-type="JTA">

       <provider>org.apache.openjpa.persistence.
         PersistenceProviderImpl</provider>

       <jta-data-source>
   ```

```
   osgi:service/javax.sql.XADataSource/
      (osgi.jndi.service.name=jdbc/demoxa)
</jta-data-source>
<non-jta-data-source>
   osgi:service/javax.sql.DataSource/(transactional=false)
</non-jta-data-source>

<class>com.packt.jpa.demo.entity.Recipe</class>
<exclude-unlisted-classes>true</exclude-unlisted-classes>
```

After switching the transaction type, we need to add a `jta-data-source`. The previous example registers `jdbc/demoxa` as a service with JNDI. The `non-jta-data-source` used in the previous recipe is retained to help show the progression from the basic design to container-managed transactions; it may be removed during development.

2. The next step is updating the Blueprint descriptor. Switching our transaction type from `RESOURCE_LOCAL` to `JTA` changes how we will wire our `RecipeBookService` class. This is shown in the following code:

```
<!-- Define RecipeBookService Service, and expose them. -->
<bean id="recipeBookService" class="com.packt.jpa.demo.dao.
  RecipeBookServiceDAOImpl">
  <tx:transaction method="*" value="Required" />
  <jpa:context property="entityManager" unitname=
    "recipe" />
</bean>
```

We change the `jpa` property to reference the context instead of the unit and now add in a reference to the container-provided `entityManager` interface. The presence of JTA-style transactions also means that we can now include definitions for XA-capable data sources. Consider the following code:

```
<bean id="xaDataSource" class="org.apache.derby.jdbc.
  ClientXADataSource">
  <property name="databaseName" value="demo"/>
  <property name="createDatabase" value="create" />
</bean>
```

We wire together data-source-specific XA drivers with `XADataSource` service instantiations as follows:

```
<service ref="xaDataSource"
        interface="javax.sql.XADataSource">
  <service-properties>
    <entry key="osgi.jndi.service.name"
      value="jdbc/demoxa"/>
```

```
        <entry key="transactional" value="true"/>
    </service-properties>
</service>

<!-- JTA Transaction Manager setup. -->
<reference id="txManager"
            interface="javax.transaction.TransactionManager"
            availability="mandatory"/>
```

Finally, we add a service reference for the container-provided `TransactionManager` interface, and set its presence to `mandatory`.

3. The next step is updating the service DAO. The changes to our persistence and Blueprint configuration to JTA-style transactions necessitates changes to our DAO service implementation. Our service does not need to create and manage its own transactions, as entities are now accessed through the container-provided `EntityManager` function. Consider the following code:

```
public class RecipeBookServiceDAOImpl implements RecipeBookService
{

    private EntityManager em;

    public void setEntityManager(EntityManager em) {
        this.em = em;
    }

    @Override
    public List<Recipe> getRecipes() {
        List<Recipe> result = new ArrayList<Recipe>();
        result = em.createQuery("select r from RECIPE r",
            Recipe.class).getResultList();
        return result;
    }

    @Override
    public void addRecipe(String title, String ingredients) {
        em.persist(new Recipe(title, ingredients));
    }

    @Override
    public void deleteRecipe(String title) {
        em.remove(em.getReference(Recipe.class, title));
    }
}
```

A result of this subtle change is that our service methods are simplified.

4. The next step is deploying the project into Karaf. Deploying our application into Karaf will require two steps (in addition to those outlined in the *Building a project with a persistence layer for deployment in Karaf* recipe): installing transaction support and adding our project bundle to the container. JTA will require a container-based transaction manager; we can install one using the following command:

```
karaf@root()> feature:install transaction
```

Once installed, we can now deploy our project bundles using the following command:

```
karaf@root()>  install -s mvn:com.packt/jpa-jta/1.0.0-SNAPSHOT
```

We can verify the installation by executing the `list -t 0 | grep -i JPA-JTA` command, which will list the bundle state of our project.

5. The final step is testing the project. We've now deployed a large collection of bundles into the Karaf container; we can test our integration using the supplied Karaf test commands as follows:

```
karaf@root()> test:addrecipe "Recipe-Title" "Ingredients."
Executing command addrecipe
Recipe added!
karaf@root()>
```

In the previous code, we have added a simple placeholder entry into our recipe's data store. Now, consider the following command line snippet:

```
karaf@root()> test:listrecipes
Executing command list recipes
Recipe-Title Ingredients.
karaf@root()>
```

Issuing the `listrecipes` command, we retrieve our previous entry.

 See the JDBC feature note in the *Building a project with a persistence layer for deployment in Karaf* recipe for Karaf console commands to verify data source information.

How it works...

The operation of this persistence-enabled bundle is very similar to that of our previous recipe. The vital changes being the introduction of the JTA transaction manager, updating the persistence unit to JTA, adding the XA datasource, then wiring an `EntityManager` function into the DAO service implementation and requiring the transaction manager's availability.

Operationally, transactions are coordinated by the container's transaction manager—this allows for more complex transactions with more varied enlisted resources than standard JPA-style transactions.

See also

▶ For an alternative persistence layer approach, see *Chapter 8, Providing a Big Data Integration Layer with Apache Cassandra*.

8
Providing a Big Data Integration Layer with Apache Cassandra

In this chapter, we will cover the following topics:

- ▶ Installing Cassandra client bundles in Apache Karaf
- ▶ Modeling data with Apache Cassandra
- ▶ Building a project with a persistence layer for deployment in Karaf

Introduction

As illustrated in the previous chapters, persistence is a large part of most deployments and applications. So far, we've focused on relational databases. Let's start off with some history.

In 1970, IBM published a paper named *A Relational Model of Data for Large Shared Data Banks*. This paper became the foundation for RDBMS and modern relational databases in that it described joins and relationships between entities. From this work, followed SQL (1986), ACID (Atomic, Consistent, Isolated, and Durable), schema design, and sharding for scalability.

Let's fast forward to the advent of social networks; a term called **WebScale** was coined based on Reed's law that states:

"The utility of large networks, particularly social networks, can scale exponentially with the size of the network."

Does this mean that RDBMS cannot be scaled? No, but it led to the development of NoSQL. NoSQL is usually based on the following definitions:

- It was originally coined by Carlo Strozzi who developed the Strozzi NoSQL database in 1998
- It typically has the key/value style of storage in columns/tables
- It is generally schema-less, or each row can contain a different structure
- It does not require SQL as a language; thus the name *NoSQL*
- Many support BASE consistency
- Most are distributed and fault-tolerant in nature

Apache Cassandra was originally developed at Facebook, then released as open source in 2008, incubated at Apache in 2009, and became a top-level Apache project in 2010. Through rapid adaptation and features desirable in many use cases, Apache Cassandra has rapidly gained traction and wide distribution. Today's versions of Cassandra have a slightly stricter schema orientation with the introduction of **Cassandra Query Language** (**CQL**), a way of helping to drive transition from traditional RDBMS models to a more unstructured key/value pair storage model while retaining a structure and data model familiar to users in general. For an annotated history of the transition of Apache Cassandra, see `http://www.datastax.com/documentation/articles/cassandra/cassandrathenandnow.html`.

CQL is the default and primary interface into the Cassandra DBMS. Using CQL is similar to using SQL. CQL and SQL share the same abstract idea of a table constructed of columns and rows. The main difference is that Cassandra does not support joins or subqueries, except for batch analysis through Apache Hive. Instead, Cassandra emphasizes denormalization through CQL features like collections and clustering specified at the schema level.

What this basically means is that there are other client APIs—they are, as of Cassandra release 2.x, actively discouraged from use by the Cassandra community. A healthy debate over the usage of schema modeling versus column family is still quite active on mailing lists and in user communities.

Installing Cassandra client bundles in Apache Karaf

Before we begin to explore how to build Cassandra-backed applications, we must first install all the required client modules into the Karaf container.

Getting ready

The official *GettingStarted* document from the Cassandra community can be found at `http://wiki.apache.org/cassandra/GettingStarted`.

The ingredients of this recipe include the Apache Karaf distribution kit, access to JDK, and Internet connectivity. We also assume that an Apache Cassandra database is downloaded and installed. Apache Cassandra can be downloaded and installed as RPMs, Debian `.deb` packages, or `.tar` archives. In a binary `.tar` archive, you'll have to open and change two configuration files: the `cassandra.yaml` and the `log4-server.properties` files of the `conf` folder. The changes pertain to where you store data, which is by default in the `/var/lib/cassandra/*` folder for the data backend and in the `/var/log/cassandra/*` folder for the system log. Once these changes are done, you can start Cassandra using the `bin/cassandra -F` command.

How to do it...

Cassandra's drivers aren't part of the standard Karaf feature library; so, we either have to write our own feature or manually install the necessary bundles for the client to run.

We use the following commands to install Apache Cassandra's driver and supplemental bundles into Karaf:

```
karaf@root()>install -s mvn:io.netty/netty/3.9.0.Final
karaf@root()>install -s mvn:com.google.guava/guava/16.0.1
karaf@root()>install -s mvn:com.codahale.metrics/metrics-core/3.0.2
karaf@root()>install -s mvn:com.datastax.cassandra/cassandra-driver-
   core/2.0.2
```

We can verify the installation by executing the `list -t 0 | grep -i cass` command, which will list the DataStax driver bundle.

With this, we have access to the Cassandra driver from our own bundles.

Modeling data with Apache Cassandra

Before we start writing a bundle using Apache Cassandra, let's look a little at how we model data in Cassandra using CQL 3.x.

Getting ready

Let's define a very simple schema, and as we are using CQL, Cassandra isn't schema-less from a client perspective even if the data storage internally works slightly differently.

We can reuse the `RecipeService` class from the previous chapter. We will just modify it slightly for our Cassandra integration. The original entity (and by virtue of using JPA) provides a basic table definition, which is as follows:

```
@Id
@Column(nullable = false)
private String title;

@Column(length=10000)
private String ingredients;
```

So, we have two fields in this table: an ID field named `title` and a data field we call `ingredients` for consistency and simplicity.

First, we need a place to store this. Cassandra partitions data in keyspaces at the top level. Think of a keyspace as a map containing tables and their rules.

How to do it...

We'll need to perform the following two steps:

1. The first step is starting the Cassandra client. The basic creation command in Cassandra's client, `cqlsh`, is shown as follows:

    ```
    ./bin/cqlsh

    Connected to Cluster at localhost:9160.

    [cqlsh 4.0.1 | Cassandra 2.0.1 | CQL spec 3.1.1 | Thrift protocol
    19.37.0]

    Use HELP for help.
    ```

2. The next step is creating our data store. Now that we have started the interactive client session, we can create a keyspace as shown in the following command:

    ```
    cqlsh> CREATE KEYSPACE karaf_demo WITH replication = {'class'
      :'SimpleStrategy', 'replication_factor':1};
    ```

    The previous command-line prompt returns no response indicating that we have successfully created a new keyspace where we can store data. To use this keyspace, we need to tell Cassandra that this is where we'll be working right now.

We rely on SimpleStrategy as we only have one Cassandra node, we don't have a real cluster defined, nor do we have multiple data centers. If this was the case, we could change the strategy class for replication. We also set the `replication_factor` value to 1; this can be set to more replicas and certainly should be done in security-related contexts where you, for instance, store account information.

To switch the keyspace, we issue a `USE` command as follows:

```
cqlsh> USE karaf_demo;
cqlsh:karaf_demo>
```

The preceding command prompt indicates that we are in the `karaf_demo` keyspace. Consider the following command:

```
cqlsh:karaf_demo> DESCRIBE tables;

<empty>

cqlsh:karaf_demo>
```

As the preceding command indicates, we have nothing defined schema-wise in this keyspace, and so we need to define a table. This can be done as follows:

```
cqlsh:karaf_demo> CREATE TABLE RECIPES (title text PRIMARY
KEY,ingredients text);
cqlsh:karaf_demo> DESCRIBE TABLES;

recipes

cqlsh:karaf_demo>
```

We now have a defined table and the columns in this table are defined as the storage type `text` and the primary key and retrieval token as the `title`.

How it works...

It is beyond the scope of this book to explore the under-the-hood functioning of Apache Cassandra. However, you can examine its source code at `http://git-wip-us.apache.org/repos/asf/cassandra.git`.

In terms of our data store, we can let Cassandra describe exactly what is being stored. Consider the following command-line snippet:

```
cqlsh:karaf_demo> DESCRIBE TABLE recipes;

CREATE TABLE recipes (
    title text,
    ingredients text,
    PRIMARY KEY (title)
) WITH
    bloom_filter_fp_chance=0.010000 AND
    caching='KEYS_ONLY' AND
    comment='' AND
    dclocal_read_repair_chance=0.000000 AND
    gc_grace_seconds=864000 AND
    index_interval=128 AND
    read_repair_chance=0.100000 AND
    replicate_on_write='true' AND
    populate_io_cache_on_flush='false' AND
    default_time_to_live=0 AND
    speculative_retry='NONE' AND
    memtable_flush_period_in_ms=0 AND
    compaction={'class': 'SizeTieredCompactionStrategy'} AND
    compression={'sstable_compression': 'LZ4Compressor'};
```

As you can see, there are quite a few options you, as a data modeler, can work with. These will affect replication, caching, lifetime, compression, and several other factors.

Building a project with a persistence layer for deployment in Karaf

Application developers often need to make use of a persistence layer in their projects; one of the preferred methodologies to perform this in Karaf is to make use of the Java Persistence API. As we are building on the existing JPA project, we will try and set up a new service layer and reuse (copy) the same project model while moving over the storage backend to Apache Cassandra. This is not a complete refactoring nor a reuse of code. Technically, we could have moved the API parts from *Chapter 7, Providing a Persistence Layer with Apache Aries and OpenJPA*, into a new module and then refactored the chapter to have the Cassandra-related dependencies and a slightly different set of imports. This isn't really in the scope of a Cookbook, hence the copied structure.

In the *Installing Cassandra client bundles in Apache Karaf* recipe, we learned how to install the necessary JAR files into Karaf. Continuing with this recipe, we'll make use of the drivers to build a simple application that persists recipes to a database using the `RecipeBookService` class, which will hide the complexities of data storage and retrieval from its users.

Getting ready

The ingredients of this recipe include the Apache Karaf distribution kit, access to JDK, and Internet connectivity. The sample code for this recipe is available at `https://github.com/jgoodyear/ApacheKarafCookbook/tree/master/chapter8/chapter8-recipe1`. Remember, you need both the drivers installed and Apache Cassandra running for these recipes to work!

How to do it...

Building a project with a JPA persistence layer will require the following eight steps:

1. The first step is generating a Maven-based bundle project. Create an empty Maven-based project. A `pom.xml` file containing the essential Maven coordinate information and bundle packaging directives will suffice.

2. The next step is adding dependencies to the POM file. This is shown in the following code:

```
<dependencies>
  <dependency>
    <groupId>org.osgi</groupId>
    <artifactId>org.osgi.core</artifactId>
    <version>5.0.0</version>
  </dependency>
  <dependency>
    <groupId>org.osgi</groupId>
    <artifactId>org.osgi.compendium</artifactId>
    <version>5.0.0</version>
  </dependency>
  <dependency>
    <groupId>org.osgi</groupId>
    <artifactId>org.osgi.enterprise</artifactId>
    <version>5.0.0</version>
  </dependency>
  <!-- Cassandra Driver -->
  <dependency>
```

```
        <groupId>com.datastax.cassandra</groupId>
        <artifactId>cassandra-driver-core</artifactId>
        <version>2.0.1</version>
    </dependency>
    <!-- custom felix gogo command -->
    <dependency>
        <groupId>org.apache.karaf.shell</groupId>
        <artifactId>org.apache.karaf.shell.console</artifactId>
        <version>3.0.0</version>
    </dependency>
</dependencies>
```

For Karaf 3.0.0, we use the OSGi Version 5.0.0. The Cassandra driver only depends on three external projects. We are in luck as all of these are available as bundles—there isn't going to be much difficulty in deploying this in any version of Karaf. The majority of our dependencies are now related to our commands.

3. The next step is adding build plugins. Our recipe requires only one build plugin to be configured, which is the bundle plugin. We configure the `maven-bundle-plugin` to assemble our project code into an OSGi bundle. We add the following plugin configuration to our POM file:

```
<plugin>
    <groupId>org.apache.felix</groupId>
    <artifactId>maven-bundle-plugin</artifactId>
    <version>2.4.0</version>
    <extensions>true</extensions>
    <configuration>
        <instructions>
            <Bundle-SymbolicName>
                    ${project.artifactId}
            </Bundle-SymbolicName>
            <Bundle-Activator>
                    com.packt.cassandra.demo.Activator
            </Bundle-Activator>
            <Export-Package>
                    com.packt.cassandra.demo.api.*
            </Export-Package>
            <Import-Package>
                org.osgi.service.blueprint;resolution:
                  =optional,
```

```
        org.apache.felix.service.command,
        org.apache.felix.gogo.commands,
        org.apache.karaf.shell.console,
        *
      </Import-Package>
    </instructions>
  </configuration>
</plugin>
```

The Felix and Karaf imports are required by the optional Karaf commands.

Once again, compared to the JPA project, we have less complexity in the `pom.xml` file as we are relying on fewer external resources. We only make sure that we have the correct Karaf and Felix imports to activate our commands.

4. The next step is creating a Blueprint descriptor file. Create the directory tree as `src/main/resources/OSGI-INF` in your project. Then, create a file named `blueprint.xml` in this folder. Consider the following code:

```xml
<?xml version="1.0" encoding="UTF-8" standalone="no"?>
<blueprint default-activation="eager"
  xmlns="http://www.osgi.org/xmlns/blueprint/v1.0.0"
>
  <!-- Define RecipeBookService Services, and expose them.
    -->
  <bean id="recipeBookService"
    class="com.packt.cassandra.demo.dao.RecipeBookService
    DAOImpl" init-method="init" destroy-method="destroy"/>

  <service ref="recipeBookService"
    interface="com.packt.cassandra.demo.api.
    RecipeBookService"/>

  <!-- Apache Karaf Commands -->
  <command-bundle xmlns="http://karaf.apache.org/xmlns
    /shell/v1.1.0">
    <command>
      <action class="com.packt.cassandra.demo.
        commands.AddRecipe">
        <property name="recipeBookService"
          ref="recipeBookService"/>
      </action>
    </command>
    <command>
```

```
        <action class="com.packt.cassandra.demo.
          commands.RemoveRecipe">
          <property name="recipeBookService"
            ref="recipeBookService"/>
        </action>
      </command>
      <command>
        <action class="com.packt.cassandra.demo.
          commands.ListRecipes">
          <property name="recipeBookService"
            ref="recipeBookService"/>
        </action>
      </command>
    </command-bundle>
</blueprint>
```

In the preceding Blueprint structure, we ended up removing the transaction manager. Remember, Cassandra doesn't work in the same way as a traditional relational database.

5. The next step is developing an OSGi service with a new Cassandra backend. We've created the basic project structure and plumbed in configurations for Blueprint descriptors. Now, we'll focus on the underlying Java code of our Cassandra-backed application. We break down this process into three steps: defining a service interface, implementing the service DAO, and implementing a very simple class that we will use as an entity.

In this recipe, we will be using the raw CQL driver in a more extensive project. It is highly likely that something like a DataMapper or another ORM-like solution will be of benefit. A higher level library will help hide type conversion between Cassandra and Java, manage relations, and help generalize data access.

The following is a brief list of CQL-friendly libraries to use as a starting point:

- **Astyanax**: This is available at `https://github.com/Netflix/astyanax`
- **Spring data-cassandra**: This is available at `http://projects.spring.io/spring-data-cassandra/`
- **Hecate**: This is available at `https://github.com/savoirtech/hecate`

1. The first step is defining a service interface. The service interface will define the user API to our project. In our sample code, we implement the `RecipeBookService` class, which provides the methods required to interact with a collection of recipes. Consider the following code:

   ```
   package com.packt.cassandra.demo.api;
   ```

```
import java.util.Collection;
import com.packt.jpa.demo.entity.Recipe;

public interface RecipeBookService {

    public Collection<Recipe> getRecipes();

    public void addRecipe(String title, String ingredients);

    public void deleteRecipe(String title);

}
```

The interface's implementation follows standard Java conventions, requiring no special OSGi packages.

2. The next step is implementing the service DAO. Now that we have defined our service interface, we'll provide an implementation as a DAO. By using Cassandra, we don't necessarily need to follow a DAO pattern, although this isn't a bad idea, as this will make refactoring existing JPA code fairly simple and approachable. We use the same interface and accommodate the implementation to work with the Cassandra CQL syntax instead. Consider the following code:

```
public class RecipeBookServiceDAOImpl implements
RecipeBookService {

    private Cluster cluster;
    private Session session;

    public void connect(String node) {
        cluster = Cluster.builder().addContactPoint
            (node).build();
        Metadata metadata = cluster.getMetadata();
        System.out.printf("Connected to cluster: %s\n"
            , metadata.getClusterName());
        for (Host host : metadata.getAllHosts()) {
            System.out.printf("Datacenter: %s; Host: %s
                ; Rack: %s\n", host.getDatacenter()
                , host.getAddress(), host.getRack());
        }
        session = cluster.connect("karaf_demo");
    }
```

```java
    public void destroy() {
      cluster.close();
    }

    public void init() {
      connect("127.0.0.1");
    }

    @Override
    public List<Recipe> getRecipes() {
      List<Recipe> result = new ArrayList<Recipe>();
      ResultSet results = session.execute("SELECT * FROM
        karaf_demo.recipes;");

      for (Row row : results) {
        Recipe recipe = new Recipe();
        recipe.setTitle(row.getString("title"));
        recipe.setIngredients(row.getString("ingredients"));
        result.add(recipe);
      }
      return result;
    }

    @Override
    public void addRecipe(String title, String ingredients) {

      ResultSet resultSet = session.execute("INSERT INTO
        karaf_demo.recipes (title, ingredients) VALUES
        ('" + title + "', '" + ingredients + "');");
      System.out.println("Result = " + resultSet);
    }

    @Override
    public void deleteRecipe(String title) {
      ResultSet resultSet = session.execute("DELETE from
        karaf_demo.recipes where title='" + title + "';");
      System.out.println("Result = " + resultSet);
    }
  }
```

Our Cassandra class is now pretty much self-contained. On startup, we print out some information about where we are connected and which rack and datacenter our cluster node exists in.

3. The next step is implementing entities. These entities in the Cassandra case are just plain old POJO classes. They no longer contain persistence information. We utilize them to conform to the existing API and ensure that we hide the underlying Cassandra implementation from the end user. Consider the following code:

```java
public class Recipe {
    private String title;
    private String ingredients;
    public Recipe() {
    }
    public Recipe(String title, String ingredients) {
        super();
        this.title = title;
        this.ingredients = ingredients;
    }
    public String getTitle() {
        return title;
    }
    public void setTitle(String title) {
        this.title = title;
    }
    public String getIngredients() {
        return ingredients;
    }
    public void setIngredients(String ingredients) {
        this.ingredients = ingredients;
    }
    public String toString() {
        return "" + this.title + " " + this.ingredients;
    }
}
```

This class is now just a plain old POJO class that we use to transport data in accordance with the already established API. For more complex mapping and ORM-like structure, there are several DataMappers that are built on top of the existing Cassandra data drivers. As they are not standardized as JPA, recommending one in particular isn't as easy. They all have their little quirks.

6. The next step is the optional creation of Karaf commands to directly test the persistence service. To simplify manual testing of our `recipeBookService` instance, we can create a set of custom Karaf commands, which will invoke our Cassandra storage and retrieval operations. The sample implementations of these optional commands are available in the book's code bundle. Of particular interest is how they obtain a reference to the `recipeBookService` instance and make calls to the service.

Now, we must wire the command implementation into Karaf via Blueprint as shown in the following code:

```
<!-- Apache Karaf Commands -->
<command-bundle xmlns="http://karaf.apache.org/
  xmlns/shell/v1.1.0">
  <command>
    <action class="com.packt.cassandra.demo.commands
      .AddRecipe">
      <property name="recipeBookService" ref=
        "recipeBookService"/>
    </action>
  </command>
  <command>
    <action class="com.packt.cassandra.demo.commands.
      RemoveRecipe">
      <property name="recipeBookService" ref=
        "recipeBookService"/>
    </action>
  </command>
  <command>
    <action class="com.packt.cassandra.demo.commands.
      ListRecipes">
      <property name="recipeBookService" ref=
        "recipeBookService"/>
    </action>
  </command>
</command-bundle>
```

Each of our custom commands implementation classes are wired to our `recipeBookService` instance.

7. The next step is deploying the project into Karaf. We install our project bundle by executing the `install` command on its Maven coordinates as follows:

```
karaf@root()> install -s mvn:com.packt/chapter8-
  recipe1/1.0.0-SNAPSHOT
```

 This demo will require a running instance of Cassandra!

8. The final step is testing the project. As soon as the bundle is deployed, you'll see some startup information; it'll be something like the following:

```
karaf@root()> Cassandra Demo Bundle stopping...
Cassandra Demo Bundle starting...
Connected to cluster: Cluster
Datacenter: datacenter1; Host: /127.0.0.1; Rack: rack1
```

Consider the following commands:

```
karaf@root()> test:addrecipe "Name" "Ingredients"
karaf@root()> test:listrecipes
```

When you run the preceding commands, you'll have the stored recipe displayed on the console as output!

How it works...

Our persistence layer works with the official Apache Cassandra driver in a Karaf container. Providing access to Cassandra is quite simple; we only need to look at one external project and make sure that we have two dependencies and that we can connect to an existing Cassandra cluster. The key to using Cassandra lies more in data modeling, structuring of clusters, amount of read/writes, and the size of clusters and participating nodes and their usage and storage patterns.

The data driver we connect with will provide us with cluster awareness, failover, and high availability as well as the features necessary to control replication factors and cluster behavior of our data. The official Cassandra documentation can be found at http://cassandra.apache.org/.

An extremely useful resource to get the historical context of the evolution of Cassandra can be found at http://www.datastax.com/documentation/articles/cassandra/cassandrathenandnow.html. This will show and explain why things have changed, how CQL came about, and why certain designs were chosen.

9

Providing a Big Data Integration Layer with Apache Hadoop

In this chapter, we will cover the following topics:

- ▶ Installing Hadoop client bundles in Apache Karaf
- ▶ Accessing Apache Hadoop from Karaf
- ▶ Adding commands that talk to HDFS for deployment in Karaf

Introduction

To continue building on data storage models that aren't as inflexible as traditional RDBMS structures, we will look at Apache Hadoop. Hadoop was created by Doug Cutting and Mike Cafarella in 2005. Cutting, who was working at Yahoo! at the time, named it after his son's toy elephant. It was originally developed to support distribution for the Nutch search engine project.

Hadoop followed the ideas published by Google in the papers pertaining to Google File System and Google MapReduce. With over a decade of use, Hadoop has grown to a very large and complex ecosystem with a projected revenue of around $23 billion in 2016. Hadoop drives everything from repackaged distributions to full database implementations, analytics packages, and management solutions.

Hadoop has also started changing the way startups look at their data models, allowing new companies to make Big Data part of their overall strategy.

At the core of Hadoop, you have **Hadoop Distributed File System** (**HDFS**). This mechanism is what allows the distribution of data. It evolved from a potential single point of failure scenario to having competing implementations from companies like DataStax and RedHat with Cassandra FS and RedHat Cluster File System, respectively.

In the arena of complete product offerings, you'll find MapR Cloudera, Hortonworks, Intel, and IBM, to name a few as alternatives to the Apache Hadoop distribution.

If you ponder the future, it does seem that the marriage of SQL-like techniques with a distributed store is where the majority of use cases are headed. This allows users to, at the very least, leverage the RDBMS ideas that are already tried in combination with practically unlimited storage for data mining, social networking aspects, monitoring, and decision making.

With YARN (Cluster Resource Management) becoming part of the Hadoop infrastructure, HDFS is taken from just storage and MapReduce to an environment that can handle batch, interactive, and streaming as well as application deployment.

Starting a standalone Hadoop cluster

To start this all off, we'll begin by setting up a simple standalone cluster. We'll need to download and configure an Apache Hadoop release and make sure that we can use it. Then, we will move on to configuring the same configurations and access methods in an Apache Karaf container. We will utilize an external cluster to show how you can utilize Apache Karaf to spin up a new job engine against a large existing cluster. With the features we have and will deploy, you can also embed an HDFS filesystem from a Karaf container.

Download a Hadoop release from one of the Apache mirrors at `http://hadoop.apache.org/releases.html#Download`. At the time of writing this book, the latest release is 2.4.0. A full walkthrough of setting up a cluster can be found at `http://hadoop.apache.org/docs/current/hadoop-project-dist/hadoop-common/SingleCluster.html`.

The following are the changes you need to make to get HDFS up and running and talking to a locally installed node, replication handler, and job tracker.

Expand the downloaded archive and modify the files in the `etc/hadoop/*` folder. The `core-site.xml` file needs to be modified as follows:

```
<configuration>
  <property>
    <name>fs.defaultFS</name>
    <value>hdfs://localhost:9000</value>
  </property>
</configuration>
```

The `hdfs-site.xml` file needs to be modified as follows:

```
<configuration>
  <property>
    <name>dfs.replication</name>
    <value>1</value>
  </property>
</configuration>
```

The `mapred-site.xml` file needs to be modified as follows:

```
<configuration>
  <property>
    <name>mapred.job.tracker</name>
    <value>localhost:9001</value>
  </property>
</configuration>
```

Once this is accomplished and you can run SSH to your localhost without a password, you can start your daemons. If you cannot run SSH, run the following commands:

```
ssh-keygen -t dsa -P '' -f ~/.ssh/id_dsa
cat ~/.ssh/id_dsa.pub >> ~/.ssh/authorized_keys
```

The preceding commands will create an empty SSH key for remote login. If you already have an existing SSH key associated with your account, you only need to run the second command to make sure that you can remotely log in to your localhost.

Now, let's verify that the existing installation is accessible and we can operate against it. Once this is done, we can start all the daemons in one fell swoop using the following command:

```
./sbin/start-all.sh
```

 Keep in mind that this command will probably go away as you configure more YARN options in the future.

You should see several daemons starting and hopefully no error messages other than possible warnings pertaining to your missing native libraries. (This isn't covered in this little tutorial but pertains to IO libraries and optimized access for your particular platform.)

When we have a running HDFS system, we'll first create a directory using the following command:

```
./bin/hadoop fs -mkdir -p /karaf/cookbook
```

Then, we verify that we can read using the following command:

```
./bin/hadoop fs -ls /karaf
Found 1 items
drwxr-xr-x   - joed supergroup          0 2014-05-15 21:47
  /karaf/cookbook
```

We've created a directory in the simple single node cluster we started (we are calling this a cluster as all the components necessary to cluster are running and we are simply running them all on one node). We've also ensured that we can list the contents of the said directory. This tells us that HDFS is accessible and active.

The following is what we have accomplished so far and what we will be covering next.

> ▸ We now have a Karaf external HDFS system running. This could have been an existing deployment, an Amazon job, or a set of virtual servers. Basically, we have the fundamentals of a cluster and we know we can access it and create content.

> ▸ The next step is going to be a deep dive into transforming an existing model of deployment into an OSGi-friendly deployment.

Installing Hadoop client bundles in Apache Karaf

With Hadoop running, we are ready to start utilizing the resources from Apache Karaf.

Getting ready

The ingredients of this recipe include the Apache Karaf distribution kit, access to JDK, and Internet connectivity. We also assume that an Apache Hadoop distribution is downloaded and installed. It can be downloaded from `http://hadoop.apache.org/#Download`.

How to do it...

Hadoop's HDFS libraries aren't part of the standard Karaf feature library; so, we either have to write our own feature or manually install the necessary bundles for the client to run. Apache Camel does have this feature available via Camels HDFS2 component. We can either use Camel's existing feature or build the feature ourselves.

With the current version of Snappy Java used in the Camel feature, you will run into problems using native libraries with Java 7. This is a well-known issue and is being addressed in the 1.0.5 release of Snappy Java (https://github.com/xerial/snappy-java). To resolve this issue for all platforms, we will build a Karaf feature of our own where we can utilize all of the bundles that are in the Camel feature as well as some additional JAR files that will allow us to run the latest versions. This can be done as follows:

```xml
<features name="com.packt.chapter.nine-${project.version}">

    <repository>mvn:org.apache.cxf.karaf/apache-
      cxf/3.0.0/xml/features</repository>

    <feature name='xml-specs-api' version='${project.version}'
      resolver='(obr)' start-level='10'>
      <bundle dependency='true'>mvn:org.apache.servicemix.specs/
        org.apache.servicemix.specs.activation-api-1.1/</bundle>
      <bundle dependency='true'>mvn:org.apache.servicemix.specs/
        org.apache.servicemix.specs.stax-api-1.0/</bundle>
      <bundle dependency='true'>mvn:org.apache.servicemix.specs/
        org.apache.servicemix.specs.jaxb-api-2.2/</bundle>
      <bundle>mvn:org.codehaus.woodstox/stax2-api/</bundle>
      <bundle>mvn:org.codehaus.woodstox/woodstox-core-asl/</bundle>
      <bundle>mvn:org.apache.servicemix.bundles/
        org.apache.servicemix.bundles.jaxb-impl/</bundle>
    </feature>

    <feature name='hdfs2' version='${project.version}' resolver=
      '(obr)' start-level='50'>
      <feature>xml-specs-api</feature>
      <feature>cxf-jaxrs</feature>
      <bundle dependency='true'>mvn:commons-lang/commons-
        lang/2.6</bundle>
      <bundle dependency='true'>mvn:com.google.guava/guava/
        16.0.1</bundle>
      <bundle dependency='true'>mvn:com.google.protobuf/protobuf-
        java/</bundle>
      <bundle dependency='true'>mvn:org.apache.servicemix.bundles/
        org.apache.servicemix.bundles.guice/</bundle>
      <bundle dependency='true'>mvn:org.apache.servicemix.bundles/
        org.apache.servicemix.bundles.jsch/</bundle>
      <bundle dependency='true'>mvn:org.apache.servicemix.bundles/
        org.apache.servicemix.bundles.paranamer/</bundle>
```

```
        <bundle dependency='true'>mvn:org.apache.servicemix.bundles/
           org.apache.servicemix.bundles.avro/1.7.3_1</bundle>
        <bundle dependency='true'>mvn:org.apache.commons/commons-
           compress/</bundle>
        <bundle dependency='true'>mvn:org.apache.commons/commons-
           math3/3.1.1</bundle>
        <bundle dependency='true'>mvn:commons-cli/commons-
           cli/1.2</bundle>
        <bundle dependency='true'>mvn:commons-configuration/commons-
           configuration/</bundle>
        <bundle dependency='true'>mvn:org.apache.servicemix.bundles/
           org.apache.servicemix.bundles.commons-httpclient/</bundle>
        <bundle dependency='true'>mvn:io.netty/netty/3.9.2.
           Final</bundle>
        <bundle dependency='true'>mvn:org.codehaus.jackson/jackson-
           core-asl/1.9.12</bundle>
        <bundle dependency='true'>mvn:org.codehaus.jackson/jackson-
           mapper-asl/1.9.12</bundle>
        <bundle dependency="true">mvn:org.codehaus.jackson/jackson-
           jaxrs/1.9.12</bundle>
        <bundle dependency="true">mvn:org.codehaus.jackson/jackson-
           xc/1.9.12</bundle>
        <bundle dependency='true'>mvn:org.apache.servicemix.bundles/
           org.apache.servicemix.bundles.snappy-java</bundle>
        <bundle dependency='true'>mvn:commons-codec/commons-
           codec/</bundle>
        <bundle dependency='true'>mvn:commons-collections/commons-
           collections/3.2.1</bundle>
        <bundle dependency='true'>mvn:commons-io/commons-io/</bundle>
        <bundle dependency='true'>mvn:commons-net/commons-
           net/</bundle>
        <bundle dependency='true'>mvn:org.apache.zookeeper/
           zookeeper/</bundle>
        <bundle dependency='true'>mvn:org.apache.servicemix.bundles/
           org.apache.servicemix.bundles.xmlenc/0.52_1</bundle>
        <bundle dependency='true'>mvn:org.apache.servicemix.bundles/
           org.apache.servicemix.bundles.xerces/</bundle>
        <bundle dependency='true'>mvn:org.apache.servicemix.bundles/
           org.apache.servicemix.bundles.xmlresolver/</bundle>
        <bundle>mvn:org.apache.servicemix.bundles/
           org.apache.servicemix.bundles.hadoop-client/</bundle>
    </feature>

</features>
```

We can now utilize this feature's file to deploy a Hadoop client that is OSGi-friendly and will allow us to utilize all the functionalities in Hadoop. We do this by utilizing another project, Apache ServiceMix. Apache ServiceMix maintains a bundle repository where commonly used or sought after resources are repackaged and turned into working OSGi bundles if necessary.

The `Apache ServiceMix :: Bundles :: hadoop-client` bundle that we are using is an uber bundle containing core, YARN, HDFS, MapReduce, common client JAR files, and the Hadoop annotations in one fell swoop.

We can verify the installation by executing the `list | grep -i hadoop` command as follows:

```
karaf@root()> list | grep -i hadoop
151 | Active |  50 | 2.4.0.1     | Apache ServiceMix :: Bundles ::
  hadoop-client
```

Accessing Apache Hadoop from Karaf

In Hadoop, the core of a cluster is the distributed and replicated filesystem. We have HDFS running and can access it from our command line window as a regular user. Actually, getting to it from an OSGi container will prove to be slightly more complicated than just writing the Java components.

Hadoop requires us to provide configuration metadata for our cluster that can be looked up as file or classpath resources. In this recipe, we will simply copy the HDFS site-specific files we created earlier in the chapter to our `src/main/resources` folder.

We will also include the default metadata definitions into our resources by copying them from a dependency, and finally, we'll allow our bundle classloader to perform fully dynamic class loading. To sum it up, we have to copy the `core-site.xml`, `hdfs-site.xml`, and `mapred-site.xml` files into our classpath. These files together describe to our client how to access HDFS.

As we get to the code, there is also a step we'll perform to trick the Hadoop classloaders into utilizing our bundle classloader as well as respecting the configuration data by providing specific implementations.

How to do it...

The first thing we'll do is make sure that the necessary defaults are copied into our tutorial bundle.

1. First, we will modify the Felix bundle plugin and add the following segment:

```
<Include-Resource>
  {maven-resources},
```

```
  @org.apache.servicemix.bundles.hadoop-client-
    2.4.0_1.jar!/core-default.xml,
  @org.apache.servicemix.bundles.hadoop-client-
    2.4.0_1.jar!/hdfs-default.xml,
  @org.apache.servicemix.bundles.hadoop-client-
    2.4.0_1.jar!/mapred-default.xml,
  @org.apache.servicemix.bundles.hadoop-client-
    2.4.0_1.jar!/hadoop-metrics.properties
</Include-Resource>
```

2. Next, we will add another section for dynamic loading of classes as they are needed. This isn't necessarily best practice in OSGi, but sometimes, it is one of the few possible ways of getting bundles and JAR files not intended for OSGi to work. We do this by adding another little snippet to the Felix bundle plugin as follows:

```
<DynamicImport-Package>*</DynamicImport-Package>
```

With this addition, we tell our bundle that if you need a class at a later time, just go look it up when we need it. It is a tad more costly and certainly not recommended as a general practice as it forces the bundle to scan classpaths.

3. Finally, we pull two more tricks out of our hat inside our implementation code. We do this as the Hadoop code is multithreaded, and by default, the classloader for a new thread is the system classloader. In an OSGi context, the system classloader is going to have very limited visibility.

   1. First, we replace the `ThreadContextClassLoader` class as follows:

   ```
   ClassLoader tccl = Thread.currentThread().
     getContextClassLoader();
   try {
     Thread.currentThread().setContextClassLoader
       (getClass().getClassLoader());
       .
   } catch (IOException e) {
     e.printStackTrace();
   } finally {
     Thread.currentThread().setContextClassLoader(tccl);
   }
   ```

   2. Secondly, as we are using Maven and as Hadoop unfortunately reuses the same file for SPI depending on your implementation, we cannot simply copy resources. Our aggregate JAR file and any dependencies we import will be overwritten with the last imported version.

To get around this, we explicitly tell our `Configuration` object which implementations to use when accessing our cluster. This is shown in the following code:

```
Configuration conf = new Configuration();
  conf.set("fs.hdfs.impl", org.apache.hadoop.hdfs.
    DistributedFileSystem.class.getName());
  conf.set("fs.file.impl", org.apache.hadoop.fs.
    LocalFileSystem.class.getName());
```

With the preceding actions, we have satisfied all the classloading and instantiation issues. Now, we are actually ready to access HDFS remotely. However, we still haven't forced our bundle to import and export all of Hadoop, but we can fairly easily change versions and we can externalize the static XML files that define the cluster if needed.

How it works

We have basically tricked our bundle into being able to imitate a single monolithic classloader in a normal classpath-provided JVM. We did this by creating a bundle that dynamically imports resources it needs from the Apache Hadoop bundle, and we have ensured that our bundle can access all the necessary configuration resources. We also adjusted classloading so that the Hadoop code base uses our bundle classloader to instantiate new instances.

Adding commands that talk to HDFS for deployment in Karaf

As HDFS at its core is a filesystem, let's see how we can access that with the standard tools and the bundle we've been building up so far.

What we'll do is store one level of configuration files from our running Karaf container into HDFS. Then, we'll provide a second command to read the files back.

We've learned how to build a feature for Hadoop that takes care of all the various dependencies needed to talk to HDFS, and we have also jumped a little bit ahead and discussed classloading and a few tricks to get the Hadoop libraries we deployed to cooperate. We are now at a point where we can start writing code against Hadoop using the libraries provided.

Getting ready

The ingredients of this recipe include the Apache Karaf distribution kit, access to JDK, and Internet connectivity. The sample code for this recipe is available at `https://github.com/jgoodyear/ApacheKarafCookbook/tree/master/chapter9/chapter-9-recipe1`. Remember, you need both the drivers installed and Apache Hadoop's HDFS running for these recipes to work!

How to do it...

Building a project that can access Hadoop will require the following steps:

1. The first step is generating a Maven-based bundle project. Create an empty Maven-based project. A `pom.xml` file containing the essential Maven coordinate information and bundle packaging directives will suffice.

2. The next step is adding dependencies to the POM file. This can be done as follows:

```
<dependencies>
  <dependency>
    <groupId>org.osgi</groupId>
    <artifactId>org.osgi.core</artifactId>
    <version>5.0.0</version>
  </dependency>
  <dependency>
    <groupId>org.osgi</groupId>
    <artifactId>org.osgi.compendium</artifactId>
    <version>5.0.0</version>
  </dependency>
  <dependency>
    <groupId>org.osgi</groupId>
    <artifactId>org.osgi.enterprise</artifactId>
    <version>5.0.0</version>
  </dependency>
  <dependency>
    <groupId>org.apache.servicemix.bundles</groupId>
    <artifactId>org.apache.servicemix.bundles.hadoop-
      client</artifactId>
    <version>2.4.0_1</version>
  </dependency>
  <!-- custom felix gogo command -->
  <dependency>
```

```
      <groupId>org.apache.karaf.shell</groupId>
      <artifactId>org.apache.karaf.shell.console</artifactId>
      <version>3.0.0</version>
    </dependency>
  </dependencies>
```

For Karaf 3.0.0, we use OSGi Version 5.0.0. The Hadoop libraries require quite a few supporting bundles. The existing Camel feature was used as a starting point but doesn't actually work on all platforms, so we have to rewrite it to suit our needs.

3. The next step is adding build plugins. Our recipe requires only one build plugin to be configured, which is the bundle. We configure the `maven-bundle-plugin` to assemble our project code into an OSGi bundle. We add the following plugin configuration to our POM file:

```
<plugin>
  <groupId>org.apache.felix</groupId>
  <artifactId>maven-bundle-plugin</artifactId>
  <version>2.4.0</version>
  <extensions>true</extensions>
  <configuration>
    <instructions>
      <Bundle-SymbolicName>${project.artifactId}</Bundle-
        SymbolicName>

      <Export-Package>
        com.packt.hadoop.demo*
      </Export-Package>
      <Import-Package>
        org.osgi.service.blueprint;resolution:=optional,
        org.apache.felix.service.command,
        org.apache.felix.gogo.commands,
        org.apache.karaf.shell.console,
        org.apache.hadoop*,
        *
      </Import-Package>

      <Include-Resource>
        {maven-resources},
        @org.apache.servicemix.bundles.hadoop-client-
          2.4.0_1.jar!/core-default.xml,
        @org.apache.servicemix.bundles.hadoop-client-
          2.4.0_1.jar!/hdfs-default.xml,
```

```
        @org.apache.servicemix.bundles.hadoop-client-
            2.4.0_1.jar!/mapred-default.xml,
        @org.apache.servicemix.bundles.hadoop-client-
            2.4.0_1.jar!/hadoop-metrics.properties
    </Include-Resource>

    <DynamicImport-Package>*</DynamicImport-Package>
  </instructions>
</configuration>
</plugin>
```

The Felix and Karaf imports are required by the optional Karaf commands. We are starting to get a bit more of a complicated bundle plugin as we are enabling dynamic classloading and copying resources around so that they are available to our classloader.

4. The next step is creating a Blueprint descriptor file. Create the `src/main/resources/OSGI-INF/blueprint` directory tree in your project. We'll then create a file named `blueprint.xml` in this folder. Consider the following code:

```
<?xml version="1.0" encoding="UTF-8" standalone="no"?>
<blueprint default-activation="eager"
  xmlns="http://www.osgi.org/xmlns/blueprint/v1.0.0">
  <!-- Define RecipeBookService Services, and expose them.
    -->
  <bean id="hdfsConfigService" class="com.packt.
    hadoop.demo.hdfs.HdfsConfigServiceImpl" init-
    method="init" destroy-method="destroy"/>

  <service ref="hdfsConfigService" interface="com.
    packt.hadoop.demo.api.HdfsConfigService"/>

  <!-- Apache Karaf Commands -->
  <command-bundle xmlns="http://karaf.apache.org
    /xmlns/shell/v1.1.0">
    <command>
      <action class="com.packt.hadoop.demo.
        commands.ReadConfigs">
        <property name="hdfsConfigService"
          ref="hdfsConfigService"/>
      </action>
    </command>
    <command>
      <action class="com.packt.hadoop.demo.
        commands.StoreConfigs">
```

```
        <property name="hdfsConfigService"
          ref="hdfsConfigService"/>
      </action>
    </command>

  </command-bundle>
</blueprint>
```

5. The next step is developing an OSGi service with a new Hadoop backend. We've created the basic project structure and plumbed in configurations for Blueprint descriptors. Now, we'll focus on the underlying Java code of our Hadoop-backed application. We break this process down into two steps: defining a service interface and providing a concrete implementation.

   1. First, we define a service interface. The service interface will define the user API to our project. In our sample code, we implement the `HdfsConfigService` interface, which provides the methods required to store and retrieve the configuration files we have in our Karaf instance. This can be done as follows:

      ```
      package com.packt.hadoop.demo.api;

      public interface HdfsConfigService {

        static final String HDFS_LOCATION =
          "/karaf/cookbook/etc";

        void storeConfigs();

        void readConfigs();
      }
      ```

      The interface's implementation follows standard Java conventions, requiring no special OSGi packages.

   2. Next, we implement our communication with HDFS. Now that we have defined our service interface, we'll provide an implementation as two calls to store and retrieve the file data from HDFS. This can be done as follows:

      ```
      public class HdfsConfigServiceImpl implements
        HdfsConfigService {

        private final static String BASE_HDFS =
          "hdfs://localhost:9000";

        @Override
      ```

```java
    public void storeConfigs() {
        String KARAF_etc = System.getProperty("karaf.home"
            ) + "/etc";
    Collection<File> files = FileUtils.listFiles(new
      File(KARAF_etc), new String[]{"cfg"}, false);

    for (File f : files) {
      System.out.println(f.getPath());

      ClassLoader tccl = Thread.currentThread().
        getContextClassLoader();
      try {
        Thread.currentThread().setContextClassLoader
          (getClass().getClassLoader());
        String cfg = FileUtils.readFileToString(f);

        Path pt = new Path(BASE_HDFS + HDFS_LOCATION + "/"
          + f.getName());

        Configuration conf = new Configuration();
        conf.set("fs.hdfs.impl", org.apache.hadoop.hdfs.
          DistributedFileSystem.class.getName());
        conf.set("fs.file.impl", org.apache.hadoop.fs.
          LocalFileSystem.class.getName());


        FileSystem fs = FileSystem.get(conf);

        BufferedWriter br = new BufferedWriter(new
          OutputStreamWriter(fs.create(pt, true)));
        // TO append data to a file, use fs.append(Path f)

        br.write(cfg);
        br.close();
      } catch (IOException e) {
        e.printStackTrace();
      } finally {
        Thread.currentThread().setContextClassLoader(tccl);
      }
    }
  }

  @Override
```

```
public void readConfigs() {
  try {

    FileSystem fs = FileSystem.get(new Configuration());
    FileStatus[] status = fs.listStatus(new
      Path(BASE_HDFS + HDFS_LOCATION));
    for (int i = 0;i < status.length;i++) {
      BufferedReader br = new BufferedReader(new
        InputStreamReader(fs.open(status[i].getPath())));
      String line;
      line = br.readLine();
      while (line != null) {
        System.out.println(line);
        line = br.readLine();
      }
    }
  } catch (Exception e) {
    e.printStackTrace();
  }
}

public void init() {

}

public void destroy() {

}
}
```

6. The next step is the optional creation of Karaf commands to directly test the persistence service. To simplify manual testing of our `HdfsConfigService` interface, we can create a set of custom Karaf commands that will exercise our HDFS storage and retrieval operations. The sample implementations of these commands are available from the book's website. Of particular interest is how they obtain a reference to the `HdfsConfigService` interface and make calls to the service. We must wire the command implementation into Karaf via Blueprint. This can be done as follows:

```
<!-- Apache Karaf Commands -->
<command-bundle xmlns="http://karaf.apache.org/
  xmlns/shell/v1.1.0">
  <command>
    <action class="com.packt.hadoop.demo.
      commands.ReadConfigs">
```

```
        <property name="hdfsConfigService" ref="
          hdfsConfigService"/>
      </action>
    </command>
    <command>
      <action class="com.packt.hadoop.demo.
        commands.StoreConfigs">
        <property name="hdfsConfigService" ref=
          "hdfsConfigService"/>
      </action>
    </command>

  </command-bundle>
```

Each of our custom command's implementation classes are wired to our `hdfsConfigService` instance.

7. The next step is deploying the project into Karaf.

 This demo will require a running Hadoop cluster!

We make sure that all the Hadoop bundles are installed correctly. This can be done using the following commands:

```
karaf@root()> feature:repo-add mvn:com.packt/chapter-9-
  recipe1/1.0.0-SNAPSHOT/xml/features

Adding feature url mvn:com.packt/chapter-9-recipe1/1.0.0-
  SNAPSHOT/xml/features


karaf@root()> feature:install hdfs2
karaf@root()>


karaf@root()> list
START LEVEL 100 , List Threshold: 50
 ID | State   | Lvl | Version        | Name
----------------------------------------------------------------
126 | Active  |  50 | 2.6            | Commons Lang
127 | Active  |  50 | 16.0.1         | Guava: Google Core
   Libraries for Java
```

```
128 | Active |  50 | 2.5.0          | Protocol Buffer Java API
129 | Active |  50 | 3.0.0.1        | Apache ServiceMix ::
   Bundles :: guice
130 | Active |  50 | 0.1.51.1       | Apache ServiceMix ::
   Bundles :: jsch
131 | Active |  50 | 2.6.0.1        | Apache ServiceMix ::
   Bundles :: paranamer
132 | Active |  50 | 1.7.3.1        | Apache ServiceMix ::
   Bundles :: avro
133 | Active |  50 | 1.8.1          | Apache Commons Compress
134 | Active |  50 | 3.1.1          | Commons Math
135 | Active |  50 | 1.2            | Commons CLI
136 | Active |  50 | 1.10.0         | Apache Commons
   Configuration
137 | Active |  50 | 3.1.0.7        | Apache ServiceMix ::
   Bundles :: commons-httpclient
138 | Active |  50 | 3.9.2.Final    | The Netty Project
139 | Active |  50 | 1.9.12         | Jackson JSON processor
140 | Active |  50 | 1.9.12         | Data mapper for Jackson
   JSON processor
141 | Active |  50 | 1.9.12         | JAX-RS provider for JSON
   content type, using Jackson data binding
142 | Active |  50 | 1.9.12         | XML Compatibility
   extensions for Jackson data binding
143 | Active |  50 | 1.0.4.1_1      | Apache ServiceMix ::
   Bundles :: snappy-java
144 | Active |  50 | 1.9.0          | Apache Commons Codec
145 | Active |  50 | 3.2.1          | Commons Collections
146 | Active |  50 | 2.4.0          | Commons IO
147 | Active |  50 | 3.3.0          | Commons Net
148 | Active |  50 | 3.4.6          | ZooKeeper Bundle
149 | Active |  50 | 0.52.0.1       | Apache ServiceMix ::
   Bundles :: xmlenc
150 | Active |  50 | 2.11.0.1       | Apache ServiceMix ::
   Bundles :: xercesImpl
151 | Active |  50 | 2.4.0.1        | Apache ServiceMix ::
   Bundles :: hadoop-client
152 | Active |  80 | 1.0.0.SNAPSHOT | Chapter 9 :: Manage Big
   Data with Apache Hadoop - HDFS Client Example.

karaf@root()>
```

We install our project bundle by executing the `install` command on its Maven coordinates:

```
karaf@root()>  install -s mvn:com.packt/chapter-9-
  recipe1/1.0.0-SNAPSHOT
```

8. The last step is testing the project. We can use the following commands for this:

```
karaf@root()> test:storeconfigs
```

```
karaf@root()> test:readconfigs
```

```
karaf@root()>
```

How it works...

We have a Karaf container now communicating with an external HDFS filesystem. We can back up configuration files from Karaf to HDFS and we can read them back.

A new Karaf instance can be started to consume and copy these configurations or we can use this recipe as the basis for starting up MapReduce jobs, tasks, and batch jobs.

10
Testing Apache Karaf with Pax Exam

In this chapter, we will cover the following recipes:

- ▸ Setting up a Pax Exam test environment
- ▸ Testing Apache Karaf features
- ▸ Testing commands with Apache Karaf
- ▸ Coverage with Apache Karaf Pax exam tests
- ▸ Testing Apache Camel with Blueprint and Apache Karaf

Introduction

This chapter explains how to set up a test environment for Apache Karaf. As developing OSGi applications for Apache Karaf also needs thorough testing, an environment for integration testing is needed. Pax Exam is a powerful tool for developing integration tests and can be combined with Apache Karaf.

More details about Pax Exam can be found at the OPS4j community website at `https://ops4j1.jira.com/wiki/display/PAXEXAM3/Pax+Exam`. If help is needed, you can find a working community at `https://groups.google.com/forum/#!forum/ops4j`.

Setting up a Pax Exam test environment

This recipe will guide you through the basic setup of a Pax Exam test environment using the Felix framework as the core OSGi container. The next recipe will cover how to combine Pax Exam and Apache Karaf.

Getting ready

As usual, the sources can be found at `https://github.com/jgoodyear/ApacheKarafCookbook/tree/master/chapter10/chapter10-recipe1`.

How to do it...

To perform integration tests with Pax Exam, the POM configuration is essential, since it is already part of the build environment. For example, use the `pax-exam-container-native` artifact and of course it is mandatory to connect JUnit with Pax Exam. This can be done as follows:

```
...
<properties>
  <version.pax-exam>3.4.0</version.pax-exam>
  <junit.version>4.11</junit.version>
</properties>
...
<dependency>
  <groupId>org.ops4j.pax.exam</groupId>
  <artifactId>pax-exam-junit4</artifactId>
  <version>${version.pax-exam}</version>
  <scope>test</scope>
</dependency>

<dependency>
  <groupId>org.ops4j.pax.exam</groupId>
  <artifactId>pax-exam-invoker-junit</artifactId>
  <version>${version.pax-exam}</version>
  <scope>test</scope>
</dependency>

<dependency>
  <groupId>org.ops4j.pax.exam</groupId>
  <artifactId>pax-exam-container-native</artifactId>
  <version>${version.pax-exam}</version>
  <scope>test</scope>
</dependency>
...
```

Besides this, it is required to define the OSGi framework in which to run this test scenario. This can either be the Felix framework, Equinox, or any other framework available as a Maven dependency.

Now that we are done with the important parts of the POM configuration, let's focus on the JUnit integration test.

This test class only consists of two major methods: the test method itself where we have a minor test setup for the container to work properly, and the far more important method at this point—the configuration. Consider the following code snippet:

```java
@ExamReactorStrategy(PerClass.class)
@RunWith(PaxExam.class)
public class TestOsgiServices {

  @Inject
  protected BundleContext bundleContext;

  @Configuration
  public static Option[] configuration() throws Exception {
    return options(
      workingDirectory("target/paxexam/"),
      cleanCaches(true),
      junitBundles(),
      frameworkProperty("osgi.console").value("6666"),
      frameworkProperty("osgi.console.enable.builtin")
        .value("true"),
      frameworkProperty("felix.bootdelegation.implicit")
        .value("false"),
      systemProperty("org.ops4j.pax.logging.DefaultServiceLog.
        level").value("DEBUG"));
  }

  @Test
  public void test() {
    assertNotNull(bundleContext);
  }
}
```

The unit test class needs the `@RunWith(PaxExam.class)` annotation to make clear it is a Pax Exam test. The `@ExamReactorStrategy` annotation lets you define a strategy for testing, either `PerClass`, `PerMethod`, or `PerSuite`, where you also need to define the test classes to run with. In our test, it is sufficient to run with the `PerClass` strategy as it starts the container only once per class, whereas the `PerMethod` strategy starts the test and its setup for each method invocation. The `PerSuite` strategy starts and configures the test setup for a suite of tests.

For details about the test strategies, refer to the Pax Exam documentation at `https://ops4j1.jira.com/wiki/display/PAXEXAM3/Pax+Exam`.

A Pax Exam test class always needs a `configuration` method annotated with the `@Configuration` annotation. This is needed for Pax Exam to know the configuration needed to run the test. For example, it is best to give a `workingDirectory` method, otherwise the working directory is placed in the temporary directory of the system. With the `junitBundles` method, the JUnit bundles are included so Pax Exam is capable of running JUnit tests. To run the tests with TestNG, it is required to add the dependencies of TestNG to the `configuration` method as follows:

```
mavenBundle("org.testng", "testng", "6.3.1")
```

With the `frameworkProperty("osgi.console")` property, you're able to add an OSGi console to the test; if you run the test in debug mode, you're able to access this console via port `6666`. This completes the basic setup of a Pax Exam test where we already have one test method that checks whether the injected (`@Inject`) bundle context is available.

How it works...

As Pax Exam finds its own modules on the classpath through Maven, it starts the container by itself. This is true for either a Felix or Equinox or any other kind of container supplied to Pax Exam by the POM configuration. Everything else needs to be specified using the `configuration` method. If you are using other bundles in your test scenario, you also need to specify their Maven coordinates. It's usually best to specify the version of the bundle in question in your POM configuration, and reuse this version in your configuration. You'll find more on this in the upcoming recipes.

So how does Pax Exam compare with a standard unit test? While testing on a unit level, maybe even with mocks, the tests are about the unit alone. Integration tests usually cover a wider range or a bigger scope with more units under test. Integration tests might be run as external tests against an externally available API. This is a bit hard if your APIs are services within a container. Pax Exam works with and within the container. The test class will be part of the deployed artifacts. In an OSGi environment, Pax Exam builds a dynamical bundle containing your test class, even with package imports. These bundle manifest headers can also be manipulated by the test; more details are available in the next recipe.

There's more...

An integration test usually tests an already built artifact, but sometimes it is essential to either alter the artifact or to test not after the artifact is built but when building this artifact. For this scenario, it is possible to build a *dynamic* bundle on the fly by configuring a `streamBundle`. This can be done as follows:

```
streamBundle(bundle()
  .add(Calculator.class)
  .add(CalculatorImpl.class)
  .add(CalcActivator.class)
  .set(Constants.BUNDLE_SYMBOLICNAME,
    "com.packt.IntegrationTest")
  .set(Constants.DYNAMICIMPORT_PACKAGE, "*")
  .set(Constants.BUNDLE_ACTIVATOR, CalcActivator.class.getName())
  .set(Constants.EXPORT_PACKAGE, "com.packt")
  .build()).start());
```

This example shows how to build a dynamic bundle including an activator and exporting the right packages and other manifest header entries. The registered service can be directly imported into the test and used.

 You might also be interested in using Pax Exam with other environments; it also supports Tomcat, Jetty, or JEE servers as backend for the runtime.

Testing Apache Karaf features

After going through the *Setting up a Pax Exam test environment* recipe, you should be ready to test OSGi applications in general. Now, let's take a closer look at what is needed to run a test with Apache Karaf as the container.

Getting ready

As in the previous chapters, the sources are available at `https://github.com/jgoodyear/ApacheKarafCookbook/tree/master/chapter10/chapter10-recipe2`. To fully understand this recipe, it is best to have gone through the previous recipe.

How to do it...

In the *Setting up a Pax Exam test environment* recipe, we defined the Felix framework as the runtime container. Now, we need to change this to Apache Karaf, so the first changes need to be done to the POM configuration. Pax Exam needs to know that it needs to run with Apache Karaf as the container; this is configured using the following:

1. The `pax-exam-container-karaf` dependency as a replacement dependency for the Felix framework.

2. The `apache-karaf` ZIP artifact to be used as the runtime container.

3. The standard features file for installing the standard features.

Consider the following code:

```xml
...
<dependency>
  <groupId>org.ops4j.pax.exam</groupId>
  <artifactId>pax-exam-container-karaf</artifactId>
  <version>${version.pax-exam}</version>
  <scope>test</scope>
</dependency>
...
<!-- framework to test with -->
<dependency>
  <groupId>org.apache.karaf.features</groupId>
  <artifactId>standard</artifactId>
  <version>${karaf.version}</version>
  <type>xml</type>
  <classifier>features</classifier>
  <scope>test</scope>
</dependency>

<dependency>
  <groupId>org.apache.karaf.features</groupId>
  <artifactId>org.apache.karaf.features.core</artifactId>
  <version>${karaf.version}</version>
  <scope>test</scope>
</dependency>

<dependency>
  <groupId>org.apache.karaf.system</groupId>
  <artifactId>org.apache.karaf.system.core</artifactId>
  <version>${karaf.version}</version>
  <scope>test</scope>
</dependency>
```

```xml
<dependency>
  <groupId>org.apache.karaf</groupId>
  <artifactId>apache-karaf</artifactId>
  <version>${karaf.version}</version>
  <type>zip</type>
  <scope>test</scope>
  <exclusions>
    <exclusion>
      <groupId>org.apache.karaf.shell</groupId>
      <artifactId>org.apache.karaf.shell.dev</artifactId>
    </exclusion>
  </exclusions>
</dependency>
...
```

After these changes are made to the POM configuration, the test itself needs to be reconfigured as follows:

```java
@ExamReactorStrategy(PerClass.class)
@RunWith(PaxExam.class)
public class IntegrationTestKaraf {

  @Inject
  protected BundleContext bundleContext;

  @Inject
  protected FeaturesService featuresService;

  @Configuration
  public static Option[] configuration() throws Exception {
    return new Option[] {
      karafDistributionConfiguration().frameworkUrl(maven()
        .groupId("org.apache.karaf").artifactId("apache-karaf")
        .type("zip").versionAsInProject())
        .unpackDirectory(new File("target/paxexam/unpack/"))
        .useDeployFolder(false),
      configureConsole().ignoreLocalConsole(),
      logLevel(LogLevel.INFO),
      keepRuntimeFolder(),
      features(maven().groupId("org.apache.karaf.features")
      .artifactId("standard").type("xml")
      .classifier("features").versionAsInProject(),
      "eventadmin")
    };
  }
```

```
@Test
public void test() {
  assertNotNull(bundleContext);
}

@Test
public void featuresAvailable() throws Exception {
  assertTrue(featuresService.isInstalled(featuresService
    .getFeature("eventadmin")));
}

}
```

The first major change should jump out at you right away: the Apache Karaf configuration, which has the `karafDistributionConfiguration` function with the Maven coordinates to an Apache Karaf ZIP file. As it is already defined in the POM configuration, the `versionAsInProject()` configuration can be used. Besides this, a feature is installed right away from the configuration and is available as soon as the container is up and running. The tests make sure the expected feature is installed.

How it works...

Pax Exam uses Karaf as container instead of a given OSGi framework. Some extra configuration is needed because the container is assembled as a ZIP file and needs to be unwrapped first. After this is done, the Apache Karaf container is started at the given location with the configured constraints, for example, to turn off the `Deploy` folder. The `versionAsInProject()` configuration needs some extra handling. For this to work, you need to make sure a Maven dependency file is generated. This can be done by configuring `depends-maven-plugin` from the ServiceMix project. This will generate a file containing all dependency information contained in the POM configuration readable by Pax Exam. Consider the following code:

```
<plugin>
  <groupId>org.apache.servicemix.tooling</groupId>
  <artifactId>depends-maven-plugin</artifactId>
  <version>1.2</version>
  <executions>
    <execution>
      <id>generate-depends-file</id>
      <phase>generate-resources</phase>
      <goals>
        <goal>generate-depends-file</goal>
      </goals>
    </execution>
  </executions>
</plugin>
```

With these configurations done, your tests are set. In the given test sample, we used an internal feature descriptor; if you want to test any other kind of custom feature, you just need to add it to the configuration and tell it which feature should be deployed. In the previous sample, it is the `eventadmin` feature.

Besides the already known simple injection of the `bundlecontext` object, it is also possible to inject any kind of service to the test that is available in the container. In the previous sample, we injected `featuresService`.

Testing commands with Apache Karaf

After you've gone through the first two recipes, you should be set for thorough testing of OSGi bundles, either standalone or in Apache Karaf. When working with Apache Karaf, it is sometimes necessary to also have new commands. This recipe will cover how to test with commands and make sure these commands are executed inside the Apache Karaf shell.

Getting ready

It's best to have gone through the *Testing Apache Karaf features* recipe before starting this recipe, as this one is a follow up. The sources can be found at `https://github.com/jgoodyear/ApacheKarafCookbook/tree/master/chapter10/chapter10-recipe3`.

How to do it...

To test the execution of an Apache Karaf shell command, you need to tweak the test class. First, you need to alter the way the test is run. For this, we add the probe builder which configures the way the test bundle is built. Consider the following code:

```
@ProbeBuilder
public TestProbeBuilder probeConfiguration(TestProbeBuilder probe) {
  //make sure the needed imports are there.
  probe.setHeader(Constants.DYNAMICIMPORT_PACKAGE,
    "*,org.apache.felix.service.*;status=provisional");
  return probe;
}
```

The following lines of code make sure the injection for the `CommandProcessor` interface works properly:

```
@Inject
protected CommandProcessor commandProcessor;
```

For the actual testing of commands, we add a convenience method that sends the command to the Karaf shell and receives the output from it. This can be done as follows:

```
protected String executeCommand(final String command) {
  String response;
  final ByteArrayOutputStream byteArrayOutputStream = new
    ByteArrayOutputStream();
  final PrintStream printStream = new PrintStream
    (byteArrayOutputStream);
  final CommandSession commandSession = commandProcessor.
    createSession(System.in, printStream, System.err);
  FutureTask<String> commandFuture = new FutureTask<String>(
    new Callable<String>() {
      public String call() {
        try {
          System.err.println(command);
          commandSession.execute(command);
        } catch (Exception e) {
          e.printStackTrace(System.err);
        }
        printStream.flush();
        return byteArrayOutputStream.toString();
      }
    });

  try {
    executor.submit(commandFuture);
    response = commandFuture.get(10000L, TimeUnit.MILLISECONDS);
  } catch (Exception e) {
    e.printStackTrace(System.err);
    response = "SHELL COMMAND TIMED OUT: ";
  }

  return response;
}
```

This string containing the response is testable for the expected output.

How it works...

The essential part of this test is the addition of the `ProbeBuilder` annotation. The `ProbeBuilder` annotation alters the way the bundle containing the test class is built. In our case, it alters the `Package-Import` header of the generated bundle. It is not only possible to alter or add manifest headers, but also to add additional classes or test classes.

Coverage with Apache Karaf Pax Exam tests

Apart from testing the application, it is usually also a requirement to know how well the unit and integration tests actually cover the code. For code coverage, a couple of technologies are available. This recipe will cover how to set up your test environment to find the coverage of the test.

Getting ready

It's best to have gone through the *Testing Apache Karaf features* recipe before starting this follow-up recipe. The sources of this recipe are available at `https://github.com/jgoodyear/ApacheKarafCookbook/tree/master/chapter10/chapter10-recipe4`.

How to do it...

To find out about the coverage of the test, a code coverage tool is needed. We will take the Java Code Coverage Library as it has a Maven plugin for automated coverage analysis. At first, the Maven coordinates for the plugin are added as shown in the following code:

```
<groupId>org.jacoco</groupId>
<artifactId>jacoco-maven-plugin</artifactId>
<version>0.7.0.201403182114</version>
```

We need to prepare the code first so it can be covered by the agent as follows:

```
<execution>
  <id>prepare-agent-integration</id>
  <goals>
    <goal>prepare-agent-integration</goal>
  </goals>
  <phase>pre-integration-test</phase>
  <configuration>
    <propertyName>jcoverage.command</propertyName>
    <includes>
      <include>com.packt.*</include>
    </includes>
    <append>true</append>
  </configuration>
</execution>
```

This will include the `com.packt` package, including subpackages. After the integration tests are done, the test report needs to be generated as follows:

```
<execution>
  <id>report</id>
  <goals>
    <goal>report-integration</goal>
  </goals>
</execution>
```

Besides these additions to the POM configuration, you need to add the VM options to the configuration of the Apache Karaf test. Without setting these options to the virtual machine, which executes the test, the executing environment doesn't know of the coverage and, therefore, no coverage is done. This can be done as follows:

```
private static Option addCodeCoverageOption() {
    String coverageCommand = System.getProperty(COVERAGE_COMMAND);
    if (coverageCommand != null) {
        return CoreOptions.vmOption(coverageCommand);
    }
    return null;
}
```

The resulting report of this coverage looks like the following screenshot. It shows the coverage of the `CalculatorImpl` class and its methods. While the `add` method has been called by the test, the `sub` method wasn't. This results in zero coverage for that method.

Element	Missed Instructions	Cov.	Missed Branches	Cov.	Missed	Cxty	Missed	Lines	Missed	Methods
sub(double, double)		0%		n/a	1	1	1	1	1	1
add(double, double)		100%		n/a	0	1	0	1	0	1
CalculatorImpl()		100%		n/a	0	1	0	1	0	1
Total	4 of 11	64%	0 of 0	n/a	1	3	1	3	1	3

How it works...

First, you need to prepare the agent for covering, this will be inserted into the `jcoverage.command` property. This property is passed to the test by adding the `vmOption` directory. This way the coverage agent is added to the Java Virtual Machine and it tracks the coverage of the test execution. After the test is run successfully, the report is generated by the `jacoco-maven-plugin`. All of this works fine with a single Maven module. A multimodule project setup will require additional work, especially if you want to combine unit and integration test coverage. More details can be found at `http://www.eclemma.org/jacoco/index.html`.

Testing Apache Camel with Blueprint and Apache Karaf

This recipe will cover how to test a Camel Blueprint definition. The focus of this recipe will be on the test and how it differs from the *Testing Apache Karaf features* recipe.

Getting ready

It's best to have gone through the *Testing Apache Karaf features* recipe and the *Creating a Blueprint-based Camel Router for deployment in Apache Karaf* recipe before starting this follow-up recipe. The sources of this chapter are available at `https://github.com/jgoodyear/ApacheKarafCookbook/tree/master/chapter10/chapter10-recipe5`.

How to do it...

Since we have based this recipe on the *Testing Apache Karaf features* recipe, we already have a basic setup containing the setup of the Apache Karaf container. Additionally, we need the Apache Camel feature for Karaf. This way all the bundles required for testing a Camel route are present. The test itself requires the Camel Context of the `blueprint.xml` definition to attach itself to its mock object. This can be done as follows:

1. The test class itself inherits from the `CamelTestSupport` class for easier testing of Camel:

    ```
    …
    @RunWith(PaxExam.class)
    public class TestCamelInKaraf extends CamelTestSupport {

      @Inject
      protected FeaturesService featuresService;

      @Inject
      protected BundleContext bundleContext;

      @Inject
      @Filter(value="(camel.context.name=blueprintContext)",
        timeout=10000)
      protected CamelContext testContext;
    …
    ```

    To have access to the mock contained in the Camel route, we make sure the Camel Context is injected. The `@Filter` annotation makes sure only the desired Camel Context is injected within the given timeout.

2. The configuration contains the targeted Karaf runtime and installs the required `camel-blueprint` and `camel-test` features as shown in the following code:

```
@Configuration
public static Option[] configure() throws Exception {
  return new Option[] {
  karafDistributionConfiguration().frameworkUrl(
  maven().groupId("org.apache.karaf")
.artifactId("apache-karaf")
.type("zip").versionAsInProject()).useDeployFolder(false)
.karafVersion("3.0.1")
  .unpackDirectory(new File("target/paxexam/unpack/")),
  logLevel(LogLevel.WARN),
  features(
maven().groupId("org.apache.camel.karaf")
.artifactId("apache-camel").type("xml")
.classifier("features")
.versionAsInProject(),
"camel-blueprint", "camel-test"),
  keepRuntimeFolder(),
  streamBundle(
    bundle().add(HelloBean.class)
  .add("OSGI-INF/blueprint/blueprint.xml",
  new File("src/main/resources/OSGI-
    INF/blueprint/blueprint.xml")
  .toURL())
.set(Constants.BUNDLE_SYMBOLICNAME, "com.packt.camel-test")
  .set(Constants.DYNAMICIMPORT_PACKAGE, "*").build())
  .start() };
}
```

3. Additionally, the `HelloBean` class and `blueprint.xml` file are wrapped up in a streamed bundle so the test is runnable inside the same module. As the last specialty to the test, we make sure the Camel Context is only created once per class creation. This can be done as follows:

```
@Override
public boolean isCreateCamelContextPerClass() {
  return true;
}
```

This completes the setup for testing a Camel route with Pax Exam inside the Karaf container.

4. In the `Test` method, we make sure that the required features are installed, the Camel Context has been injected, and that the mock is satisfied. Consider the following code:

```
@Test
public void test() throws Exception {
  assertTrue(featuresService.isInstalled(featuresService.
    getFeature("camel-core")));
  assertTrue(featuresService.isInstalled(featuresService.
    getFeature("camel-blueprint")));

  assertNotNull(testContext);

  MockEndpoint mockEndpoint = (MockEndpoint)
    testContext.getEndpoint("mock:result");
  mockEndpoint.expectedMessageCount(1);

  assertMockEndpointsSatisfied(100001,
    TimeUnit.MILLISECONDS);

}
```

How it works...

As in the previous recipes, Pax Exam makes sure Apache Karaf is run as the basic container. With the feature configuration inside the `@Configuration` method, we install the `camel-blueprint` and `camel-test` features. The test makes sure those features are indeed installed and running. To verify that the `HelloBean` class has actually sent a message to the mock endpoint, the test gets the mock endpoint from the injected Camel Context and expects at least a message count of one. Pax Exam injects the Camel Context used by the `blueprint.xml` file into the test class. To make sure it is the context that is actually needed, the `@Filter` annotation given with the LDAP filter syntax for OSGi services is used. While the `blueprint.xml` file containing the Camel Context is started, the Camel Context itself is registered as a service in the OSGi registry with the Camel Context ID registered as the `camel.context.name` property.

Because of the inheritance and the overridden `isCreateCamelContextPerClass` method, the Camel Context is only created once during the test execution. This is essential for running the Camel tests with Pax Exam because the container is only created once in the test. Otherwise, the Camel Context would be created a couple of times resulting in various errors.

To assert the successful execution of the test and to verify the expected message count, you are required to call the `assertIsSatisfied` method on the mock instead of calling the `assertMockEndpointsSatisfied` method. The latter method asserts all mock endpoints of the Camel Context bound to the test itself, while the former one asserts the mock that is contained in the Camel Context created by the Blueprint handler.

Index

Symbols

@ExamReactorStrategy annotation 223
@Produces annotation 140

A

ActiveMQ 69
activemq command 78
ActiveMQ
  dstat command, using 79, 80
  list command, using 78
  purge command, using 81, 82
  query command, using 73-77
Apache ActiveMQ modules
  installing, into Apache Karaf 71-73
Apache Aries JTA modules
  installing, in Apache Karaf 166, 167
Apache Camel
  testing, with Apache Karaf 233-235
  testing, with Blueprint 233-235
  URL 38, 49
Apache Camel modules
  installing, into Apache Karaf 34-36
Apache Cassandra
  data, modeling with 189-192
  history 188
  URL 188
Apache CXF modules
  installing, in Apache Karaf 131-134
Apache Derby
  installing, URL 178
Apache Hadoop
  accessing, from Karaf 209-211

Apache Hadoop distribution
  URL 206
Apache Karaf
  administering, JMX used 23-25
  Apache ActiveMQ modules,
      installing into 71-73
  Apache Aries JTA modules,
      installing 166, 167
  Apache Camel modules, installing into 34-36
  Apache Camel, testing with 233-235
  Apache CXF modules, installing 131-134
  Apache Karaf Cellar modules,
      installing into 150-152
  Camel Context information, displaying 38-40
  Camel Contexts, listing 36, 37
  Camel Contexts, starting 41
  Camel Contexts, stopping 41
  Camel CXF web service, building 142-148
  Camel CXF web service, deploying 142-148
  Cassandra client bundles, installing 188, 189
  CDI web application, creating with 128-130
  commands, testing with 229, 230
  endpoints, listing 46
  extended Http Service, installing 100, 101
  Hadoop client bundles, installing 206-209
  Http Service project, building 104-107
  installing, as service 27, 28
  JTA Feature, installing into 166, 167
  logging mechanism, configuring 8-11
  master/slave broker, configuring with 87-91
  master/slave broker, deploying with 87-91
  monitoring, JMX used 23-25
  OpenJPA modules, installing 164, 165

Pax modules, installing 98, 99
Pax Web modules, configuring 102-104
RESTful service, building 138-141
RESTful service, deploying 138-141
route information, displaying 43, 44
routes, listing 42
routes, resuming 44-46
routes, starting 44-46
routes, stopping 44-46
routes, suspending 44-46
Servlet 3.0 annotated web application,
    building with 126-128
setting up, for High Availability 29-31
SSH access, reconfiguring to 25, 26
Apache Karaf Cellar
    commands, using 152-157
Apache Karaf Cellar modules
    installing, into Apache Karaf 150-152
Apache Karaf console
    branding 14-17
Apache Karaf features
    testing 225-229
applications
    building, with custom HttpContext 113-116
    deploying, as feature 18-23
astyanax
    URL 196

B

Blueprint
    Apache Camel, testing with 233-235
Blueprint-based Camel Router
    Configuration Admin service, adding 54-58
    creating, for deployment in Apache
        Karaf 52-54
browse command 86
BundleActivator interface 49

C

camel:context-start contextName
    command 41
camel:context-stop contextName
    command 41
camel:endpoint-list command 47
camel:route-info routeId command 43

camel:route-list command 42
camel:route-resume routeName command 45
camel:route-start routeName command 45
camel:route-stop routeName command 45
camel:route-suspend routeName
        command 45
Camel Context information
    displaying, in Apache Karaf 38-40
Camel Contexts
    listing, in Apache Karaf 36, 37
    starting, in Apache Karaf 41
    stopping, in Apache Karaf 41
Camel CXF web service
    building, in Apache Karaf 142-148
    deploying, in Apache Karaf 142-148
Camel library
    features 34
Camel Router
    managed service factory implementation,
        creating 59-67
Cassandra client bundles
    installing, in Apache Karaf 188, 189
Cassandra documentation
    URL 201
Cassandra Query Language (CQL) 188
CDI web application
    creating, with Apache Karaf 128-130
Cellar
    distributed architecture, building
        with 158-162
    distributed architecture, deploying
        with 158-162
cellar-dosgi feature 159
cluster:bundle commands 156
cluster configuration commands 155-157
cluster:feature commands 156
cluster:service-list command 159, 161
cluster:sync command 155
Command annotation 14
commands
    testing, with Apache Karaf 229, 230
commands, Apache Karaf Cellar
    cluster configuration commands 155-157
    group commands 152, 153
    node commands 154
config:list command 157

Configuration Admin service
  adding, to Blueprint-based Camel
    Router 54-58
context-info command 40
Contexts and Dependency Injection (CDI) 128
custom HttpContext
  application, building with 113-116
custom Karaf command
  creating, Maven archetype used 12-14
CXF list-endpoints command
  using 134-136
CXF start command
  using 136-138
CXF stop command
  using 136-138

D

DAO service
  feature 181
data
  modeling, with Apache Cassandra 189-192
deleted method 65
distributed architecture
  building, with Cellar 158-162
  deploying, with Cellar 158-162
Distributed OSGi (DOSGi) 158
dstat command, ActiveMQ 79, 80

E

embedded ActiveMQ
  versus standalone ActiveMQ 70
endpoints
  listing, in Apache Karaf 46
Enterprise Integration Patterns (EIPs) 34
EntityManagerFactory function 181
error page mapping
  defining 110
error pages
  registering 109
extended Http Service
  installing, in Apache Karaf 100, 101

F

feature
  applications, deploying as 18-23
feature:install 22
feature:repo-add command 35
File Install
  URL 10

G

group commands 152-154
group-list command 151, 153

H

Hadoop 203
Hadoop access
  project building, for obtaining 211-220
Hadoop client bundles
  installing, in Apache Karaf 206-209
Hadoop Distributed File System (HDFS) 204
Hadoop release
  URL 204
Hazelcast
  about 151
  URL 151
hecate
  URL 196
HelloDispatcher object 65
HelloFactory class 63
High Availability
  Apache Karaf, setting up for 29-31
hosting, Apache Karaf
  standard web project, building for 117-119
Http Service
  building, with Whiteboard pattern in Apache
    Karaf 107-112
Http Service project
  building, in Apache Karaf 104-107

I

installation, Apache Karaf Cellar modules
  into Apache Karaf 150-152

J

Java Authentication and Authorization Service (JAAS) 120
Java-based Camel Router
  developing, for deployment in Apache Karaf 47-51
Java Management Extensions. *See* **JMX**
Java Persistence API (JPA) 163
JavaServer Pages. *See* **JSP**
Java Transaction API (JTA) 163
Java transaction support
  adding 182-186
jetty.xml file configuration
  URL 102
jms:create command 86
JMS browse command
  using 86, 87
JMS commands
  using 82-85
JMS send command
  using 85, 86
JMX
  used, for administering Apache Karaf 23-25
  used, for monitoring Apache Karaf 23-25
jndi:names command 178
JPA persistence layer
  project, building with 167-201
JSP
  registering 111, 112
JTA Feature
  installing, into Apache Karaf 166, 167

K

Karaf
  Apache Hadoop, accessing from 209-211
KAraf aRchive (KAR) 23
Karaf's console
  URL 14
keytool 123

L

list command, ActiveMQ 78
list-endpoints command 139

listrecipes custom command 179
list -t 0 | grep -i JPA-JTA command 185
list -t 0 | grep -i OpenJPA command 165
logging mechanism
  configuring, in Apache Karaf 8-11

M

managed service factory implementation
  creating, of Camel Router 59-67
manifestFile attribute 119
master/slave broker
  configuring, with Apache Karaf 87-91
  deploying, with Apache Karaf 87-91
Maven archetype
  used, for creating custom Karaf command 12-14

N

NCSA log format
  URL 103
Network of Brokers (NoB)
  configuring, with Apache Karaf 92-96
  deploying, with Apache Karaf 92-96
node commands 154
node-list command 154
NoSQL
  defining 188

O

openjpa-maven-plugin 169
OpenJPA modules
  installing, in Apache Karaf 164, 165
OPS4J Pax Logging 9
OSGi Alliance website
  URL 60
OSGICommandSupport class 14

P

Pax CDI project page
  URL 130
Pax Exam
  URL 221

Pax Exam documentation
  URL 224
Pax Exam test environment
  setting up 222-225
Pax modules
  installing, in Apache Karaf 98, 99
Pax Web
  installation options 98
Pax Web modules
  configuring, in Apache Karaf 102-104
persistence layer
  project, building with 182-186
PID 62
ProbeBuilder annotation 230
project
  building, for accessing Hadoop 211-220
  building, with JPA persistence layer 167-201
  building, with persistence layer 182-186
purge command, ActiveMQ 81, 82
PurgeCommand class 82

Q

query command, ActiveMQ 73-77

R

remote access
  URL 26
RESTful service
  building, in Apache Karaf 138-141
  deploying, in Apache Karaf 138-141
route-info command 43
route information
  displaying, in Apache Karaf 43, 44
route-list command 42
route-resume command 46
routes
  listing, in Apache Karaf 42
  resuming, in Apache Karaf 44-46
  starting, in Apache Karaf 44-46
  stopping, in Apache Karaf 44-46
  suspending, in Apache Karaf 44-46
route-start command 45
route-suspend command 46

S

security
  configuring, for web application in Apache
    Karaf 120-124
send command 86
service
  Apache Karaf, installing as 27, 28
service bundle
  producing 159-161
service consuming bundle 161, 162
Servlet 3.0 annotated web application
  building, with Apache Karaf 126-128
Snappy Java
  URL 207
SoapUI
  URL 146
specific HTTP connector
  web project, binding to 124-126
spring data-cassandra
  URL 196
SSH access
  reconfiguring, to Apache Karaf 25, 26
standalone ActiveMQ
  versus embedded ActiveMQ 70
standalone Hadoop cluster
  starting 204-206
standard web project
  building, for hosting in Apache Karaf 117-119

T

test environment
  setting up, for finding test coverage 231, 232

U

updated method 64
users.properties file 24

W

WAR feature
  prerequisite, for installation 120
web:list command 101

web application, Apache Karaf
  security, configuring for 120-124
Web Application Archive (WAR) 98
Web Application Bundle (WAB) 98
web console
  URL 17
web project, Apache Karaf
  binding, to specific HTTP connector 124-126
WebScale 187
welcome page
  registering 110, 111
Whiteboard pattern, Apache Karaf
  Http Service, building with 107-112
  URL 100
wrapper:install command 27

Thank you for buying
Apache Karaf Cookbook

About Packt Publishing

Packt, pronounced 'packed', published its first book "*Mastering phpMyAdmin for Effective MySQL Management*" in April 2004 and subsequently continued to specialize in publishing highly focused books on specific technologies and solutions.

Our books and publications share the experiences of your fellow IT professionals in adapting and customizing today's systems, applications, and frameworks. Our solution based books give you the knowledge and power to customize the software and technologies you're using to get the job done. Packt books are more specific and less general than the IT books you have seen in the past. Our unique business model allows us to bring you more focused information, giving you more of what you need to know, and less of what you don't.

Packt is a modern, yet unique publishing company, which focuses on producing quality, cutting-edge books for communities of developers, administrators, and newbies alike. For more information, please visit our website: www.packtpub.com.

About Packt Open Source

In 2010, Packt launched two new brands, Packt Open Source and Packt Enterprise, in order to continue its focus on specialization. This book is part of the Packt Open Source brand, home to books published on software built around Open Source licenses, and offering information to anybody from advanced developers to budding web designers. The Open Source brand also runs Packt's Open Source Royalty Scheme, by which Packt gives a royalty to each Open Source project about whose software a book is sold.

Writing for Packt

We welcome all inquiries from people who are interested in authoring. Book proposals should be sent to author@packtpub.com. If your book idea is still at an early stage and you would like to discuss it first before writing a formal book proposal, contact us; one of our commissioning editors will get in touch with you.

We're not just looking for published authors; if you have strong technical skills but no writing experience, our experienced editors can help you develop a writing career, or simply get some additional reward for your expertise.

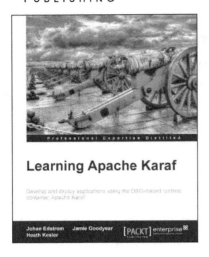

Learning Apache Karaf

ISBN: 978-1-78217-204-8   Paperback: 128 pages

Develop and deploy applications using the OSGi-based runtime container, Apache Karaf

1. Understand Apache Karaf's commands and control capabilities.

2. Gain familiarity with its provisioning features.

3. Explore various application deployments targets experientially.

Instant Apache ServiceMix How-to

ISBN: 978-1-84951-966-3   Paperback: 66 pages

Learn to create simple ServiceMix-based integration solutions using short, practical, hands-on recipes

1. Learn something new in an Instant! A short, fast, focused guide delivering immediate results.

2. Leverage OSGI to speed up the ESB deployment.

3. Define message flow with Camel DSL.

Please check **www.PacktPub.com** for information on our titles

Instant Apache Camel Messaging System

ISBN: 978-1-78216-534-7   Paperback: 78 pages

Tackle integration problems and learn practical ways to make data flow between your application and other systems using Apache Camel

1. Learn something new in an Instant! A short, fast, focused guide delivering immediate results.

2. Use Apache Camel to connect your application to different systems.

3. Test your Camel application using unit tests, mocking, and component substitution.

Apache Camel Developer's Cookbook

ISBN: 978-1-78217-030-3   Paperback: 424 pages

Solve common integration tasks with over 100 easily accessible Apache Camel recipes

1. A practical guide to using Apache Camel delivered in dozens of small, useful recipes.

2. Written in a Cookbook format that allows you to quickly look up the features you need, delivering the most important steps to perform with a brief follow-on explanation of what's happening under the covers.

3. The recipes cover the full range of Apache Camel usage from creating initial integrations, transformations and routing, debugging, monitoring, security, and more.

Please check **www.PacktPub.com** for information on our titles